A
HISTORY OF
THE CHARTIST
MOVEMENT

A
HISTORY OF
THE CHARTIST
MOVEMENT

BY

JULIUS
WEST

WITH AN INTRODUCTORY
MEMOIR BY J. C. SQUIRE
CONSTABLE & COMPANY LIMITED
LONDON

Published 1920

Printed in Great Britain by Butler & Tanner, *Frome and London*.

INTRODUCTORY MEMOIR

JULIUS WEST was born in St. Petersburg on March 21 (9th O.S.), 1891. In May, when he was two months old, he went to London, where from that time onwards, his father, Mr. Semon Rappoport, was correspondent for various Russian papers. At twelve years of age West entered the Haberdashers' (Aske's) School at Hampstead. He left school in 1906, and became a temporary clerk in the Board of Trade, assisting in the preparation of the report on the cost of living in Germany, issued in 1908. On leaving the Board of Trade, he became a junior clerk in the office of the Fabian Society, then in a basement in Clement's Inn. (It was there that in 1908 or 1909 I first saw him.) To get to the Secretary's room one had to pass through the half-daylight of a general office stacked with papers and pamphlets, and on some occasion I received the impression of a new figure beyond the counter, that of a tall, white-faced, stooping youth with spectacles and wavy dark hair, studious-looking, rather birdlike. The impression is still so vivid that I know now I was in a manner aware that he was unusual long before I was conscious of any curiosity about him. I had known him thus casually by sight for some time, without knowing his name; I had known his name and his repute as a precocious boy for some time without linking the name to the person. He was said to read everything and to know a lot of economics; a great many people were getting interested in him; he was called West and was a Russian, a collocation which puzzled me until I learned that he was a Jew from Russia who had adopted an English name. Although still under twenty, he was already, I think, lecturing to small labour groups when I got to know him more intimately. He knew his orthodox economics inside out, and was

i

in process of acquiring a peculiar knowledge of the involved history of the Socialist movement and its congeners during the last hundred years.

He was, in fact, already rather extraordinary. His education had been broken off early, and he always regretted it ; but I have known few men who have suffered less from the absence of an academic training. Given his origins, his early struggle, his intellectual and political environment, the ease with which he secured some sort of hearing for his first small speeches to congenial audiences, one might have expected a very different product. It would not have been surprising, had he, with all his intellect, become a narrow fanatic with a revoluntionary shibboleth ; it would not have been strange if, avoiding this because of his common sense, he had been drawn into the statistical machine and given himself entirely to collecting and digesting the materials for social reform. He took a delight in economic theory and he had a passion for industrial history ; the road was straight before him. But the pleasure and the passion were not exclusive. Although it is possible that his greatest natural talents were economic and historical, and (as I think) likely that had he lived his chief work would have been along lines of which the present book is indicative, he was in no hurry to specialize. He had a catholic mind. Behind man he could see the universe, and, unlike many Radicals of his generation, behind the problems and the attempted or suggested solutions of his time, he could see the wide and long historical background, the whole experience of man with the lessons, moral, psychological and political, which are to be drawn from it, and are not to be ignored. You may find in his early writings (though not in this book) all sorts of crudities, flippancies and loose assertions ; he was young and impulsive, he had been under the successive influences of Mr. Shaw and Mr. Chesterton, and lacked their years and their command of language ; he had a full mind and a fluent pen which, when it got warm, sometimes ran away. But at bottom he was unusually sane ; and his sanity came in part from the intellectual temper that I have sketched, but partly from a sweet, sensitive and sympathetic nature which made injustice as intolerable to him as it was unreasonable. He did not always (being young and having had until the last year or two little experience of the general world of men) realize how people would take his words ; but I never knew a man who more quickly or more girlishly blushed when he thought he had said or written something wounding or not quite sensible.

Julius West's life was conspicuously a life of the mind. But if the reader understands by an intellectual a man to whom books and verbal disputations are alone sufficient, reservations must be made. It is true that he was a glutton for books : he collected a considerable library where Horace Walpole, Marx, Stevenson, Mr. Conrad, Mr. and Mrs. Sidney Webb and Marlowe stood together. His father writes : " He was a great reader, and his literary taste even as a schoolboy was remarkable. He scorned to read books written specially for children, but used to enjoy the reading of classical writers even at the age of seven or eight years, and his knowledge of all Shakespeare's dramas was astonishingly complete." But he was restless and roving rather than sedentary. He was capable of running great physical risks and enduring hardships beyond his strength ; he travelled as much as he could, and had the authorities admitted him into the Army, he would, unless his body had given out, have made a good soldier. He did not mistake books for life ; but one had the feeling that life to him was primarily a great book. His nature was emotional enough : he fell in love ; he was deeply attached to a few intimate friends ; and there was an emotional element in his politics and his reactions to all the strange spectacles he saw in his last years of life. But ordinarily what one thought of was his curiosity rather than his emotions ; his senses not at all. If at one moment one had peeped into his affectionate nature the next one was always carried off into some " objective " discussion. His curiosity about things, his love of debate, gave him a refuge during trouble and an habitual resort in ordinary times. He seemed incapable of any idle thing. Most of us, with varying frequency, will make physical exertions without obtaining or desiring reward beyond the effort and the fatigue ; or we will lie lapped in the gratification of our senses, happy,

without added occupation, to drink wine or sit in silence with
a friend and tobacco, or encumber a beach and feel the hot
sun on our faces, or loll in a green shade without even a green
thought.   Or we will travel and see men and countries, or take
part in events for the mere exhilaration of doing it.   But whatever his physical activity, Julius West would always have been
the curious spectator, observing and learning, recording and
deducing, with history in the making around him ; and,
whatever his physical inactivity, his brain would never have
been asleep, or his senses dormant.   If one walked with him,
there were few silences ; a punt on the river with him would
have meant (unless he were reading) eager, peering eyes and
speculations either about the surrounding objects, and what
people had said about them, or else about Burke, Bakunin or
some such thing.   For all his energy, I never knew his ambition, or was clearly convinced that he had any other ambition
than to see and learn all he could, and produce his results.

He attempted all sorts of literary work ; parodies, short
stories, criticism.   It was to be expected that the criticism
would be chiefly concerned with doctrine, and that the other
work would be defective and full of ideas.   Partly, I suppose,
all this writing was the by-product of an intellectual organ
which could not stop working but demanded a change of work ;
partly his very curiosity operated : he saw what other men
had written, and he wanted to find out what it would be like
to write this, that and the other thing.   But he had neither
the sensuousness nor the selfishness (if that hard word may be
used of that detachment and that preoccupation) of the artist,
nor the reverence for form that demands and justifies an intense
application to general detail which is not, to the hasty eye,
very significant.   As a rule he was exclusively preoccupied
with the general purport of what he wanted to say.   But it
was not unnatural that a young man with his heart, his imagina-
tive intelligence and his wide reading, should have begun his
career as an author with a book of poems.   (The book published
by Mr. David Nutt in 1913 was called *Atlantis and Other Poems.*)
It was ignored by the reviewers and the public ; he would not
have denied that it deserved to be ; but it was very interesting

to any one interested in him. A great part of it (remember, most of the verses had been written by a boy under twenty-one) was very weak ; short poems about mermaids, sunken galleons, maidens, dreams, ghosts and witches, written in rhythms which are lame, but displaying in the ineffective variety of their form the restless ingenuity, the hunger for experiment of this young author ; and here and there lit up by a precocious thought or phrase. A man with a greater share of the poetic craft was likely to do better with a larger subject and a looser structure, and much the best poem in West's book is *Atlantis*, a narrative in about five hundred lines of blank verse, with a few songs embedded in it. The blank verse is as good as most ; few men of West's age could write better ; and he could without contortion move in it, and make it say whatever he wanted it to say. He represents the Lost Continent as dwindled to a small island and inhabited by people conscious of their impending doom, weighed down with the memory of what their country's forests and fields and birds were like before the last wave. The subject offered an obvious chance as a visible spectacle, and the poet (feeling this) made an attempt to paint the features of the city, describing its houses and temples and festivals. The attempt was unsuccessful ; it was when he reached more congenial ground that West showed his originality and his power. With one of the most alluringly " picturesque " and melodramatic subjects in the world under consideration, he put all the obvious things behind him and spent his time considering what effects such a situation as that of the doomed remnant of Atlanteans would have had upon the minds of men. Passionate love became almost extinct :

> and 'twas thought 'twas well
> No helpless childish hands there were to pull
> Their elders' heartstrings, making death seem hard
> And parting very bitter, and the end
> A bitter draft of pain, poured by a hand
> Unpitying, a draft of which the old
> Were doomed to drink more than a double share.

The poets

> Did all but cease th' eternal themes to sing
> And in their place sang songs about the End.

The philosophers ran to strange doctrines about the perfectibility of the survivors from the next deluge or starkly expounded the End, or were

> Buffoons who sought to turn the End a thing
> For jest;

and across the city sometimes flashed a band of fanatics proclaiming this shadowed life to be an illusion from which those who had courage and faith could escape. Voices spoke, sad or resentful, of men cheated out of their due years; one fierce

> For us an aimless life, an aimless Death . . .
> That I should have the power for once to *live*,
> To be a creature strong with power to kill,
> To stay, but for a little while, the strength
> That hems us in! That I might taste the joy
> Of conflict with an equal force to mine,
> Conflict of life and death, not purposeless,
> Not vain, as we now feebly struggle on. . . .
> That I could have the gift of knowing hate,
> Black hate that animates before it kills. . . .
> O, to do aught with force, not rest supine.

In this boyish poem we can see West's mind trying to realize Atlantis as a whole community, where characters vary and doctrines clash; as a vessel holding, at a certain position in time and space, the human spirit.

Whether he would have written more poetry I do not know. I doubt it; at all events he had little time and many distractions, and he looked like growing confirmed in other pursuits. In 1913 he went into the office of the *New Statesman*, for which, intermittently, he wrote reviews (usually of books about Eastern Europe) and miscellaneous articles until he died. He remained in the office for a few months; then left, and became a free lance writing for various papers, lecturing, and starting work on the present book and others. I think his second publication was a tract, notable for its sagacity and its wit, on John Stuart Mill. He was busy with several books when the war broke out, which in the end was to kill him at twenty-seven.

I forget if it was in August, 1914, that he first tried to join the Army. A layman might have supposed that both his eyes and his lungs were too weak, but a doctor told him that he was good for active service. Whenever it was that he volunteered— his first attempt was early, and there were others after his short visit to Russia and Warsaw in 1914–15—he made a discovery. He had not realized—if he had ever known it the conception had dropped out of his mental foreground—that he was not a British subject. But they told him so, and said that his status must be settled before he could have a commission. He had arguments : his parents were Russian subjects and he himself was born in Russia ; but his parents were merely visiting Russia when he was born, and he submitted that he was at that time really domiciled in England. The argument, it seemed, had no legal validity ; and, denied citizenship in the only home he knew or wanted, he at once went, very set and intent, to a solicitor's office in Lincoln's Inn Fields where I had the odd experience of assisting, as I believed, to naturalize a man I had never thought of as a foreigner. This, he thought, would settle it ; he would soon be in the Army. But no. The hierarchy at this point thought of something new. He was a Russian, an Ally of military age ; if he wished to fight he must join the Russian army ; we would not naturalize him here. It would have been difficult to conceive a more grotesque suggestion, if one knew the man. He had left Russia when a baby in long clothes ; he spoke Russian (at that time) with difficulty ; he looked at Russia and her institutions from an English point of view ; he was married (he had been con- firmed in the Church of England) to the daughter of an English clergyman ; all his friends were English and most of them in uniform : and it was suggested that if he really desired to serve the Allied cause he should divest himself of all his ties and go off to mess in the snows of Courland or Galicia with bearded strangers from the Urals and the Ukraine. The sug- gestion was repulsive to him, quite apart from the fact that it might mean years of unbroken exile. He was, however, allowed to join an ambulance corps in London.

Before long he was off to Petrograd on a flying tour as a corre- spondent; thence to Moscow and Warsaw, within sound of which the German guns were booming : Russian Warsaw with enemy aeroplanes overhead and expensive Tsarist officers revelling in the best hotels. He saw the Grand Duke Nicholas on November 17, 1914, in the greatest Cathedral of Petrograd at a gorgeous service of commemoration of the miraculous preservation of the Tsar Alexander II : that was six years ago ! He returned, and for a year and more was in England, editing *Everyman* and writing books at a great pace. Then his wife died. Another opportunity of going to Russia offered, and a man always restless took it as a means of escape from himself. He was in Petrograd in the early months of the Bolshevik regime. He lived (a few letters came through) in a state of high excitement, seeing everything he could, visiting the Institute and the Bolshevik law courts, attending meetings at which Lenin and Trotsky spoke, dogged everywhere, for he was suspected, daily expecting to be shot from behind. Being a democrat and a believer in ordered progress he was very angry with the Bolsheviks ; having a zest for queer manifestations of life he found an immense variety of interest and amusement in their conduct. When he returned he was full of stories of rascality. Lenin, on the point of character, was in many ways an exception ; but he was tricked wholesale by German Jew agents disguised as Bolsheviks. One of them, high in the Bolshevik Foreign Office, had even judiciously edited the Secret Treaties, the publication of which so edified the Bolshevik public and so surprised the world. Daily great stacks of documents were served out to the Bolshevik press, a dole for this paper, a dole for that ; but the busy German spy had taken the last precaution to ensure that the documents which involved the Allies should come out, and that those which most seriously compromised Germany should not. West became pretty familiar with many of the revolutionary figures, and enjoyed working in such an extraordinary scene. But he recognized that his excitement was hectic and bad for him ; he suffered to some extent from the famine conditions of Petrograd ; the cold was terrible, and that and the indoor stuffiness which it led to affected his chest. He had to get away. In February, 1918, he left with a party of English governesses and elderly invalids. He was not an old man nor a governess ; he was in effect an English journalist of fighting age who might be carrying valuable information ; but he was fortified with some lie or other, and with the rest of the pathetic caravan he went over the ice and through the German lines. The enemy were at that time in occupation of the Aland Islands, and West told a romantic story of the night he and his companions spent in a village there guarded by the German soldiers : a night filled with snow, a silence broken by guttural voices talking of home and the fortunes of the war in Flanders.

He got through to Stockholm and from there home, where, unexpected and unannounced he floated in on me, keen and volatile as ever, but looking ill. He ought then to have taken a long rest ; but he was asked to go off to Switzerland—then a hotbed of enemy and pacifist intrigue—and he thought that with his experience and his knowledge of languages (he now knew Russian, French, German, Dutch, and Roumanian) it was his duty to go. But it killed him. He came back, hollow-eyed and coughing, and went first to an hotel in Surrey, and then to a sanatorium in the Mendips. His friends did not know how ill he was ; he wrote cheerfully about books and politics, asked for more books, was glad he had found an invalid officer or two with cultivated tastes. But he just saw the war out. A complication of influenza and pneumonia developed, and he died.

During the war he had published several books. Two— *Soldiers of the Tsar* and *The Fountain*—were issued by the Iris Publishing Company, the proprietor of which, now dead, deserves a book to himself. The first was a collection of sketches written mostly in Russia in 1914 ; the second a tumultuous race of satires and parodies probably modelled on *Caliban's Guide to Letters*. The aged Reginald at the end observes :

And oh, my children, be not afraid of your own imaginations. Once in the distant ages before our universe was born, when Time was an unmarked desert, and God was lonely, He let the fountain of His fancies play, and life began. Be you, too, creators, for there is none, even among my own grandchildren, who has not in him a vestige of that impulse which made the earth.

The book was written on this principle ; perhaps the fountain

played too fast ; but its many-coloured spray shows how various
was the manipulator's knowledge and how active his mind.
The other books were *G. K. Chesterton : a Critical Study* (Secker),
an abridged translation of the de Goncourt *Journal*, published
by Nelson's, and translations of three plays by Tchekoff and
one by Andreieff. The translation from the Goncourts, produced at a great pace, is really good : lively, vivid, idiomatic.
The monograph, though independent and containing plenty of
reservations, was an exposition of the theory that Mr. Chesterton " is a great and courageous thinker." West, though not
blind to his subject's genius as artist and humorist, characteristically concentrated on his opinions about religion and politics ; his own were revealed *en passant*. " The dialogues on
religion contained in *The Ball and the Cross* are alone enough
and more than enough to place it among the few books on
religion which could safely be placed in the hands of an atheist
or an agnostic with an intelligence." *Magic* and *Orthodoxy*
together " are a great work, striking at the roots of disbelief."
During the war " those of us who had not the fortune to escape
the Press by service abroad, especially those of us who derived
our living from it, came to loathe its misrepresentation of the
English people. . . . Then we came to realize, as never before,
the value of such men as Chesterton." It was an impulsive
book, but there was a great deal of very acute analysis in it.
The one book, however, which has a reasonable chance of long
survival is the present *History of Chartism*.

Now it really is rather remarkable that this book should
have come from the same man, the same very young man, as
the works mentioned above. We still produce, and it is a good
thing we do, men who take an interest in everything and talk,
whether shallowly or with the instinct of genius, or both, about
literature, science and politics, relating them all. But if a
man does this, one can never expect him to be also a specialist
(except, rarely, in some literary subject) who is capable of
research and loves documents. An essay on *Chartism* we
might expect ; an exposition of its real or supposed principles ;
an idealization of the movement. But we do not expect a
man with the habits of the literary-political journalist to grub

for years amongst pamphlets and manuscripts in the British Museum, and produce a chapter of history containing and relating a "mass of new facts." But that is what West did, and he did it concurrently with his other miscellaneous work ; editing, reviewing, translating, speaking, and the rapid composition of topical books. The Chartists were especially interesting as being in some sort pioneers of the modern Labour movement in which West had grown up ; but he might have been drawn to any other such subject had he found another that had been so neglected by English historians. It did not take him long to discover that some current opinions would have to be revised ; that the physical menace of the Chartist movement had often been exaggerated, and its historical importance generally ignored. But, whatever might have been his conclusions, he loved finding things out ; almost anything would do. He had a prodigious memory that would enable him to correct at a moment's notice a misstatement as to the percentage of one-roomed tenements in Huddersfield, or the name of the Chancellor of the Duchy of Lancaster in Mr. Gladstone's first Government. He could read anything with interest and he forgot nothing that he read. At the British Museum he went through all the available Chartist literature like a caterpillar. Then one day, with great excitement and amusement, he came to tell me that he had discovered at the Hendon annexe scores of manuscript volumes put together by Francis Place which had never been examined by any previous English writer. Every sort of Chartist trifle had been " pasted up " by the industrious tailor ; the obscurer the newspaper from which Place's cuttings came, the greater West's pleasure. He liked them for their own sakes ; but he retained his sense of proportion, and I do not think that those more competent to judge than I, who read this book, will think that West swamped his general outline with his own lesser discoveries. And he had none of the jealous greed of the baser kind of research worker. He would have given his results to any one. When he was nearly through his book, there was announced a book on somewhat similar lines by another young student, the late Mr. Hovell. West showed no fear that his own work might be rendered worthless, but (I think) volunteered to assist in preparing it for the press.

I will add no more, for his most important achievement and his memorial are here—except that the proofs of the volume have been read by myself, no expert ; and that had he lived to revise them himself he would probably have removed what errors may be found.

J. C. SQUIRE.

PREFACE

THE Chartist movement occupies a position of exceptional importance in the social history of England. The People's Charter was the basis of the first working-class agitation to take place in this country on a national scale. This fact alone makes the movement a prominent feature in the political education of the English people. Historians, nevertheless, have consistently refused to study Chartism, or to see in it much more than a demonstration which attempted to overawe Parliament on April 10, 1848, and failed ignominiously. For the most part the standard histories of the last century have done little more than to copy one another's inaccuracies. Thus, Miss Martineau, Molesworth, Justin McCarthy, and innumerable lesser writers, repeat the story that Daniel O'Connell handed the Charter to Lovett, remarking solemnly, " There, Lovett, is your Charter . . ." etc. The fact that Lovett was the principal author of the document in point would alone disqualify the story; the facts that O'Connell took no part in its composition, that his immediately subsequent actions belied the remaining sentiments attributed to him, that he and Lovett were in a state of chronic mutual dislike, condemn the tale beyond all hope of acquittal. A few facts, a few conventional comments, and a piously expressed gratitude that the English were not as other people in 1848, generally complete the tale of references to Chartism. In his preface to the English translation of *The Right to the Whole Produce of Labour*, by Anton Menger, Professor Foxwell has some striking things to say about the Chartist period and the treatment it usually receives. " It is notorious that all the great remedial measures which have proved the most effective

5   B

checks against the abuses of capitalistic competition are of English origin. Trade Unions, Co-operation, and Factory Legislation are all products of English soil. That the revolutionary reaction against capitalism is equally English in its inspiration is not so generally known." The great interest of the Chartist period is the active quest for ideas which was then being carried on, and its first results. Within a few years working men had forced upon their attention the pros and cons of trade unionism, industrial unionism, syndicalism, communism, socialism, co-operative ownership of land, land nationalization, co-operative distribution, co-operative production, co-operative ownership of credit, franchise reform, electoral reform, woman suffrage, factory legislation, poor law reform, municipal reform, free trade, freedom of the press, freedom of thought, the nationalist idea, industrial insurance, building societies, and many other ideas. The purpose of the People's Charter was to effect joint action between the rival schools of reformers ; but its result was to bring more new ideas on to the platform, before a larger and keener audience.

This teeming mass of ideas, inspired with nascent energy, is the most striking characteristic of the Chartist movement. To the working men who listened to William Lovett and Feargus O'Connor, ideas mattered more than to any succeeding generation. Lovett's autobiography is a curious piece of evidence, showing its writer's obsession with ideas. More than one-half of that substantial book consists of manifestos and addresses drafted by its author. To Lovett the idea was as important as the deed, He and his generation really did believe in the prevailing power of truth.

At the present moment there is no history of Chartism in print in the English language. R. G. Gammage's book once held the field undisputed, but its value has diminished with its age, as generations have arisen with no first-hand knowledge of the subject, and therefore unable to fill in the gaps from memory. Gammage's prolix account of meetings, personalities, squabbles, and prosecutions, would be of more interest to Chartists themselves than to those ignorant of the underlying forces and ideas of the movement, which the author scarcely explains. Prof. Dolléans' massive *Le Chartisme* is also more concerned with men than with ideas, and is quite extraordinarily diffuse. Perhaps the best existing account of the subject is contained in M. Beer's *Geschichte des Socializmus in England*.[1] Herr Schluter's *Die Chartisten-Bewegung*, completed, as the author alleges, in order to rectify the errors of the former writer, is a comparatively inferior work, based upon a smaller amount of research but an infinitely stronger sentimentality. Chartism has long been a favourite subject of German students, who have produced several short works on it, down to the inevitable philological study on *Der Flugschriftenliteratur des Chartistenbewegung*. Other works on the subject are to be had in Italian and Russian.

The author of the present work can claim to have one considerable advantage over his predecessors, of whatever nationality. This has been his access to the Place Collection at the British Museum. It appears that in 1866, on the death of Joseph Parkes, the Museum bought from his library 180 volumes, mainly consisting of press cuttings, which had come into his possession on the death of Francis Place. Among these volumes (a list of which is to be found in the bibliography) a set of twenty-eight consists of materials for a history of Chartism down to 1847. Place himself attempted to write a history of Chartism, but had to give it up. This particular set contains many otherwise inaccessible pamphlets, with correspondence, memoranda, and annotations. The Place Collection is at present kept in the British Museum Repository at Hendon, and was first catalogued only in 1913. Its value to a student of the first half of the last century cannot be over-estimated. The Collection should not be confused with the ninety-three volumes of the Place MSS. at the British Museum, which have been well known to historical students since the publication in 1898 of *The Life of Francis Place*, by Mr. Graham Wallas.

---

[1] *The first volume of an English translation of this work has now appeared.—J.C.S.*

CONTENTS

CHAPTER I

THE EARLY RADICAL MOVEMENT

CHARTISM is the name generally applied to a democratic movement which came to a head in this country about 1840. It was distinguished by certain specific demands, which came to be both its objects and its insignia. In the course of its existence, the movement, while adhering closely to its original ends, underwent a number of changes within itself. From a purely middle-class agitation, it developed into a working-class campaign; woman suffrage entered to a certain extent into the programme; many of the present-day problems of trade unionism, industrial unionism, and syndicalism took shape; and organized labour became for the first time a factor of importance in the life of the nation.

The beginnings of a political movement may generally be traced, with a modicum of ingenuity, to Plato's *Republic* by those historians who wish to describe their subject *ab ovo*. But a dawn in history differs from the dawn of the meteorologist; it may be fixed arbitrarily. So we shall place the beginning of our movement in the year 1776, without apologies to those numerous students who have found, and will continue to find, Radicalism already existing before that year. Since 1776, the movement we shall describe has been continuous; before that date it was sporadic. When the Metropolitan Parliamentary Reform Association came into being in 1842, it published an *Address* in which 1776 was stated to be the date of the new birth. " The first attempt," it said, " free from all party bias, to induce the people to concur in efforts to obtain a radical reform of the Commons House of Parlia-

11

ment, was made by the late Major John Cartwright in the year 1776, in a pamphlet entitled *Take your Choice.*"[1]   Although students of Major Cartwright's *Life and Letters* will find a letter addressed to him by Lord Stanhope[2] (the third Earl, the scientist and inventor with the revolutionary sympathies), claiming that the first writing published in support of parliamentary reform was by himself, in 1774, we may nevertheless neglect his claim.   The succession does not date from him, a mere voice in the wilderness.[3]

A slight glance at the state of thought during 1776 may be helpful.   Voltaire and Rousseau were in the ascendant.   Adam Smith published *The Wealth of Nations*, and a part of Gibbon's *Decline and Fall of the Roman Empire* had appeared.   The Declaration of Independence was another event of the year. North's Ministry was in power.   Dr. Johnson still dogmatized his listeners out of breath.   Louis XVI had but just ascended the French throne, and Turgot had not yet lost his control of the French finances.   Neither William Godwin nor Mary Wollstonecraft had published anything.   John Wilkes had triumphed, and, after having been Lord Mayor of London, had without opposition just succeeded in regaining his seat as member for Middlesex.   The spirit of religious toleration had made itself felt within the Houses of Parliament ; the Roman Catholic Relief Act was in sight.   Bentham had published his *Fragment on Government*, and Cartwright issued the tract we have already mentioned.

This tract appears to have succeeded in making a certain impression, for in 1777 we have a revised and enlarged second edition, bearing the title *The Legislative Rights of the Commonalty Vindicated : or, Take your Choice !* which contains Cartwright's replies to some arguments adduced by opponents. That the publication was read at all is only to be accounted for on the ground that it fell in with prevalent opinion, for,

---

[1] Place MSS. 27,810 contains copies of this *Address*.

[2] Edited by his niece, Miss F. D. Cartwright   Vol. I, p. 82.

[3] It should be noted that in April, 1776, a few months before the publication of Cartwright's tract, Wilkes moved a reform resolution in the House of Commons : this was negatived without a division.

in common with all Cartwright's works, it is intolerably dull,
and very long-winded. But the train had been laid.

Cartwright lived to become a figurehead among the Radical
reformers by sheer weight of years (he died in 1824, aged eighty-
four), and by dint of saying the same thing for just under
fifty years. His mind possessed a certain originality, which,
however, expended itself almost invariably upon trifling and
inessential matters. He used to invent great schemes of
national defence, based upon his ideas of what existed in
the Golden Age, which in his belief was somewhere about the
reign of King Alfred. He designed a new form of pike to
take the place of bayonets—also based, of course, on Anglo-
Saxon examples—and later spent some considerable energy
in inducing the Greeks to use it in their struggles against the
Turks. Francis Place refers to him as " the old gentleman."[1]
He appears to have been universally loved by the younger
generation of Radicals, for the old bore possessed a childlike
simplicity that was not the mere accompaniment of second
childhood. His *Take your Choice* put the case directly for
universal suffrage and annual parliaments—two points which
remained in the forefront of the Radical programmes until
the end of the Chartist movement. The term " universal
suffrage," the most common of all the shibboleths of this
long agitation, had not then attained to its present meaning ;
it simply meant manhood suffrage. It was never the intention
of the early Radicals to allow women to be participants in
the extended franchise. When the Dean of Gloucester (Josiah
Tucker) criticized *Take your Choice* on the ground that if all
men were to be given a vote, soon all the women would demand
their enfranchisement, Cartwright angrily replied in the second
edition : " For want of *arguments* against an equality of representation, some authors have been driven to the sad expedient
of attempting to be *witty* on the subject. A dignitary of our
Church . . . has been pleased to advance that, provided this
equality be due to men, it must equally appertain to the
women . . . etc."[2] We need not proceed to quote the now

[1] Wallas, *Life of Francis Place*, p. 63.
[2] *The Legislative Rights of the Commonalty Vindicated*, p. 45.

familiar argument that Scripture demands that the husband should be the head of the family. In common with certain anti-Suffragists of our own day, Cartwright preserves a discreet silence as to the spinsters and widows whom Scripture does not appear to have inhibited from voting.

During the next few years reform ideas spread with great rapidity, especially in Middlesex and Yorkshire. Inside the House of Commons, Burke was labouring at schemes to abolish sinecures and corruption, but without success. Delegate meetings were held in many towns, and " conventions " met at the Thatched House Tavern and the St. Alban's Coffee House, both in St. James's Street. Pitt, Burke, and Sheridan were among the Members of Parliament who attended these meetings. Petitions to Parliament began to pour in, and the whole existing system of representation was subjected to raking criticism. A majority of the House of Commons was returned by only 11,000 electors.[1] Sir Philip Francis, in a letter to his sister, describes his election for Appleby in this ludicrous strain :[2] " I was unanimously elected by one elector to represent this ancient borough in Parliament . . . there was no other Candidate, no Opposition, no Poll demanded, Scrutiny or Petition. So I had nothing to do but to thank the said Elector for the Unanimous Voice with which I was chosen. . . . On Friday morning I shall quit this triumphant scene with flying colours and a noble determination not to see it again in less than seven years . . . my Elector intends to hang himself in November, and then I shall elect myself : and that will do as well." Where the electorate was more numerous and less unanimous, bribery used to take place upon a most expensive scale. The reformers had not to seek far for ammunition, but the enemy's defences were strong.

At a meeting held in Westminster at the beginning of 1780, a committee was appointed to draw up a programme for the reformers. This formulated the following demands, which remained the basis of the Radical agitation for many years :

[1] *Wyvill Papers*, Vol. III, App. 195.
[2] *Francis Letters*, II, 493 ; quoted by G. S. Veitch in *The Genesis of Parliamentary Reform*, p. 9.

(1) Annual Parliaments, (2) Universal Suffrage, (3) Voting by Ballot, (4) Equal Polling Districts, (5) No Money Qualifications for Members, (6) Payment of Members for their Attendance. " At this time there was no political public, and the active friends of Parliamentary Reform consisted of noblemen, gentlemen, and a few tradesmen. . . . Their proceedings were neither adapted for, nor were they addressed to the working people, who, at that time, would not have attended to them."[1] The Radical movement was essentially a middle-class movement, and, although the working class was not excluded to the extent indicated by our last quotation, when victory was at last achieved, it was the middle class that received the greater part of the satisfaction.

Many years before the events of 1780, a Bill of Rights Society had been formed for the purpose of helping Wilkes with money, and for the propagation of his opinions. This still existed ; so also did the Constitutional Society, which had seceded from it. This last combined the functions of a study circle, a dining club, and a charitable body. Some of the more advanced members of the latter body again broke away and formed the " Society for Promoting Constitutional Information " ; its members were to be chosen by ballot, each person on becoming a member was to subscribe not less than one guinea, but as much more as he pleased, and five guineas each per annum. A considerable number of tracts were published, recommending Annual Parliaments, Universal Suffrage, and Voting by Ballot.[2] The first President[3] appears to have been Sir Cecil Wray, M.P. for East Retford from 1768–80, who had wrested the representation of that borough, on the nomination of the Bill of Rights Society, from the Duke of Newcastle and the corporation. This new Society was, as we may gather from the subscription, scarcely proletarian either in its membership or its aspirations. R. B. Sheridan was one of the original members, as were a large number of Whig M.P.'s. In its first existence, from 1780

---

[1] *Address of the Metropolitan Parliamentary Reform Association.*

[2] Place MSS. 27,808.

[3] According to Place MSS. 27,810, fo. 142, the Duke of Richmond was the first President.

to 1783, the Society did little more than to bear witness to the prevalence of a sentiment, and three years after its formation it was shut down by the North-Fox coalition. But the French Revolution stimulated the dead bones into an avatar in 1791, when more was heard of it. This Society was but one of the outward and visible signs of a movement, not yet sufficiently conscious of its own objects to be democratic, and not yet completely divorced from the Tory creed of the necessity of class subordination. But in Parliament matters were moving in a manner all the more remarkable when the times are considered. The anti-Catholic riots of 1780, under the leadership of the mentally defective Lord George Gordon, were an anticipation, on a large scale, of Mafeking night. After a week's experience of entirely unprecedented mob law, the reformers in Parliament found their faith unshaken. On the first day of serious rioting, Friday, June 2, the Duke of Richmond was actually bringing in a motion in the House of Lords in support of universal suffrage and annual parliaments. " But no serious discussion was possible. Pale, bruised, and agitated, with their wigs torn off, their hair dishevelled, their clothes torn and bespattered with mud, the peers of England sat listening to the frantic yells of the multitude who already thronged the lobbies."[1] So Lecky describes the scene. But no revolution was at hand. Richmond's motion was negatived without ostentation, the riots died out, and England was herself again. The next positive advance of the reform movement took place in 1782, and carried things to a point which was not passed for almost fifty years.

On March 27 of that year, Edmund Burke became Paymaster-General in the Rockingham Ministry, and promptly introduced measures to abolish sinecures, to reduce the Pensions List, and to guard against the possibility of corruption. At the moment it seemed necessary to both Lords and Commons to keep the Rockingham Ministry alive at all costs. Nothing therefore was done to impede the progress of the Bill in which these reforms were embodied, and it passed both Houses with

[1] W. E. H. Lecky, *A History of England in the Eighteenth Century*, Vol. IV, p. 311.

flying colours to the accompaniment of scarcely muffled exe-
crations.   A few weeks afterwards,[1] Pitt[2] introduced an important resolution in a powerful speech : " That a committee be
appointed to inquire into the present state of representation
of the Commons of Great Britain in Parliament, to report
the same to the House, and likewise which steps in their opinion
it may be proper for Parliament to take concerning the same."
The extent to which the myth of a perfect constitution had
gripped the imagination of all politicians is nowhere better
illustrated than in the reports of the debate which followed
this resolution.   Proposals of reform were, as it were, apologized for ; they were, it was strenuously maintained, not incompatible with the myth.   Pitt himself kotowed before
the fetish, declaring that " he was afraid that the reverence
and the enthusiasm which Englishmen entertained for the
constitution would, if not suddenly prevented, be the means
of destroying it ; for such was their enthusiasm, that they
would not even remove its defects, for fear of touching its
beauty."   In the course of the debate the defenders of the
status quo were easily out-talked, but the myth won on a
division.   For the resolution, 141 voted ; against, 161.   This
majority of only twenty votes was not diminished till 1831.
Between 1782 and 1785, Pitt several times brought up the
subject, but in vain.   His acceptance of the Premiership in
1783 made him fearful of rebuffs, and, a few years later, his
views on democracy and reform came to be overshadowed by
the fear of revolution.

In July, 1782, the Society for Constitutional Information
addressed an appeal " to the people of Great Britain of all
denominations, but particularly to those who subsist by honest
industry."   This would appear to be the first invitation to
the wage-earning classes to participate in the reform movement.   About this date we find a large number of county
associations had sprung up, especially in Yorkshire.   Here an
indefatigable clergyman, one Christopher Wyvill, was organizing middle-class opinion with remarkable success.   Although

[1] *Parliamentary History*, May 7, 1782.
[2] He had only become an M.P. the previous year.

his cloth prevented him from entering Parliament at any time, he took a prominent part in the politics of Yorkshire, where he owned considerable property, and as early as 1779 he became Secretary of the Yorkshire Association, a body with reformist objects. He then began, by correspondence and personal effort, to secure the formation of no less than twenty-five county associations. The six volumes of Political Papers, chiefly respecting the Attempt of the County of York, and other Considerable Districts, commenced in 1779, and continued during several subsequent years, to effect a Reformation of the Parliament of Great Britain, collected by the Rev. Christopher Wyvill, Chairman of the late Committee of Association of the County of York, contain evidence of a remarkable mass of activities. The associated counties, however, were far from Radical in their demands. Yorkshire in 1781 merely required (1) support of the " economical Petition " (carried in 1782 by Burke), (2) the addition of at least one hundred county members, (3) duration of Parliament not to exceed three years. Wyvill gives a list of the associations which more or less agreed with these objects ;[1] they number seventeen. Here, too, Demos does not appear to have been welcomed. The American War had undoubtedly given these bodies a great stimulus. Wyvill could triumphantly and frequently point to the fact that while the county representatives approved of the war, the county associations did not. Now, however, that the American War was ended, that economical reform was a fact, and that Pitt was in a position of responsibility, Wyvill suddenly found himself deserted by his former associates and supporters. The landed interest—or that portion of it that had once helped him—crumbled away. The county associations went to pieces.

The year 1788, the centenary of the Revolution, saw a revival of sorts. But the revival was less in the nature of a national movement than of a celebration. Such political impetus as the reform movement gathered was materialized ignobly into dining clubs. A few of the reformers—Cartwright, for example—were in deadly earnest, but to large numbers reform

[1] Wyvill, *Political Papers*, Vol. I, pp. 381–383.

was merely a toast.   The following year saw the outbreak of
the French Revolution.   Only a few observers understood
that the National Assembly was not to be the end ; the majority
of Whigs welcomed the new development, while few, Whigs
and Tories, actually disapproved.   " Cautious and reflecting
politicians like Grenville, the Secretary for Foreign Affairs—
afterwards, indeed, to be swept along unresisting in the race
of political reaction—looked on with the placid content of
some petty tradesman who sees his rival's premises destroyed
by fire ; and his view was typical of the prevailing orthodoxy."[1]
The first Englishman to adopt the view which afterwards
became orthodox—detestation of the Revolution—was Edmund
Burke.   He could not sympathise with those who believed
with Fox that the taking of the Bastille was " the greatest
and the best event that ever happened in the world," and
broke his friendship with Fox on account of the difference of
opinion.   Alarmed at the spread of Radical societies in this
country with avowedly revolutionary sympathies, Burke
published, in November, 1790, his *Reflections on the Revolution
in France*.   This was, despite its name, largely a glorification
of the British *status quo*, alleging a perfect constitution, a wise
distribution (*i.e.* concentration) of property and power, and a
necessary and beneficent Church in close combination with
the sovereign power.   The book evoked an extraordinary
outburst of applause and brickbats.   In the dispatch of the
latter a number of those who were to give the Radical and,
later, the Chartist movements their ideas first emerged into
publicity.

An American writer [2] has counted up no less than thirty-
eight replies to Burke's *Reflections*.   The first in the field was
Mary Wollstonecraft, whose *Vindication of the Rights of Man*
even to-day reads freshly.   On sheer points of reasoning, of
keenness of assault, of clear-cut statement of contending principles, the statesman is unmistakably second to the schoolmis-
tress.   Only a few months later she followed up her attack
on the fastnesses of the conservative intellect by what must

[1] G. S. Veitch, *The Genesis of Parliamentary Reform*, p. 112.
[2] Walter Phelps Hall, *British Radicalism*, 1791–1797, p. 75.

be regarded (considering its time) as one of the most daring political essays ever penned. *A Vindication of the Rights of Woman* remains a standard textbook of feminism to this day. It contains the first plea—left undeveloped, however—for the political enfranchisement of women, and much other matter accurately calculated to shock.

The Rights of Man, by Thomas Paine, published in 1791, had an enormous and immediate influence. This was far less revolutionary than Mary Wollstonecraft's reply, and is to-day frankly out of date. But its racy style, its positive proposals for amending the Poor Law and reducing taxation, made the book extraordinarily popular. Paine received no less than £1,000 in royalties from the first part, which he handed over to the Constitutional Society for the further dissemination of the book. The second part (1792) was equally successful. " In the end it was adopted by the Constitutional Society as a kind of democratic Magna Charta, and sent by them to all the Corresponding Societies in England, France, and Scotland."[1] Before Paine fled for France in September, 1792, he had collected round himself a small circle of Radicals who were greatly to influence the events of the coming years. Godwin (who became Mary Wollstonecraft's husband), Horne Tooke, Holcroft (the dramatist), William Blake, John Frost, Romney, and Lord Edward Fitzgerald were among his close friends.

Side by side with this development of Radical theory, societies had been springing up to carry the new doctrines into effect. About this time we begin to notice the first signs of the working-class Radical, although the movement remained almost completely in middle-class hands. On April 11, 1792, a new body was formed, calling itself The Friends of the People, associated for the Purpose of Obtaining a Parliamentary Reform.[2] Erksine, the barrister who made so brilliant a reputation by his defence of Horne Tooke a few years later, was perhaps the most important promoter of the new society. This too was bourgeois—with a vengeance. Election was by ballot, and the annual subscription 2½ guineas. It had a

---

[1] C. R. B. Kent, *The English Radicals*, p. III.
[2] Place MSS. 27,808.

general declaration, which was signed on admission to membership. " First, to restore the Freedom of Election and a more equal representation of the people in Parliament. Second, to secure to the people a more equal and more frequent exercise of their right of electing their Representatives." It is interesting to note that the Friends of the People disclaimed all connexion with the Society for Constitutional Information, although their membership was largely duplicate. This Society was to a very large extent merely a pious Whig body, and its members, though distinguished, were never unduly strenuous. The indefatigable Major Cartwright was, as ever, one of the founders. A mildly reformist petition to the House of Commons presented by this society in 1795, found only forty-two supporters.[1]

The society of which most was heard during this period was the London Corresponding Society.[2] This differed essentially from all the bodies of which we have been speaking. Its aims were similar, but its membership was largely plebeian. The subscription was one penny a week. The first secretary was Thomas Hardy, an ex-shoemaker. The L.C.S. came out into the open about the beginning of 1793. Branches sprang into existence all over the country. The greater part of Hardy's work consisted of correspondence with these local societies. Leaflets were scattered broadcast. The Journal of the L.C.S. and Hardy's incomplete manuscript history of it are in the Place MSS. at the British Museum. They are interesting reading, and are written with a flow of optimism for which we to-day cannot account. The conquest of England seemed easy to those pioneers. The trumpets had but to be blown, and the walls of Jericho would collapse, surely enough. " Clergy and courtiers are not so numerous as they appear," Hardy cheerfully remarks in a personal letter to a faint-hearted

---

[1] *The Wyvill Papers*, Vol. III, Appendix, pp. 132–292, contains the complete history of the Friends of the People.

[2] Its original name, as recorded in its first minute book was The Corresponding Society of the unrepresented part of the People of Great Britain. Place MSS. 27,811, fo. 2.

editor.[1]   The reformers of the old school, Major Cartwright for example, had on the whole a clear notion of what reform would mean. But not so the new enthusiasts. The London Corresponding Society's Addresses and Resolutions (1794) contains a large instalment of that enticing utopianism which, in the long run, was to destroy the Chartist movement. " Numerous as our grievances are, reform one alone and the others will disappear. What we must have is—

> An Honest Parliament,
> An Annual Parliament,
> A Parliament where each individual will have his repre-
> sentative.

Soon then we shall see our liberties restored, the press free, the laws simplified, judges unbiassed, juries independent, needless places and pensions retrenched, immoderate salaries reduced, the public better served, and the necessaries of life more within the reach of the poor."[2]   This, as we shall see, was the type of thing which the movement of fifty years ahead suffered from, more, perhaps, than any other cause. The Radicals accepted the constitutional myth so sedulously cherished by Burke and Blackstone, and dressed it up in clothes of their own fashioning. " Return to us the true English constitution," they cried, " and the Golden Age will be with us again."

Events altered their course when, after the execution of Louis XVI, war broke out between England and France, on February 1, 1793. Many of the Corresponding Societies had carried their sympathy with the French Revolution farther than was to the taste of the authorities. They had corresponded with French societies ; their principal source of inspiration, the author of *The Rights of Man*, had had French citizenship conferred upon him, and had actually been elected a member of the Convention. The Whig reformers, be it noted, had gradually withdrawn their sympathy from the

[1] Place MSS. 27,814, fo. 187.
[2] P. 15.

Revolutionary cause, until the execution of Louis changed them to active opponents. But the working-class members of the L.C.S., numbering certainly not less than 10,000,[1] had cut themselves adrift from Whig opinion. Numbers of societies sprang up in London and the provinces, willing and anxious to make trouble. Subscriptions were collected for the Jacobin army, and addresses of congratulation poured in upon the Convention.[2] The Government began to take action.

On May 21, 1792, a royal proclamation [3] had already been issued against " seditious practices," " all proceedings tending to produce riots and tumults," and " seditious writings,' [4] but no deliberate efforts at repression were made for over a year. In the meantime the movement among the working class spread, and, as it grew, it acquired a distinct individuality, which, allied with its Jacobin sympathies, caused in the end the L.C.S. to be disowned by the Friends of the People. In December, 1793, the first severe blow was struck. A " British Convention " was held in Edinburgh, attended by a hundred and fifty-three delegates, two of whom, Margarot and Gerrald, had been sent to represent the L.C.S. The proceedings adopted a French phraseology, delegates addressed each other as Citizen, and matters were conducted with a solemnity beside which a modern Labour Party Congress assumes an almost frivolous aspect. But " Convention " was now a word that stank in official noses. Margarot, Gerrald, and three Scotsmen (Muir, Palmer and Skirving) were arrested and tried for sedition. The unlucky five were most unfairly treated ; [4] and were sentenced to transportation to Botany Bay for fourteen years, with the exception of Palmer, whose sentence was seven years. But only Margarot, the least reputable of them all, survived the sentence and returned to his own country. It seems fairly certain, from the line taken by the prosecution, that the Government of the day had overestimated the quantity of revolutionary sentiment, and sincerely believed that it

---

[1] Hardy somewhere asserts that there were 20,000 members.
[2] G. S. Veitch, *Genesis of Parliamentary Reform*, p. 230.
[3] *Annual Register*, 1792, Part 2, p. 192.
[4] For a full report of the case, see *State Trials*, Vol. XXIII.

might overflow and plunge the nation into confusion.   Gerrald
had published a pamphlet in 1793,[1] in which he had suggested
the formation of a legislative assembly, on the lines of the
French Convention.   But the Government, after all, is not
greatly to be blamed for taking the Radicals as seriously as
they took themselves.   A few months later Pitt introduced a
Bill to suspend the Habeas Corpus Act.   This passed through
both Houses with large majorities.   It is specially to be noted
that in the speech introducing the Bill, Pitt referred at great
length to the London Corresponding Society, for whose particular benefit the measure was intended.   He made the extraordinary statement that the Society wished to upset law and
order, property and religion, and generally indicated a belief
in the extreme gravity of the situation.

A few days before the introduction of this Bill, thirteen
members of the London Corresponding Society had been
arrested in London on a charge of high treason.   Only three
were eventually brought to trial.   These were Thomas Hardy,
Horne Tooke, and John Thelwall.   The three were tried separately and all enjoyed the defence of the brilliant Erskine.
Hardy's case came first—the report of it covers 1,208 pages
of *State Trials*.   Erskine's cross-examination of some of the
witnesses for the prosecution practically settled the case.
They were forced to admit to such a depth of their own rascality that the jury had no alternative but to return a verdict of
" not guilty."   The case of Horne Tooke was far more piquant,
and less voluminous.   This man was a philologist on the one
hand, and a champion of fair play on the other, and his life
appears to have been evenly divided between these two pursuits.   He entered upon a stormy political career by embracing
the cause of Wilkes thirty years previous to the trial of which
we are speaking.   He had founded the Constitutional Society
in 1771, to uphold the rights of Wilkes and the American colo-
nists.   He had served two sentences of imprisonment in
connexion with his political activities.   Now, in the dock,
after Erskine had once more rent to pieces the characters of
some of the witnesses for the prosecution, Tooke asked the

[1] *A Convention the Only Means of Saving Us from Ruin.*

embarrassed Prime Minister, cited as a witness, " whether or
no he had been present, with the prisoner himself, at a meeting
at the Thatched House Tavern in 1780, which was a ' Convention of delegates from great towns and counties of England,
. . . with the object of animating the people to meet in districts and petition Parliament for a reform.' Pitt awkwardly
responded to his shrewd questioner that ' he had no distinct
recollection of the composition of the meeting.' "[1] And Tooke
was found " not guilty."

Lastly came the trial of Thelwall. This man was a type
altogether different from either Hardy or Tooke, although the
latter had so far recognized his abilities as to have offered his
help to Thelwall on several occasions. He became a peripatetic lecturer who preached the extremest Radicalism, and
delighted in clothing his sentiments in parables. He thus
secured the applause of audiences keenly alert for the concealed
sting, while the police officers—always in attendance at his
lectures—listened in vain for an indisputably seditious phrase.
He had the gifts of the mob-orator to an altogether exceptional
extent. In writing to his wife he says : " Two lectures in
particular . . . have shaken the pillars of corruption till every
stone of the rotten edifice trembled. Every sentence darted
from breast to breast with electric contagion, and the very
aristocrats themselves—numbers of whom throng to hear me
—were frequently compelled by irresistible impulse to join in
the acclamations, however they disliked the doctrine."[2] He
had gone farther than his fellow-prisoners. His sentiments
may have been the same as theirs, but his allusions—not in
the best of taste—to George III and the desirability of his
removal from this earth were entirely his own. But the
witnesses for the prosecution had been discredited, Erskine
was as convincing as before, and, for the third time, the jury
returned a verdict of " not guilty." The incendiary powers of
Thelwall thus received an enormous advertisement, of which
he fully availed himself for three or four years. He then
dropped politics and taught elocution.

[1] C. Cestre, *John Thelwall*, p. 109.
[2] *Life of John Thelwall*, 1837, p. 367.

The effect of these trials was, in the first place, to direct the attention of the country to the Radical movement. The London Corresponding Society enjoyed an unprecedented accession of members, Francis Place amongst them. In the second place, the movement was made to appear as supplying the only possible escape from the apparent economic impasse into which the revolutionary war had already led the country. The year 1795 was one of the most trying in the history of England. It was during this year that the extraordinary distress among agricultural labourers found a solution that was no solution in the " Speenhamland Act of Parliament," which brought almost the whole population of the South of England on the rates within the next thirty years.   Enclosures were also beginning their dislocation of village life.   High prices of food prevailed [1]—the invariable concomitant of working-class unrest.   When George III went to the House of Lords to open Parliament on October 29, he was hooted the whole way from Buckingham House and back again.   The mob was so dense as actually to impede the progress of the state coach.   The cries raised were, " Bread !   Peace ! " and one man was taken up for shouting, " No King." [2]   The struggle between the Government and the Radicals was distinctly embittered as a result of these events. [3]   The fight on the Radical side was concentrated on the London Corresponding Society, for the Friends of the People evaporated in 1795, and the Society for Constitutional Information melted away rather than face prosecution.   A few great meetings were held by the L.C.S., which insisted on demonstrating its growing vitality.   Pitt passed the " Two Acts," which extended the definition of treasonable practices, and placed obstacles in the way of public meetings.   There is no doubt that he, and the Government generally, had been really frightened by what appeared to them to be preparations

[1] According to the *Annual Register* for 1795, prices had been rising steadily during the preceding ten years, and were now at a record.

[2] *Annual Register*, 1795, p. 38.

[3] See *William Pitt and the Great War*, by Dr. Holland Rose, pp. 282–285.

for an armed rising. The L.C.S, adroitly reconstituted itself
to escape the penalties prescribed by the new Acts. A comic
interlude is supplied by the Reeves affair—the one event of
1795 at which the reformers could afford to laugh. John
Reeves was a worthy civil servant who founded and became
chairman of a comic opera Association for preserving Liberty
and Property against Levellers and Republicans. This was
all very well, but Reeves allowed his enthusiasm to make him
plus royaliste que le roi. He published an anonymous pamphlet,
Thoughts on the English Government, which was so *royaliste*
as to suggest the superfluousness of Parliament, all authority
resting with the King. The House of Commons regarded this
as a breach of privilege, and, praying in an undertone for
deliverance from its friends, caused Reeves to be tried for
libel. He was not convicted, however ; the jury applauded
his motive and forgave his indiscretion. But the whole case
must have been an immense source of delight to the Radicals.[1]

The events of the year led the L.C.S. to issue, on November 23,
*An Explicit Declaration of the Principles and Views of the
London Corresponding Society.*[2] This document is of special
interest, as showing both the theoretical position of the Radicals
and the direction into which persecution was already beginning
to force the movement. "In their ideas of equality, they
have never included (nor, till the associations of alarmists
broached the frantic notion, could they ever have conceived
so wild and detestable a sentiment could have entered the
brain of man) the equalization of property, or the invasion
of personal rights and possessions. This levelling system they
know, and all rational men must immediately perceive, to
be equally unjust and impracticable." Having thus obliquely
dealt with Reeves, the manifesto proceeds : " Peaceful reform,
and not tumultuary revolt, is their object ; and they trust
to the good sense and candour of the nation that something
more than vague accusations and *interested calumny* will be
expected to discredit their protestation that *They abhor alike*

---

[1] The Reeves affair was debated in the Commons from November 23
to December 15.

[2] Place MSS. 27,815.

the FANATICAL ENTHUSIASM *that would plunge into a sea of anarchy in quest of speculative theories, and the Villainous Hypocrisy that would destroy the very essence of existing institutions, under pretence of preserving them from destruction ! ! !*" Here the existence of "Fanatical Enthusiasm" is at any rate admitted. But, such as it was, it was certainly not fomented by the Committee of the L.C.S. In 1796, their principal action was the sending out of two missionaries to address meetings (limited now by Pitt's "Two Acts" to audiences not exceeding forty-nine) up and down the country. John Gale Jones and John Binns both did much this year to strengthen the provincial Corresponding Societies; both men were arrested in Birmingham, but when, after a long delay, they were brought to trial, one was acquitted and the Court released the other after he had been found guilty. This year and the next efforts appear to have been made by the L.C.S. to obtain the sympathy of the army and navy. But the evidence is inconclusive; it is tolerably certain that both services were growing heartily sick of the war, and were consequently becoming disaffected, especially in Scotland. It also appears from recent research that the naval mutinies of 1797, off Spithead and the Nore, were spontaneous; and not, as was believed, encouraged by the L.C.S. But no unqualified assertion is possible. The Government about this time began to discover "plots." We cannot take the evidence in support of their existence very seriously. Pikes and battle-axes were found in the houses of suspected persons, and were regarded as proof positive of preparations for an attempt at armed insurrection. The conquest of Britain with a handful of battle-axes may be dismissed as a notion that would appeal to a hero of a novel by Mr. G. K. Chesterton, rather than to any conspirator in possession of his senses. But, little by little, the London Corresponding Society was beaten down. In 1797 a number of its more thoughtful members left it in protest against the Committee's decision to hold meetings in defiance of the law.[1] The secretarial work was conducted incapably. Funds were low. On April 19, 1798, the Committee—or

[1] Place MSS. 27,808 and 27,815.

what remained of it—was arrested *en masse,* and the Society may be said to have come to its end. Not until 1801 were the prisoners released. By that time O'Coigley, an Irish priest, who had attempted to reanimate the dead bones of the Society, had been hanged for treason, and the L.C.S. was all but forgotten. " The close of the eighteenth century marks an epoch in the history of the Radicals. They were then at their nadir of depression."[1] The Combination Acts of 1799, amended in 1800, were further blows struck at political organization in general. Although the Combination Acts were intended to suppress trade unions and working-class associations in particular, yet in general they extended to all combinations whatsoever. The intention, however, was revealed in the administration of the Acts. During the whole epoch of repression, whilst thousands of journeymen suffered for the crime of combination, there is absolutely no case on record in which an employer was punished for the same offence."[2]

With the turn of the century the whole movement changes. Francis Place, the greatest organizer English democracy has ever known, had retired from public life after the closing up of the London Corresponding Society. He did not emerge from his tailor's shop in Charing Cross at all between 1800 and 1805, but stuck to his business and built up that material security which was later to enable him to give up his whole energies to the movement. Major Cartwright, almost alone of the first radical generation, kept the old flag flying. He was now over sixty years of age, and as active and as hopeful as ever. But his propaganda, as in former years, was confined to the upper and middle classes. His niece illustrates his activities and the responses they earned. " In the month of October (1805) Major Cartwright wrote to the Dukes of Norfolk, Northumberland, Bedford, to Lord Dundas, to the Earls of St. Vincent and Stanhope, to Messrs. Grey, Fox, etc., etc., urging the necessity of calling another meeting of the county of Middlesex ![3] From most of these distinguished

---

[1] C. B. R. Kent, *The English Radicals,* p. 157.
[2] Sidney and Beatrice Webb, *History of Trade Unionism,* p. 64.
[3] I.e., the freeholders of the county.

persons he received very flattering replies, but they seemed generally to have adopted an opinion that it was not the time to agitate the question, and Mr. Fox in particular observed, that ' to stir it at that time would not only be highly prejudicial to the interests of reform itself, but to every other measure that could be taken for the general good, in this critical and disastrous state of public affairs.' "   Then follows the pathetic comment, " It is a little remarkable, that during so long a life as that of Major Cartwright, he never, in the opinion of some persons, found out the happy moment for agitating a question which they acknowledged to be of the highest importance, and that whenever he proposed any public measure, the country should be either in a state too apathetic and prosperous, or else too critical and disastrous." [1]

A figure curiously characteristic of these disheartening times is that of Thomas Spence (1750–1814). This man was the author of a scheme of land nationalization and social reform, the diffusion and acceptance of which, in view of its crudeness, is a valuable illustration of that strange combination of mental receptivity and uncritical outlook that was the bane of so many of the Radical reformers.   Spence wished the inhabitants of each parish to be a corporation in whom the land should be vested, while his scheme of social reform embraced a five-day week.   About 1780 he came to London from his native New-castle and opened a bookstall, at which, however, the principal commodity sold was saloop.   This appears to have been a sassafras tea, considered a sovereign remedy for drunkenness. The books sold were frequently " seditious," and Spence was imprisoned for a few months in 1794, and for a year in 1801. It is curious to note that Spence invented a simplified spelling system, on phonetic principles.   But as he had a Newcastle accent, the scheme was promptly disqualified.[2]   Two years

---

[1] *Life of Major Cartwright*, p. 327.

[2] Attempting to improve the English language appears to have been the recognized hobby of the early Radicals.   Thelwall tried to write poetry without the use of sibilants ; Horne Tooke was, of course, a philologist of some distinction and Burdett was his pupil.   Cobbett wrote an *English Grammar*, etc.

after his death, evidence as to the widespread currency of his views was furnished by the formation of the Society of Spencean Philanthropists, which had several branches in London. The period was one of inquiry, and in the country of the blind, the one-eyed are leaders.

A far more exhilarating personality is that of William Cobbett (1762–1835), who returned to England from America in 1800, preceded by a strong Tory reputation. The same year he started *The Porcupine*, a daily paper with anti-republican, anti-Gallican, and anti-reform politics. The views expressed in the paper were extreme ; it stood practically alone among the opposition periodicals in deriding the Peace of Amiens, which gave the country a moment's breathing-space. For which reason Cobbett's house was mobbed, and publication was suspended. When resumed the paper soon had to be dropped. " He who has been the proprietor of a daily paper for only one month wants no Romish priest to describe to him the torments of purgatory,"[1] said Cobbett, whose talent for locating wasps' nests was not compensated by any power of destroying them. Then, curiously enough, the views of this sturdy bull-like publicist began to undergo a change. From 1802 to 1835 he edited the *Political Register*, which, always independent, veered gradually from an almost entirely negative to an advanced reformist standpoint. After 1806, Cobbett is perhaps the most influential exponent of the popular demand.

Between 1800 and 1806 the reform movement, with the exceptions we have named, was all but inarticulate. Among the people the coercive measures of Pitt's Government had suppressed the outward signs of Radicalism. Industrial conditions were such as to leave little room for hope in the minds of the most ardent reformers. The price of provisions had doubled between 1783 and 1803, and the poor rates had more than doubled within the same period.[2] Every now and again the police were alarmed at the possible consequences of a popular demonstration against high prices ; the French

[1] Quoted in *William Cobbett, a Biography*. By Edward Smith. Vol. I, p. 278.
[2] Wm. Smart, *Economic Annals of the Nineteenth Century*, pp. 94, 95.

Revolution was still recent enough to make any popular outbreak appear an embryonic national catastrophe. On December 3, 1800, a royal proclamation exhorted the public to exercise the utmost care in the use and consumption of grain of all kinds. At the end of 1802, the Despard conspiracy, with its chimerical projects for seizing the reins of government, showed the extent of the terror that was beginning to brood over the country. Not until the Napoleonic spectre had been finally disposed of did the reform movement find the necessary psychological atmosphere for a successful fruition. The period provides a unique quantity of material to the student of psychology who would attempt an estimate of the dependence of belief upon terror, for there is no doubt that many of the most fundamental tenets of the ruling class underwent an essential transformation by the fear of a revolution. The accentuated cleavage between the ruling and the ruled classes has been observed and described [1] But perhaps the most significant fact illustrating the new relationship is that the ancient virtue of working-class thrift was discouraged in many quarters, lest more power be added to the labourers.[2]

During such a period, where all was incoherence, there is no simple series of finger-posts to guide the direction taken by the reform movement. Certain general tendencies are all that can be noted ; there is little to be gained by drawing a chart of the sporadic outbreaks that may or may not have been connected with the reform agitation. The first fact that is to be borne in mind is that the burden of life was pressing with ever-growing intensity upon the working classes.[3] This was the cause of a restlessness that, inchoate and at first undirected, found expression at the start in a long series of riots, and later in the reform movement. The internal history of England, from 1795 to 1832, is virtually a long tale of riots, the objects of which were diffused in the beginning among a whole array of grievances, and later came to be concentrated

[1] Especially well in *The Village Labourer* 1776–1832, by J. L. and Barbara Hammond.

[2] B. Kirkman Gray, *A History of English Philanthropy*, p. 256.

[3] In 1812 the price of wheat per quarter rose to £6 10s. and upwards.

upon parliamentary reform. The following quotation conveys an idea of the diversity of the irritants and the area of disturbance in 1815 and 1816 alone : " In London and Westminster riots ensued, and were continued for several days whilst the (Corn) Bill was discussed ; at Bridport, there were riots on account of the high price of bread ; at Bideford, there were similar disturbances to prevent the exportation of grain ; at Bury, by the unemployed, to destroy machinery ; at Ely, not suppressed without bloodshed ; at Newcastle-on-Tyne, by colliers and others ; at Glasgow, where blood was shed ; at Preston, by unemployed weavers ; at Nottingham, by Luddites, who destroyed thirty frames ; at Merthyr Tydvil, on a reduction of wages ; at Birmingham, by the unemployed ; and at Dundee, where, owing to the high price of meal, upwards of one hundred shops were plundered."[1] Elsewhere the enclosure movement [2] and municipal corruption [3] were also responsible for riots. It became a capital offence to preach reform to a soldier or to smash a frame. The cure for all these things, in the eyes of working-class leaders, was reform, and by degrees they managed to convert a large number of their followers. " Quoting scripture, we did in fact say, first obtain annual parliaments and universal suffrage, and ' all these things shall be added unto you.' "[4] Thus Bamford, who was at one time a sort of link between the middle-class body of reformers—Cobbett, Cartwright, Hunt, etc.—and the trades clubs, where annual parliaments and universal suffrage were discussed in an atmosphere of beer and cheap tobacco. Bamford (1788–1872) lived to be a patriarch of the labour movement, acquiring a prestige entirely unaccountable on any theory of deserts.

A chapter of the reform agitation that should not be overlooked is the peculiar series of election campaigns which took place in Westminster between 1807 and 1815. This enabled

---

[1] Samuel Bamford, *Passages in the Life of a Radical*, Vol. II, p. 11.

[2] J. L. and B. Hammond, *The Village Labourer*.

[3] S. and B. Webb, *English Local Government*, Vols. II and III. *The Manor and the Borough*.

[4] *Passages in the Life of a Radical*, Vol. II, p. 14.

Francis Place to make his reputation as an organizer of victory, by securing the return of Sir Francis Burdett for the constituency.   Burdett was a pugnacious Whig with much wealth[1] and high principles.[2]   He had to undergo a large number of prosecutions in the course of his long parliamentary career (1796–1844).   But it has rightly been said of him, that, after the repressive measures of the early years of Radicalism, it was he who restored the right of free speech.

A middle-class movement with working-class ramifications that was to achieve a great deal was the Hampden Club, which came into being on April 20, 1812.   British political movements, we may note, appear generally to select a tavern for their birthplaces.   The Thatched House Tavern fathered this one.   The first Hampden Club was brought into existence through the energies of the inexhaustible Major Cartwright, although, as his niece tells us, he left at once on hearing that certain influential persons were refraining from membership because he himself was a member.   The original papers of this Society show unmistakably that its prime object was purely to benefit the freeholding class.[3]   The original Rules and Regulations made one of the qualifications for membership £300 a year in land, or heirship to as much ; there were to be half-yearly dinners ; and the annual subscription was fixed at £2.   The statement of principles made the wonted reference to King Alfred.   The work of the Club consisted in organizing and financing missionary tours through the country, to get petitions sent to Parliament.   Cartwright, though not a member, also undertook distant journeys with the same purpose.   More popular Hampden Clubs were opened on the model of the original.

The *Annual Register* for 1816 is largely a list of riots.   The best known of these was the Spa Fields meeting on December 2,

---

[1] He had married Miss Coutts, whose name will be sufficient.

[2] See Graham Wallas, *Life of Francis Place*, chap. ii, " Westminster Politics."

[3] The British Museum contains a number of these papers in volume form, as presented by Thomas Cleary, the first secretary, to Joseph Hume in 1854.

noteworthy because it seems to have been the first deliberate
effort of the Whig reformers to obtain the support of the working classes.   It was addressed by Hunt,[1] Cartwright, and an
inflammatory doctor named Watson, and his son.   The military and the police assembled in large numbers, whereupon
the meeting dispersed into small gangs, which spent the night
in terrifying the City.[2]   Another such fiasco in the early part
of 1817 was followed by a second suspension of Habeas Corpus.
Incidentally the Seditious Meetings Act was hurried through
both Houses, and made all public meetings and most lectures
illegal.   This measure, introduced by Castlereagh, stiffened
up all the preceding legislation of repression, but, in the end,
overreached itself by its severity.   However, the danger of
being known to be a Radical became so great that Cobbett
promptly fled to America.   But when the Act came to be
put into operation, the patent vindictiveness of some of the
prosecutions, no less than the calibre of one of the accused,
resulted in a temporary reaction against the Government.[3]

A climax was reached in 1819.   During the early months of
this year numerous mass meetings were held all over the
country, especially in Lancashire and the Midlands.   The
crowds present were frequently very large ; one meeting near
Leeds is said to have been attended by 35,000 persons.   We
have the authority of the *Annual Register*—whose bias at this
time was distinctly Tory—for the somewhat striking statement,
in view of the line taken by the Government, that : " Not the
slightest breach of the peace occurred on any of these occasions,
for the leaders were strenuous in their exhortations to the
people to preserve an inoffensive demeanour."[4]   A meeting was
organized to take place at St. Peter's Fields, Manchester, on
August 16, with Hunt in the chair.   The magistrates decided
to prohibit the meeting, then, finding this impossible, to arrest
the speakers.   Large numbers of soldiers and special con-

[1] Late parliamentary candidate for Bristol ; later M.P. for Preston.
[2] *Annual Register*, 1816, p. 190.
[3] Lord Ellenborough, Lord Chief Justice, resigned in disgust at the
triple acquittal of Hone, who was tried for " seditious libel."
[4] *Annual Register*, 1819, p. 103.

stables were assembled, and made virtually to surround the place of meeting. No sooner had Hunt stepped to the front of the hustings than the military began to clear the square. Although it is improbable that bloodshed had been intended from the outset, yet the soldiers, as usual on such occasions, got out of control. Five or six lives were immediately lost, some thirty persons were seriously wounded, while at least forty others required medical assistance for their injuries. Hunt was arrested with some others ; Bamford, who had been present, was also taken up, a week later. After much delay Hunt was sentenced to two years' and Bamford to one year's imprisonment. The principal outcome of the " Manchester Massacre," or of " Peterloo," as the affair came to be called, was that reformers of all shades of opinion coalesced into an unanalysable conglomerate. Whig Radicals,[1] incipient Chartists, Socialists, Spenceans, and the most Utopian of dreamers were forced into association, from the sheer necessity of self-defence. To this day traces remain of the cohabitation of Socialist and Chartist. Adult suffrage, an invariable item of Socialist programmes, obviously proceeds from the time when franchise and freedom were held to be synonymous. In point of fact, it is fairly certain that Socialism would stand to gain less from the granting of adult suffrage than the other political parties.

About 1818 the woman suffrage movement appears to have first taken root. At a small reform meeting in Yorkshire, addressed by Bamford, the women present were invited, on his initiative, to take part in the vote on the resolution. The men present made no objection, and the women were much pleased with the suggestion. After this, the participation of women in votes, and even in discussions, became general.[2] Although Bentham, the " Grand Old Man " of Philosophic Radicalism, was a supporter of woman suffrage, Cobbett

---

[1] Strictly speaking, the term Radicals only came into general use about this time. See Harriet Martineau, *History of the Peace*, Vol. I, p. 292.

[2] Bamford, *Passages*, Vol. II, p. 141.

violently dissented.[1]   But the most startling development of
this side of the reform movement is that which the *Annual
Register* for 1819 describes, with bated breath, as follows :[2]
" An entirely novel and truly portentous circumstance was the
formation of a Female Reform Society at Blackburn, near
Manchester, from which circular letters were issued, inviting
the wives and daughters of workmen in different branches of
manufacture to form sister societies, for the purpose of co-
operating with the men, and of instilling into the minds of
their children ' a deep-rooted hatred of our tyrannical rulers.'
A deputation from this society attended the Blackburn reform
meeting, and, mounting the scaffold, presented a cap of liberty
and an address to the assembly.   The example of these females
was successfully recommended to imitation by the orators of
other meetings."

In terror at the possibilities of an operative Habeas Corpus
Act,[3] Sidmouth, then Secretary of State for Home Affairs,
rushed the Six Acts through Parliament in the autumn of
1819.   At no other time have Englishmen ever been deprived
of so many of their privileges.   The possession of arms, and
military training were both interdicted.   Public meetings were
only to be held subject to extremely difficult conditions, until
1824.   Seditious libels could be punished by banishment, a
stamp duty was imposed upon small pamphlets, and powers of
summary judgment were given to magistrates.   The discovery
of the Cato Street Conspiracy in 1820, the object of which was
the assassination of George IV, only a few months after his
accession, and the execution of Thistlewood, the chief conspirator, embittered the situation still more, as Thistlewood was
well known as a Spencean and the organizer of the Spa Fields
demonstration in 1816.   About the same time the authorities
were frightened by the reports of attempts to force a revolution, which had been taking place in Scotland.   Something
like a pitched battle took place at Bonnymuir, between cavalry
and Radicals, ending in the capture of several alleged conspira-

[1] Martineau, *History of the Peace*, Vol. I, p. 264.
[2] P. 104.
[3] The Act had come back into operation in 1818.

D

tors and the execution of three of them. Before we pass on to another subject it may be added that at the end of 1819 Cobbett had returned to England, to continue his campaign. Incidentally he had, at the time, added enormously to the gaiety of nations by bringing back with him the bones of Thomas Paine. Cobbett would have given sepulture on a national scale to the corpse, but everybody refused to take him seriously, and Paine's relatives themselves professed to be annoyed.

The reform movement after 1820, as far as the working classes were concerned, sank underground for a time. Cobbett continued to influence his readers to an extent which has been equalled by few subsequent journalists. The greatest event between the years of suppression and the passing of the Reform Act was the repeal of the Combination Laws in 1825. The credit for this is very largely due to Place. He played his moves with the deadly accuracy of a champion chess player who meets a novice, and with the assistance of Joseph Hume and a handful (a small one) of M.P.'s this revolutionary measure was carried. Combinations of workmen were now permitted, and the right of collective bargaining was recognized. The story of the way in which the strings were pulled is contained in the Place MSS. in the British Museum.[1] This measure, the increasing prosperity of the country, and the prominence given to reform by Whig Members of Parliament, together took the edge off the working-class agitation. And it remained off. As 1832 drew closer it was the middle-class campaign that stimulated the working-class agitation back into life. The *Annual Register* from 1825 to 1831 mentions no serious insurrectionary outbreaks. The economic justification of such movements had receded from its former prominence. The working classes looked with approval and admiration upon the conduct of the struggle in Parliament by Lord John Russell, Brougham, Hume, and others. Not until the Reform Bill was very nearly an accomplished fact do we once more have signs of organized working-class participation in the reform movement. And that is so largely due to the influence of a

[1] No. 27,798.

new generation that we may defer the consideration of this new factor until the next chapter, which will, in effect, largely deal with the new doctrines.

There is no need to describe the final victory of the middle-class Radical reformers. The Reform Act of 1832 is, of course, a landmark of the first importance, but the details of its passing do not concern us here. The tactics, the excitements, the failures of 1830–32, the studied histrionics of Brougham, and the ineffectual opposition of Wellington, have little immediate relation to the working-class movement which is our subject.

The generation that had achieved the Reform Act differed entirely in its personnel from the pioneers who had struggled for the suffrage in the years immediately following the French Revolution. Thomas Hardy, the secretary of the London Corresponding Society, just lived to see the Reform Act carried, and died four months afterwards, aged eighty years. Cartwright had also passed away in 1824, aged eighty-four. Only three years before his death the indomitable old man had managed to get himself fined £100 for sedition. The working life of Bentham, the philosopher of the movement, exactly coincides with the agitation. He had published his first book in 1776 ; he died two days after the Reform Act had been carried through the House of Lords, and on the eve of the Royal Assent.

An older generation had led men's attention to certain theories of government ; economic distress had emphasized their teachings. Born of the industrial revolution, a new type of man was arising who was to attempt to put the theories into practice. Chief among them was Robert Owen.

CHAPTER II

THE FOLLOWERS TAKE THE LEAD

WE have seen that Labour, scarcely organized, had at this time a political programme too heterogeneous to be practicable, an inchoate mass of aspirations, and was at the same time faced by the triumphant philosophy of the successful middle classes, the *laissez faire*-creed, to which the answer was not yet understood. Consequently personalities came to matter more than theories. They at any rate provided something tangible even if inconsistent.

It would be useless to attempt to understand the history of this period without taking into account the life and ideas of Robert Owen. Although he was not directly concerned with the Chartist movement, yet Owen's views were a permanent feature in the background of industrial politics for many years after his death. He always held a patriarchal position : a " thing to wonder and admire." He was born in 1771, began to earn his living at an extremely early age, exercised his intelligence, and by the time he was nineteen years of age found himself in charge of a cotton mill employing five hundred persons. Improvements suggested by him enormously increased the output of his firm, then he went into business on his own account, and by 1800 he had become principal partner and manager of mills at New Lanark. Here he proceeded to put into practice his theories of education and management, although it was not until 1814 that he had bought out the other partners and could do what he liked. He established infant schools, reduced hours of labour and succeeded in greatly strengthening the financial position of his business. By 1824 he had left New Lanark to give full play to his theories.   In a vague sort of way Owen had anticipated most if not all of the theories which have been under discussion since his time.   But so far as political economy was concerned, Owen was entirely uneducated.   His views were of the crudest.   He believed that labour was the standard of value and made a local effort to supersede currency by paper " labour notes."   He attempted to found self-supporting communities in Scotland and the United States, and reaped the inevitable failure which comes to those who try to bring Socialism about by private enterprise.   The peculiarity of many of his views—he was antipathetic to all religion and privately believed that marriage was an unnecessary institution—caused him to quarrel time and again with those who were most inclined to aid him in his schemes.   Yet with all his theoretical crudities and practical failures, he succeeded in influencing the Socialist and Co-operative movements as no other man has done.   He was on the whole inclined to deprecate the value of political action ; hence he was not directly connected with Chartism.   His peculiar glory lies in two things : first, he upset the theory of *laissez-faire* by making a fortune under conditions the reverse of those advocated by the philosophers of that unholy doctrine ; in the second place, he produced a body of ideas, which came to be superseded, it is true, but which nevertheless gave people a clue to the future of working-class movements at a time when such a clue was badly needed.[1]

An illustration of the material bent of Owen's theories is afforded by his cordial reception of phrenology.   " There can be no doubt whatever that Phrenology is founded in fact : the functions and manifestations are truly found in present society to the extent represented ; the question, however, is, how we came by them, and whether with or without the knowledge of Phrenology it is not practicable so to train human beings from infancy upwards, that in all the ordinary instances of organization they shall become highly intelligent and greatly conducive to their own and to others' happiness ?   The Phreno-

[1] There are two excellent books on Owen : *Life and Labours of Robert Owen* by Lloyd Jones, and *Robert Owen* by Frank Podmore.

logists probably will not dispute this, but may insist further that their science will make such result the more certain, forasmuch as they bring into operation additional facts to assist the development when weak, and to correct where it is most liable to deviation."[1]   These sentiments are, of course, only those to be expected of a paper which bore on its title-page the motto " The character of man is formed for him—not by him."

At New Lanark Owen had been brilliantly successful.   He had anticipated in experiment what is being done in our own day.   He made New Lanark a kind of Bourneville under infinitely more difficult conditions than those which Messrs. Cadbury had to overcome.   His educational schemes have a touch of the Montessori Method, and we have not yet caught up with his views on the treatment of crime.   Between Owen's experiments and his theories a sharp line draws itself.   Owen saw the world as a larger New Lanark, to be managed on much the same lines.   His ideas ran away with him.   He insisted that " circumstances "—or what we now call environment—determined everything in the life of the individual, and that it was therefore impossible for improvement to come as the gradual outcome of individual efforts.   In other words, the method of political democracy was not likely to give results as efficacious as those of informed and benevolent autocracy.   Perhaps this needs a little qualification.   The force of " circumstances " could be altered by education, and Owen never ceased to persuade all with whom he came in contact to adopt some system of education.   The pages of the numerous periodicals conducted by Owen are full of the need for universal and free education.

The early Radicals made occasional endeavours to gain the support of Owen.   But his aloofness from working-class politics was unconquerable.   He was by nature an autocrat, longing to impose a system upon the world, and not in the least anxious that the world at large should have the opportunity of examining it before its wholesale imposition.   He regarded the middle and governing classes as his most natural

[1] *New Moral World* for August 13, 1836, p. 335.

audiences.   The annual subscription to the Institution in the
Gray's Inn Road was a guinea and upwards, well above what
a working man would be likely to pay.[1]   This criticism is
contained in a few tactful phrases in a letter to Owen from
Bronterre O'Brien, dated May 27, 1832, begging him to use
his influence to stimulate working-class opinion in London in
favour of the Reform Bill.   The letter goes :   " To you who
know human nature so well, and whose writings afford abundant
evidence that you are as well conversant with the nature of
existing governments, I need not say that these governments
have ultimately no other basis of support than public opinion.
Be they ever so complicated or simple, be they monarchical
or Republican, they stand or fall, move retrograde or forward,
solely in obedience to Public Opinion.   It is therefore of
vital importance to gather up this Public Opinion, to concentrate it on the social system and make it bear irresistibly on
the government, by the weight, unity of direction and simultaneous action of all its parts.   With this view I respectfully
suggest that the Association in Gray's Inn Road should be
made of a more popular character.   I would in fact recommend
you to . . ." [2]

It need hardly be said that the writer's suggestions for the
democratization of Owen's Institution were not attended to.
Owen would almost certainly have refused to accept the theory
that Public Opinion greatly mattered.   He considered it his
mission to change rather than to convert, to mould the public
and let its Opinion look after itself.

The word Socialism, as far as can be ascertained, originated
in 1837, and was used as label for the whole bulk of Owen's
theories.   His followers annexed the use of the word Socialists
to themselves, in contradistinction to the believers in political
reform, especially of the franchise, *who had long been known
as Radicals*.[3]   The two sections soon began to show signs of

[1] Podmore, *Life of Robert Owen*, Vol. II, p. 426.
[2] Ib., quoted from letter in Manchester collection.
[3] It is important to remember that the words Radical and Socialist
were not invented in order to make such a contradistinction.   The first
use of the word Socialist in the English language appears to be in a

divergence, although to the outside world Radicals were Socialists, and Socialists were Chartists for many years to come.
A leading article in Owen's *New Moral World* [1] declares that
the Radicals blame the Socialists for not exerting themselves
in obtaining universal suffrage, etc., as a part of the objects
they have in view, or a step towards the realization of these
objects. But, "when the Socialists know that the whole
jar of sweetmeats could more easily be obtained, by perseverance in their measures, than a few of the sweetmeats could
be wrung from the grasp of enemies of freedom, by the proceedings of the Chartists—when they knew that the whole
journey can be accomplished, with far less time and fatigue,
by the superior roads they propose, than by the obstacle-
encumbered roads to universal suffrage—knowing this, would
it be wise in them to consume in pursuit of the fraction, more
time and energies than would suffice to place them in possession
of the whole? We say, without fear of refutation, that, if
the individuals who are now straining every nerve in the
righteous cause of giving to the working classes those rights
and privileges which have so long been most unjustly withheld
from them—were to apply their zeal and energies to the
establishment of *Union* among the workng classes themselves—with the co-operation of the numerous bodies from
the other classes who are willing to make common cause with
them—*for the purpose of establishing communities*—they possess
amply sufficient of talent and influence to secure the accomplishment of that great object ; and by so doing, to obtain at
once far more than all the advantages which they are now
struggling for, by more difficult and circuitous proceedings."

Owen, in fact, believed in the possibility of changing the
whole composition of human society and the abolition of every

signature to a letter in *The Poor Man's Guardian*, August 24, 1833 ;
it appears to have been in use in France a year or two earlier. Radical
is some years older. The earliest example of its use, supplied by the
New English Dictionary, is from an article in the *Morning Post*, June 17,
1809, and there is another somewhat unsatisfactory reference to its
employment in 1802.

[1] March 2; 1839.

human evil at a single stroke. The two-and-a-half sentences quoted above, however, contain a promise to the Radicals. For Owen's invincible optimism and his faith in the ready malleability of humanity communicated itself even to his opponents. If the " whole jar of sweetmeats " was to be obtainable virtually for the asking, not all his ponderous eloquence could make a Chartist believe that one particular sweetmeat could not be had. Owen's unfaith in political evolution—as we now regard the idea—made him regard the creation of political societies much as his contemporaries regarded the creation of the animal world. A society, like an elephant, entered the world as the outcome of an order given by a higher authority. The idea of time as a factor necessary for the stability of political changes had not yet been formed. Just as Plato was quite prepared for the acceptance of the constitution of his Republic by any State, so Owen readily believed that the transition from the " Old Immoral World " to the " New Moral World " would be a mere shifting of scenery between the acts of a drama. The Chartists shared his absence of a sense of time, probably acquiring the mental characteristic subconsciously from Owen. This explains their keenness, their faith in the vast and radical changes to be instantly effected by universal suffrage, and their willingness to sacrifice themselves for its achievement. And because their belief in the instant and permanent changeability from one state of civilization to a very different one was implicit and nor brought out and argued about, it was tacitly accepted by the enemies of Chartism and embittered their opposition.

About the time of the Reform Act, Owen's life was being spent mainly in the delivery of interminable addresses on what he called Co-operation, a theory bearing a distant relation, which we need not stop to examine, with the practice of the co-operative movement of to-day. These lectures attracted to themselves all the young men in whose minds ideas of social and political betterment were beginning to arise. These came, listened, met one another, found congenial spirits, and substituted for their attention to Owen's theories the founda-

tion of their own.   One little group of young men who had been
brought together by an interest in Owen's lectures became,
as we shall see, the intellectual centre of the Chartist movement.
Their names were Lovett, Hetherington, Cleave, Watson, and
a young man named Richard Moore.   They came together
from all ends of England, attracted to London and to one
another through a variety of reasons.

Some time in the second decade of the eighteenth century
a young man named Richard Carlile had come up to London
from his native village in Devonshire, and earned his living
as a tinman.   Extreme radicalism and atheism soon claimed
him for their own.   Carlile began to sell unstamped periodicals
and to publish anti-Christian works.   This, in 1817, cost him
eighteen weeks' imprisonment ; and in 1819 he was sentenced
to three years' imprisonment and a fine of £1,500.   As he
was unable to pay this amount, Carlile remained in prison
until 1825.   His publications, his works composed in his
cell, and the report of his three days' trial, gained him a widespread popularity, and the sympathy of innumerable persons
who had never even seen him.   During his second incarceration
his business was carried on by his wife and sister.   In 1821
the Government, after a period of quietness, took up the prosecution of blasphemy with greater vigour than ever.   Carlile,
fearing that his business would now certainly succumb, called
for volunteers to serve in the bookshop.   The first to sacrifice
himself in this manner was promptly arrested and sentenced
to eighteen months' imprisonment.   The second volunteer
was James Watson, a young man of twenty-three.   A few
months afterwards he was arrested and sentenced to one
year's imprisonment, during which he read prodigiously.   Soon
after his release he returned to Carlile's shop, and managed
it until its master's liberation at the end of 1825.   These
experiences determined Watson's subsequent career.   To the
end of his long life he fought, in every possible manner, for
the freedom of the press.   Through the kindness of Julian
Hibbert, who held the same views, Watson was able subsequently to set up as a printer and publisher, specializing, of
course, in Radical and freethought works.   He became note-

worthy as a publisher who took special pains with the type and appearance of the works (mostly pamphlets) he put on the market.

In 1825 Watson was introduced into Owenist circles,[1] and gave up his whole time from April, 1828, to May, 1830, in the propagation of Owen's co-operative associations. During the first year of his employment in this capacity, he was agent of the Co-operative Store at 36, Red Lion Square.

In the course of this work, Watson must have become acquainted with William Lovett. Born in 1800, a cabinet-maker by profession, Lovett came to London from Cornwall at the age of twenty-one, and soon found himself in touch with Owen and his followers. He also met many of the more serious working-class leaders of the time. His allegiance seems to have been peculiarly divided between Owenism and Radicalism for some years, and his autobiography contains little to enable us to understand the evolution of Lovett's political views earlier than 1833 or so. He was a man of extraordinary tenacity of purpose and of thorough sincerity. From him proceeded many of the ideas which dominated the moral-force Chartists, a few years later. Lovett gained the friendship and confidence of Place, and had great discussions with him, opposing the opinions he had acquired from Owen to those which Place had inherited from Bentham. The following is an extract from one of those few letters of Place which lead one to conclude that his character had its softer side. " You can hardly sufficiently appreciate the pleasure I should receive on observing that you were happy. I conclude that the causes of your disposition towards despondency date from two causes : (1) Your health not being robust, (2) that you dwell too much on the misfortunes and miseries of your fellow-men."[2]

Watson had two great friends, with whom he " made up an inseparable triad."[3] These were Richard Moore (who subsequently married Watson's niece), a woodcarver, born in 1810, and Henry Hetherington. The latter was the eldest of the

---

[1] W. J. Linton, *Life of Watson*, p. 21 (1880 edition).
[2] British Museum, Place MSS. 35,150, fo. 224.
[3] W. J. Linton, *Memories*, p. 38.

three, having been born in 1792. He was a printer and, like
the others, an atheist. Like Watson, he opened a small shop,
and sold the same class of wares. In evading the Stamp Acts
he displayed wonderful ingenuity, which did not save him,
however, from several imprisonments. In 1832 he shared a
cell with Watson for six months for the usual offence. Another
member of this group, who does not appear to have joined it
before 1830, was John Cleave, who carried on the same type
of business at 1, Shoe Lane, E.C., and was on closer terms of
friendship with Watson than with the others. He had been
a sailor, and later, the keeper of a coffee-house (as Lovett had
also been for a time). " He was a sturdy fellow, and totally
devoid of fear, and, like Lovett, ready to undergo any persecution, to bear any punishment. He was not, however, so well
informed or so placed a man as Lovett, he on the contrary was
passionate and revengeful and not at all scrupulous as to the
use of any means of accomplishing his purpose, the end of
which was improving the condition of the working people.
His notions were all vague."[1] Such is Place's verdict. Holyoake, on the other hand, tells us that Cleave did not convey
the impression that he was prepared to take risks. There
was a meeting held in 1830 to form a Metropolitan Political
Union ; on its council Cleave, Hetherington, Lovett and
Watson all had seats.[2] In a sense these men had collected
together because of Richard Carlile. This very fact brought
them indirectly into touch with the leaders of philosophic
Radicalism. Carlile's " mission was to afford a test case of
liberty of thought ; and, in that view, the advanced Liberals
stood up for him. Bentham came forward in his behalf.
John Mill's first appearance in print was to denounce the
persecution of him and his wife. I have reason to believe that
he received substantial aid in his long imprisonments from
the Bentham circle."[3] Yet the interests of this circle were
by no means limited even to the numerous ones provided by
the agitations for freedom of thought, an unstamped press,

[1] Place MSS. 27,791, fo. 67–68.
[2] Id. 27,822.
[3] Bain, *James Mill, a Biography*, p. 435.

Owenist Socialism, the individualistic Radicalism of Place, and the Reform movement. Given such teachers and such pupils, the existence of a spirit of inquiry is not to be wondered at. By 1830, when this little group was complete, its members had educated themselves in the teachings of all the heterodox economists of the day, and it so happened that these, especially Hodgskin and Thompson, were on the side of social revolution. It is not intended to convey the impression that Lovett, Watson, Hetherington and Cleave held identical views on everything. Cleave, it is fairly obvious, assented rather than believed. Lovett did not share the militant atheism of the others, and was a strong feminist. They agreed, however, on certain basic ideas. In the first place, definitely rejecting Owenism, they upheld working-class political action. They accepted Owenism, however, to the extent of refusing to regard *laissez-faire* as the highest limit of political wisdom. They shared strong views on freedom of thought and of the press. Their co-operation at first was based on this last common article of belief. They united in the fight for an " unstamped press."

In 1831, Hetherington started a weekly paper, *The Poor Man's Guardian*, which lived until 1835, in spite of endless prosecutions. Its *raison d'être* was the abolition of the " taxes on knowledge " which made newspapers a luxury the poor could not hope to enjoy. The newspaper tax had been steadily rising. It began in 1712 with a penny per copy, rose to $1\frac{1}{2}d$. in 1756, $2d$. in 1789, $2\frac{1}{2}d$. in 1795, $3\frac{1}{2}d$. in 1804, and $4d$. in 1815. In 1836 a reduction to $1d$. took place, and this was finally removed in 1855. As may be expected, infringements of the law between 1815 and 1836 were sufficiently numerous. They were also of a unanimously revolutionary tendency. Seditions and blasphemies were freely propagated by the publishers of the " unstamped " papers, who knowing that prosecutions were in any case inevitable, resolved to make the most of their delicts. *The Poor Man's Guardian* was pugnacious and provocative. It described itself as " A Weekly Newspaper for the People. Established, contrary to Law, to try the Power of ' Might ' against ' Right,' " and was sold for a penny. It was studiously offensive to the representatives and upholders of established things, and contained frequent references to " Miss V. A. Guelph " and " Mr. and Mrs. William Guelph."; There is a reference to the " profligate hypocrisy and unchristian pride of old mother church "[1]—this as a gentle comment on an official Church *pronunciamiento* against the paper. With its fifth number its price was changed to " Lent to Read, without Deposit, for an unlimited period. Charge, one penny." In it first appeared a little poem which is quoted continually in Socialist literature—a proclamation of faith and an embryonic political programme.[2]

> Wages should form the price of goods ;
> Yes, wages should be all,
> Then we who work to make the goods
> Should justly have them all ;
>
> But if their price be made of rent,
> Tithes, taxes, profits all,
> Then we who work to make the goods
> Shall have—just none at all.
>
> *One of the Know-Nothings.*

This little poem contains, in a succinct form, the whole case for " the right to the whole product of labour."

The Poor Man's Guardian was very largely concerned with the doings of the various Radical working men's societies of the time, of which a large number came into existence between 1829, and the passing of the Reform Bill.

The most important metropolitan society was the National Union of the Working Classes. This was in a sense a grandchild of Robert Owen. Several of his followers, among them Lovett, Cleave and Hetherington, had in 1829 founded the British Association for promoting co-operative knowledge in order to give currency to his ideas. But Owen's anti-parliamentarianism made him see in the reform agitation merely an obstacle to his own schemes for saving the human race, and he therefore quarrelled with some of his strongest admirers. The National Union was founded while Owen was in America.[3]

---

[1] August 6, 1831.   [2] January 7, 1832.
[3] Place MSS. 27,791, fo. 243.

As soon as he returned the original British Association broke up, and its remaining members formed the General Metropolitan Trades Union, which later merged into the National Union of the Working Classes. It will be seen that here, as it were within the four corners of a handkerchief, trade unionism, co-operation, and working class politics are united as closely as they ever have been in the course of their history. The objects of the Metropolitan Trades Union, while it lasted, were two : " first to obtain for all its members the right of electing those who make the laws which govern them, unshackled and uninfluenced by any property qualification whatsoever ; its second object, to afford support and protection, individually and collectively, to every member of the *Metropolitan Trades' Union* ; to enhance the value of labour by diminishing the hours of employment ; and to adopt such measures as may be deemed necessary to increase the domestic comfort of working men." The National Union of Working Classes, we find a little later, differed from the National Political Union. Benbow, a member of both, once moved at a Committee meeting of the former,[1] " that the Whig Union of which Sir Francis Burdett was at the head was a Jesuitical attempt to cajole the working classes to employ their moral and physical force in support of the Whig Reform Bill, and that no union deserved or ought to receive the support of the working people which did not declare its purpose to be the attainment of Annual Parliaments and Universal Suffrage." Cleave, another pluralist, and others disagreed, and Benbow withdrew the resolution at the following meeting. But the changing temper of the resolution is significant, especially in view of Benbow's subsequent career. A few days later, Burdett, Benbow's *bête noire*, resigned from the National Political Union.

The Metropolitan Reform Society, consisting " almost wholly of working men,"[2] was holding crowded meetings. Unparalleled depression in trade and agriculture prevailed at the time, and added fuel to the agitation. Moreover, the gloomy cast of things had led to searchings of heart in

---

[1] Place MSS. 27,791, fo. 94.   [2] Id. 27,789, fo. 137.

unexpected quarters. " The pension lists were dissected, the *Scotsman*, the *Times*, the *Morning Chronicle*, the *Examiner*, and several other ably-conducted newspapers made such extraordinary exposures of abuses as tended greatly to keep up the excitement and promote the demand for reform of Parliament."[1]   On March 8, a Metropolitan Union was founded. Its personnel is interesting, its influence nugatory.   Daniel O'Connell was in the chair, and Hunt was among the speakers and was appointed treasurer.   " This appointment ruined the Union . . . nobody would subscribe money to be put under the control and care of Mr. Hunt, and the Union was soon extinguished from want of money to pay its current expenses."[2]

Another body of sufficient importance to warrant its mention was the National Political Union, with which Sir Francis Burdett was at first connected, but which he left just before the passing of the Reform Bill—whether on account of an honest misunderstanding, or of the enfeebling Toryism of senility, is open question.   This association repudiated the extreme Radicalism, verging on Republicanism, of some of the existing bodies, and was more frankly bourgeois.   So it fell out with the Birmingham Union, which in spite of the more numerous social strata from which its members were derived was, in fact, far less democratically governed.   The N.P.U. was founded on October 31, 1831, and had amongst its original members, besides Burdett, Thelwall, W. T. Fox, Cleave, Place, Lovett, Benbow, and Erskine May.[3]   Its tone may be gathered from the following resolution, adopted unanimously at a meeting of the Council on November 16, 1831.

1. That all true reformers ought to rally round the throne at the present crisis, and support the King in his attempt to wrest the liberties of the people from the Boroughmongers' grasp.

2. That the increasing stagnation of trade, and the nearly exhausted patience of the nation, occasioned by the rejection of the Reform Bill, convince this Council, that it is more than ever imperative to support His Majesty's Ministers in effecting

---

[1] Place MSS. 27,789, fo. 157.   [2] Id. 27,789, fo. 145.
[3] Id. 27,791, fo. 99.

the great measure by which they have pledged themselves to stand or fall.

3. That if the arts of a faction should have triumph over a patriot King, and his present Ministry, this Council will not listen to any illusory promises of Reform that a Tory or any other Ministry may proffer to a disappointed people.

4. That if the enemies of this country should succeed in producing anarchy and confusion, this Council will devise means by which the Members of the Union may effectually protect their own lives and properties and establish the liberties of the country.

London was not the only centre of this kind of activity. The nine bulky volumes of Place's manuscript Narratives of Political Events in England, 1830–35,[1] give us an extended view of such doings all over England. Care is needed in reading these documents. Place's anxiety to record every available fact took precedence of all considerations of proportion or relevance. His tedious prolixity and his humourless and none-too-condensed summaries of innumerable unimportant speeches impede the reader's understanding of those matters reported by him which really deserve attention. Yet his MSS. are the best contemporary history of their subject, for the contemporary historians overlooked the origin of democracy, while the popular press of the time was too deeply concerned in fighting the battle for its own existence to serve as an altogether reliable record of passing events. Cobbett, for example, as energetic an editor as ever lived, made no attempts to supply his readers with news. If any was forthcoming, so much the better, otherwise the paper consisted of editorial matter, generally signed, comments, abuse, and advertisements of Cobbett's books. Cobbett was a master of the " straight talk." His readers bought the paper to enjoy his heart-to-heart chats on whatever subjects he wished to expound. For news they went elsewhere.

To begin, then, with 1830, we find that, on January 25, " The largest meeting ever assembled in this Kingdom within the walls of a building took place at Mr. Beardworth's Horse

[1] 27,789–27,797.

E

and Carriage Repository . . . there were at least from 10,000 to 15,000 persons present."[1] That those present meant business may be inferred from the fact that the meeting began at 10.30 and went on till nearly 5 p.m.   The Birmingham Union was formed, having for its first object, " To obtain by every just and legal means such a Reform in the *Commons House of Parliament* as may ensure a real and *effective representation* of the *lower and middle classes* of the *people* in that house."   The principal speaker was Thomas Attwood, to whom, more than to anybody else, the foundation of the Union may be attributed.   This was unfortunate, as Attwood belonged to the genus politician, species currency crank, and his odd and well-known views on money held off many sympathizers with reform from joining the Union, as it was believed that he would use it to propagate his own doctrine.   The Birmingham Political Union, it will be seen, was Radical in the modern sense.   Attwood began as a Tory, but, apart from his views on currency which always kept him on the circumference of any movement he supported, his opinions underwent a process of democratization as he grew older.   When the Reform Bill passed he had become enormously popular with the working classes, especially in London and Birmingham.   He entered Parliament immediately after the Bill had passed into law, and remained there for seven years.   Attwood was the member for the town who was most popular with women.   When he was canvassing they were abundant in the courts and streets. He not only kissed the children—he kissed their mothers.   At one election he was reported to have kissed 8,000 women."[2]

On the whole Thomas Attwood was the most influential extra-parliamentary protagonist of Reform.   His methods were summed up in his motto, " Peace, Law and Order."   In order to demonstrate to the House of Lords that the public enthusiasm in favour of the Bill had not abated, Attwood determined to astonish the world with the unprecedented spectacle of 100,000 undisciplined men assembled together. . . .   Hitherto no one

---

[1] Place MSS. 27,789, fo. 136.
[2] *Sixty Years of an Agitator's Life.*   By G. J. Holyoake.   Vol. I., p. 36.

had supposed it possible to bring together so huge a mass of men without the inevitable result of riot and bloodshed, but Attwood knew his power, he knew the men he had to deal with ; he decided to make the magnificent experiment, and complete success fully justified his boldness."[1]   This was the meeting held on October 3, 1831, to which J. S. Mill refers in the letter to Sterling quoted above.   The total number of those present was officially given as 150,000 ; whether or not this is an exaggeration, there is no doubt of the immense moral effect of so large and so orderly a demonstration.   In 1831, be it remembered, monster gatherings of this description were not, as now, an almost weekly affair, to which only a limited attention is paid.

We shall meet Attwood later in the course of this narrative acting as parliamentary spokesman for the Chartists.

About the same time as Thomas Attwood was agitating in Birmingham, his brother Charles was stirring up Newcastle-on-Tyne to the same ends, and less distinguished men were exciting the rest of the country.   Political Unions were being formed everywhere.   A check was placed on the multiplication of these bodies by royal proclamation issued on November 22, 1831, within a few weeks of the formation of the National Political Union.   This scarcely affected existing bodies, as it held up for reprobation and declared to be " unconstitutional and illegal " only bodies which " under the denomination of Political Associations " were " composed of separate bodies, with various divisions and sub-divisions, under leaders and with a gradation of ranks of authority, and distinguished by certain badges, and subject to the general control and direction of a superior committee or council."   The National Political Union pointed out that this did not apply to them, or, for the matter of that, to the great majority of unions in existence.[2]

Why was the Government so nervous ?   Throughout the whole course of the working-class agitation for enfranchisement there was always a section, varying in its importance, belonging

---

[1] *Life of Thomas Attwood.*   By C. M. Wakefield.   (Printed for private circulation only, 1885.)

[2] *Annual Register*, 1831, p. 297.

to what later came to be known as the " physical force party."
These, like the franchise-seekers of a later day, were more or
less completely to pin their faith to militant methods.   At the
time of which we speak these men were in a small minority,
and counted for little in the councils of the Radicals.   As a
whole the political unions stood for peaceful methods, while
their militant members must have been fully aware that while
Wellington was in existence any insurrectionary outbreaks
would be dealt with drastically.   The farm labourers' revolt in
1830, so graphically described by Mr. and Mrs. J. L. Hammond,[1]
must have still been fresh in the men's recollections, and Wellington had then identified himself with the landed interest
with an enthusiasm that approximated to ferocity.   It was in
connexion with this revolt that Cobbett secured his greatest
triumph.   Tried in July, 1831, for publishing articles in the
Political Register alleged to have had an incendiary influence
on the agricultural labourers, Cobbett put up an unexpectedly
smashing defence, and he emerged from the trial unconvicted,
with his influence enhanced enormously.   But Sir Robert
Peel and the Duke of Wellington had shown their teeth in
the most unmistakable manner, wherein lay a lesson for the
Radicals and understood by them.   For which reasons the
agitation, widespread as it was, undertaken during a period
of intense industrial depression, and with an intensely exaggerated importance attached to it by so many of its keenest participants, was nevertheless conducted on strictly constitutional
lines.   There were, of course, exceptional occurrences, which
we shall consider, but they were never the rule.   The battle
for reform was not won by militancy.

John Stuart Mill, a young man of twenty-five, in a letter to
Sterling, says : " I am convinced that we are indebted for the
preservation of tranquillity solely to the organization of people
in political unions.   All the other unions look to the Birmingham one, and that looks to its half-dozen leaders, who consequently act under a most intense consciousness of moral responsibility, and are very careful neither to do nor say anything
without the most careful deliberation.   I conversed the other

[1] *The Village Labourer*, 1760–1832, chapters xi and xii.

day with a Warwickshire magistrate, who told me that the meeting of 150,000 men a few days previous would have done *any* thing without exception which their leaders might have proposed. They would have passed any resolutions, marched to any place, or burnt any man's house. The agricultural people are as determined as the manufacturers. The West is as *exalté* as the North. Colonel Napier made a speech at the Devizes meeting the other day for the express purpose (as I hear) of letting the men in the North perceive that the West is ready to join in any popular movement if necessary ; and since that speech (which the leaders in vain attempted to prevent him from delivering) he has received numbers of letters from all parts of the country saying that they all look to him as their leader, and are ready to place themselves under his command."[1]

Yet a fortnight before Mill wrote this letter, riots had taken place in Derby and Nottingham as a result of the rejection of the Reform Bill of 1831. At Derby a mob attacked the city gaol and released the prisoners, and a few lives were lost. At Nottingham the Castle was burnt down, for which, early in 1832, three men were hanged. In London demonstrations took place. A few anti-Reform peers were recognized and mobbed, and the windows of Apsley House, the Duke of Wellington's residence, were smashed for the second time that year, but no bloodshed seems to have occurred. Mill, in fact, was a trifle too optimistic. A week after his letter had been posted, the Bristol riots broke out. This affair has been consistently held up during the last few years as a justification of militancy, and it is therefore advisable to survey what really happened, and whether the riots were, in fact, justified by their results.

The M.P. for Bristol in 1831 was Sir Charles Wetherell, Attorney-General and Recorder of Bristol. He had throughout the struggles in the House of Commons for reform shown himself a determined opponent of parliamentary reform, university reform, law reform, municipal reform, and Catholic emancipation. He had come to be accepted as a symbol of the *status*

[1] *Letters of J. S. Mill*, Vol. I, p. 7, October 20–22, 1831.

quo, a sort of embodiment of a past that refused to die.   He had never swerved from the path of resistance to proposed changes, although once, in 1817, he brilliantly defended James Watson when he was tried for high treason after the Spa Fields affair.[1]   On October 29 he made a state entry into Bristol to open the assizes.   Wetherell's reputation among the local working classes was an emphatic one, and he knew it, but he came nevertheless out of bravado.   On his arrival at the city he was greeted by large crowds, but nothing more exciting than a few hoots appeared to have been emitted.   As the procession made its way towards the Guildhall, a few stones were thrown, and one constable was struck.   The assizes were opened in the usual way, the public being restive, but tractable. After Wetherell had returned to the Mansion House, the constables bethought themselves of the stone-throwers and made several rushes upon the crowd.   The crowd, numbering about 10,000, gradually became wilder.   After four hours of skirmishing, its temper approximated to fury, while, on the other hand, some of the constables were sent home.   The Riot Act was then read by the mayor, who threatened to call out the troops.   That was the last straw.   The Mansion House was immediately attacked and all the windows and outer doors broken.   The ground floor was invaded and the furniture smashed.   Wetherell wisely beat a retreat and fled from the city.   The soldiers arrived and by midnight both troops and mob had got out of hand and a few of the latter were killed and wounded.   The next day, Sunday, the mob returned to the Mansion House, and gained admittance to the upper floors and to the cellars.   Here a large quantity of wines and spirits were found and immediately consumed.   Numbers of men and women, maddened by drink, continued the work of destruction.   When the troops arrived, the mob was on the offensive (on the previous day it had been merely on the

---

[1] The James Watson of the Spa Fields affair (1766-1838) should not be confused with the James Watson (1799-1874) who was arrested during the demonstration of March 21, 1832 (see p. 35), or with the other James Watson of Newcastle who attended the 1848 and 1851 Conventions.

defensive), and a good deal of bloodshed took place. Later on, the New Gaol was attacked, the governor's house sacked, and the prisoners set free, and the building fired. Two other prisons, the Gloucester County prison and the Bridewell, were similarly treated. The bishop's palace was next attacked and burnt to ashes. After this, nothing less than a general conflagration appeared sufficient to the insatiable mob, and a whole block of buildings in Queen's Square was destroyed. By Monday morning the riot had begun to subside and the military cleared all the streets. About a hundred had been killed or wounded.[1] The Bristol riots provided those who believed Reform was a precursor of revolution with a strong argument, of which full use was made during the final debates on Reform. The author of the *Greville Memoirs* merely expresses what was in many minds when he says : " The spirit which produced these atrocities was generated by Reform, but no pretext was afforded for their actual commission ; it was a premature outbreaking of the thirst for plunder and longing after havoc and destruction, which is the essence of Reform, in the mind of the mob."[2] About the same time other less important riots were also taking place, in Worcester, Coventry, and Bath, but they were of insignificant size when compared with the Bristol affair.

It must be conceded that these affrays did not win the Reform Act. They were engendered, for the most part, by unemployed labourers, driven to riot by the futile hope of frightening the class they held responsible for their economic distress into granting some measure of alleviation. In these riots they had not the support of the political unions. *The Poor Man's Guardian* has neither praise nor blame for the Bristol rioters. It has never been shown that any connexion existed between the political unions and the actions of the rioters. Nor has it been shown that the Reform Act was expedited by these methods. Indeed, it was claimed by Sir Francis Burdett, on behalf of the National Political Union, that " The Riots, Conflagrations, and Bloodshed at Bristol

---

[1] For fuller account see *Annual Register*, 1831, pp. 171–177.
[2] *Greville Memoirs*, Vol. II, p. 214.

have been at length arrested. By whom ? By the Bristol
Political Union, to whom the Magistrates had delegated their
authority, and whose members have been sworn in as Special
Constables."[1]

Apart from the demonstrations against the Duke of Wellington and the anti-Reform peers, London kept cool, and in doing
so disappointed those who hoped that a conflagration would
provide an opportunity for suppressing the always constitutional National Political Union and the other Radical bodies.
There is no doubt that in November, 1831, Wellington anticipated violence especially from his own side. A factitious
terror was widely advertised ; it could have had no other
motive than the encouragement of mob-violence. The King
and Queen were to have driven through the City to the Lord
Mayor's banquet on November 9, on Wellington's advice the
royal visit was postponed. " In the end the disturbances in
the metropolis proved so trifling that Ministers had to stand
ridicule, more deadly to an administration than any hatred,
for their unfounded apprehensions." [2] A few months later
something more nearly approaching an act of provocation took
place, with ludicrous results.

In 1831 an outbreak of cholera took place, with the result
that several hundreds of persons died : almost all of the working
class. As the plague gave no promise of abatement, a general
fast was proclaimed on February 6, 1832, to take place on
March 21. The suggestion met with ribaldry from a large
number of Radicals, who saw the cause of the disease in the
chronic deprivation of food under which so many of the working classes existed. Thus, a contemporary unstamped journal,
Figaro in London, published this epigram, which *The Poor
Man's Guardian* duly reprinted.

> Found lately dead, a bishop (quite aghast),—
> Verdict—The prospect of a general fast.

The same papers organized a protest against the fast, a " general
feast." A procession was to be formed and to walk round

[1] From a leaflet in Place MSS. 27,791, fo. 76.
[2] Maxwell's *Life of Wellington*, p. 256.

London in an orderly way, then disperse to various places and eat large dinners. According to *The Poor Man's Guardian* 100,000 gathered, but this is an obvious exaggeration ; it is fairly certain that not more than 1,000 took part in the march. These walked through various streets and were frequently turned aside by the police, who appeared to wish to keep the demonstrators off the main road. At no point where the police interposed was there a scrimmage. However, three arrests were made, of Benbow, Lovett, and Watson—the most prominent of the processionists. Benbow was tried, enjoyed himself a great deal making frivolous replies to his interrogators, and was finally found " not guilty." The same verdict, of course, was delivered in the other cases.

These arrests, and the general behaviour of the Government, are only to be explained by the theory that everybody believed that anything might happen at any time.

We find it difficult to-day to realize the position of the reformers of the eighteen-thirties in the face of such strange facts as that stated by Holyoake in his autobiographical *Sixty Years of an Agitator's Life*. " Only Unitarian ministers at that time would pray for Liberals, or would pray among them."[1] It is not easy to reconcile the fervent faith of so many reformers—" Mr. Owen this day has assured me, in the presence of more than thirty other persons, that within six months the whole state and condition of society in Great Britain will be changed, and all his views will be carried fully into effect "[2]—with the apathy with which the Government treated Oastler's pleas for the factory slaves. Remedies and diagnosis both were at fault.

Cobbett in his *Register* cursed Parliament for having caused prices to fall. " Such a picture of ruin no eyes ever beheld before ; no war, none of the causes of ruin in trade was ever equal in effect to the *acts of this Parliament*. If the acts had been passed for the express and avowed purpose of producing ruin, they could not have been more effectual."[3]

[1] Vol. I, p. 30.
[2] Place MSS. 27,791, January, 7, 1836.
[3] Aug. 17, 1831.

He then goes on to show how the prices of hardware, manufactured in and near Birmingham, have fallen. A quantity of ironmongery, which in 1818 fetched £15 15s. 10d., was now sold for only £6 12s. 6¾d. Cobbett demanded a paper currency to remedy this " ruin." But, apart from such impracticable prescriptions, which abounded, the sense of political perspective appears to have vanished. Long years of conflict had exaggerated the views both of the supporters and opponents of Reform. Both parties had come to expect that revolutionary changes would be the outcome of the Reform Bill. Democracy came to be synonymous with revolution. Wellington resisted the Bill almost to the bitter end, saying, on one occasion, that distribution and enfranchisement would lead to the election of " a democratical assembly of the worst description." The events of 1789 were near enough to be insistent reminders of what a revolution might involve, and yet sufficiently distant to be considerably exaggerated while the Revolution of 1830 stimulated the elements of both Radicalism and Toryism. Thus John Stuart Mill, in a news letter to John Sterling in the West Indies, wrote : " If the Ministers flinch or the Peers remain obstinate, I am firmly convinced that in six months a natural convention, chosen by universal suffrage, will be sitting in London. Should this happen, I have not made up my mind what will be best to do. I incline to think it would be best to lie by and let the tempest blow over, if one could but get a shilling a day to live upon meanwhile ; for until the whole of the existing institutions of society are levelled with the ground, there will be nothing for a wise man to do which the most pig-headed fool cannot do much better than he. A Turgot even could not do in the present state of England what Turgot himself failed to do in France—mend the old system. If all goes at once, let us wait till it is gone ; if it goes piece by piece, why, let the blockheads who will compose the first Parliament after the Bill passes do what a blockhead can do, viz., overthrow, and the ground will be cleared. . . . You will perhaps think from this long, prosing, rambling talk about politics that they occupy much of my attention ; but, in fact, I am myself often surprised how little I really care about them. The time is not yet come when a calm and impartial person can intermeddle with advantage in the questions and contests of the day."[1] If a "calm and impartial person" reared in the frigid atmosphere of Utilitarianism was thus contemplating the immediate overthrow of the established state of things, what must have been the feelings of less disciplined minds?

Another circumstance may be alluded to here. The Radical movement, and later on, and far more emphatically, the Chartist movement, were looked upon as anti-religious by the orthodox Tories, and this to a certain extent explains the bitterness of the opposition. In those days, too, it must be borne in mind that atheism was a far rarer, and also a far more strongly reprehended point of view than it is to-day. To the orthodox mind, unseasoned by any knowledge of economic fact, the French Revolution was the triumph of atheism. And it so happened that a very large number of the most prominent Radicals and Chartists were atheists, while not a few were Unitarians, who were almost as obnoxious to the orthodox. Place, Owen, Bentham and the Mills made no secret of their atheism, while of the generation that preceded them, Godwin and Paine had gone so far as to put their atheism before their Radicalism, instead of keeping it, like their successors, decently in the background. One of the results of these divergencies was that the prominent middle-class Radicals were regarded by the working-class leaders with virtual hostility, as a body of self-seekers, from whom nothing was to be expected.

The gulf between the working-class and middle-class Radicals is nowhere better illustrated than in the tone of *The Poor Man's Guardian*. In July, 1831, a dinner was held in honour of Major Cartwright, the particular occasion of the celebration being the erection of a statue to him in Burton Crescent, where he lived and died.[2] "*Hunt* is the only man in the House of Commons whom Cartwright would have called ' *consistent* ' ; he would have been ashamed to own, as his colleagues,

---

[1] *Letter of J. S. Mill*, Vol. I, p. 7.
[2] Now Cartwright Gardens, near Judd Street, King's Cross.

such a crew of *apostates* as *Burdett, Hume, O'Connell, Jones, Brougham, Grey, Denman,* etc."[1]

Working-class disapproval of the Reform Bill, in fact, began to show itself long before that measure was passed. An eruption of political associations took place from 1830 onwards, far more Radical in their objects than those supported by the main body of Whig M.P.'s. When the Bill was passing and was passed, Cobbett's *Weekly Political Register* broke into no salvos of applause ; it merely printed an article with a list of those " Die-hard " peers who had fought Reform to the bitter end, employed a great quantity of the characteristic causticity which Cobbett wielded so effectively, and passed on to the consideration of more pressing subjects. *The Poor Man's Guardian* took the new Act with equal calmness, suggesting " the following pledges to the consideration and adoption of such of our readers as will obtain the right of being represented under the Reform Bill."[2]   These may be regarded, in a sense, as the original Labour programme, and are as follows :

1. Will you pledge yourself to propose or support a measure to obtain for the nation an effectual reform in the Commons House of the British Parliament : the basis of which reform shall be short parliaments, extension of the suffrage to every adult male, vote by ballot, and especially No *Property Qualification* for Members of Parliament ?

2. Will you propose or support the total abolition of all taxes on knowledge ?

3. Will you propose or support the total abolition of tithes and the dissolution of the alliance between Church and State : thus leaving every man to adopt and pay for that religion which he most approves ?

4. Will you propose or support a measure to restore to the people the right of electing Sheriffs and Magistrates ?

5. Will you propose or support a Bill to exclude from the House of Commons placemen and pensioners ?

6. Will you propose or support a measure that will render

[1] Saturday, July 23, 1831.
[2] *Poor Man's Guardian*, July 21, 1832.

justice cheap and expeditious, so that the poor man may no longer continue the victim of oppression ?

7. Will you propose or support the abolition of all monopolies, the repeal of the corn laws, and of all the taxes pressing upon the necessaries and comforts of labouring men ?

It will be seen that this programme included not only the later Chartist proposals (except payment of members and equal electoral districts) but also several industrial reforms. The absence of factory legislation or of free education is somewhat surprising ; but none of the reforms demanded, it will be noted, call for a centralized administration, which would be needed by the two desiderata we have suggested. The first factory inspectors were appointed in 1833, before which date control from London was an impossibility.

During the years which immediately followed the Reform Act, the Government showed itself at least concerned in the state of the country. The propertied classes had had their attention occupied for so many years with the wars, and had then been so distracted by the exaggerated importance given to the Reform Agitation, that they suddenly found themselves in 1832 in a state of mind very similar to that of the working classes. They found themselves confronted with a new industrial England different in all respects from the almost wholly agricultural country of seventy years earlier. They clutched at such doctrines as seemed simplest, and the views of " Parson Malthus " were invoked to help them out of their difficulty of dealing with an immense proletariat with powers that might well be dreaded, though they were not yet understood. Almost the first action of the reformed Parliament was the appointment of a Poor Law Commission, which reported two years later, and on the strength of the recommendations of which the Poor Law was drastically reformed. The next year the Municipal Corporations Act, 1835, removed some of the outstanding abuses of town life. The Poor Law Amendment Act by no means pleased the working classes. It became the subject of much vituperation in *The Poor Man's Guardian* and elsewhere. In Bedfordshire there were numerous riots : a pamperized agricultural population rose up in revolt at out-

door relief being given in kind instead of in money as previously.[1]
At Henfield, Sussex, an attempt to limit outdoor relief resulted
in a riot which necessitated calling up the military.

Cobbett died in June, 1833, having been a member of Parliament just long enough to betray an utter incompetence in
political matters. His only success was the unmasking of
Popay, an *agent provocateur* who had actively incited to violence
against the Government the members of two political unions
in South London. Less than two years later another veteran
died. This was Henry Hunt, M.P. for Preston since 1832.
In the opinion of their common biographer, Robert Huish,
" it is scarcely possible to mention two failures more decidedly
confirmed than the parliamentary career of Hunt and Cobbett."
This condemnation, however, must be discounted by the fact
that Huish regarded the House of Commons as " the most
enlightened assembly in the world,"[2] but it is clear that the
two agitators were somewhat out of place there, and consequently ineffective. Moreover, they were in the difficult
position of having no distinct political programme to guide
them.

The Reform Act, having become law, appears to have exercised a curious psychological influence upon working-class
thought. For many years, almost for generations, Reform
had been the one subject of propaganda ; the sheer lapse of
time had given it some of the features of an established tradition. And now the tradition had been killed, beyond all
hope of resurrection. Although it was perfectly true to say
that the Reform Act had not given the working classes what
they demanded, or, indeed, anything at all, yet many who
noticed the jubilations caused by the passing of the Act, as
well as the fear-stricken opposition it had encountered,
must have felt a keen sense of disappointment, a subtle discontent due to impotence. The thousands who shouted with
Attwood must have experienced this feeling when they realized
that the middle classes alone were to benefit by the measure.
The organized working men were in the unfortunate position

[1] *Annual Register*, 1835, Part 2, p. 110.   Ib. p. 139.
[2] *Life of Henry Hunt*, Vol. II, p. 496.

of a savage tribe which has captured, at considerable cost to itself, a supposed wonder-working idol, only to find that it was a completely useless golliwog.   Some of the exasperation found a safety-valve in amorphous discontent.   In April, 1833, the National Union of Working Men indulged in a series of fierce debates, and wound them up by a fiery resolution, denouncing in the same breath " the pretended reformed House of Commons " and cursing " a pampered Monarchy, an indolent Aristocracy, and a bloated Hierarchy."   This explosion proved to be a swan-song, for the Union shortly disintegrated.   Its low subscription (2s. per annum) doubtless contributed to its decease.   The greater part of the zeal for reform, however, did not roam about in the void, but attached itself to other causes, of which there were several competing for popularity at the time.   Oastler had begun his agitation for a ten-hour day, Hetherington and Cleave exerted themselves to procure the abolition of naval and military floggings, and the Corn Law agitation began to show its head.   On August 6, 1832, the Macclesfield Political Union passed a series of resolutions demanding manhood suffrage, etc., and with this clause :

" That we further request of the electors to demand from candidates, if they are returned, that they will not absent themselves from their duty in Parliament without sufficient cause ; and when in their seat in Parliament, that they will, to the utmost of their influence or power, have the following obnoxious laws repealed, namely, the law of Primogeniture, the connexion between the Church and State, the Tithes, the Corn Laws, the East India Company's Charter, the Bank Charter, all Taxes on Knowledge, and all useless Places and Pensions under the Crown, and all other abuses, whether in Church, State, or Law, that are injurious to the people of these realms."[1]   A further resolution, we should add, declared a consumers' boycott of doctors, grocers, publicans, butchers, bakers, flour dealers, innkeepers, drapers, barbers, and all others who were known to assist any candidate who would not pledge himself to the above.   We see therefore that a

[1] *Poor Man's Guardian*, August 18, 1832.

political programme was gradually coming into being. A method of enforcing these demands also came into existence. This was the General Strike. Even before the Reform Bill had passed into law, one William Benbow had urged this method of securing the inclusion of working men within the Bill. On August 31, 1831, a large meeting of the National Union of the Working Classes took place at the Rotunda, Blackfriars Road. Benbow is reported to have said, *inter alia*,[1] that " he hoped to see a cordial co-operation among the unwashed artisans, and when so united, they had only to say, ' We must be free,' and they would be so two days after. He never did nor would recommend violence of any kind, and at the approaching conference he would advise the working classes that produces everything, and gets only the husks, to dress themselves in their Sunday clothes, and all and every one of them to take a month's holiday, and they might rest assured their rights would be quickly restored. (Great cheering.) " On November 2 he repeated his proposal, which is reported to have evoked (tremendous cheering).[2]

Benbow, in fact, has a strong claim to be regarded as the inventor of the General Strike. Owen was spending an appreciable part of his energies at the time in deprecating strikes,[3] on the grounds that they were wasteful, and that if only the strikers wished it they could do without employers. Let them but adopt Owen's plan of a " Labour Exchange " and all would be well. Benbow, on the fringe of the whirling social movement of which Owen was the centre, was thrown off centrifugally and produced a theory flatly opposed to the latter's. Little is known about Benbow. He appears to have been, in 1831, the keeper of the " Commercial Coffee House, 205, Fleet Street, London." His address and his occupation lead one to suggest the probability that Vincent, Hetherington, Cleave and Watson were known to him. In 1831 he himself printed a pamphlet, *Grand National Holiday and Congress of the Productive Classes*. This contains the General Strike scheme.

[1] *Poor Man's Guardian*, September 3, 1831.
[2] Ib., November 5, 1831.
[3] E.g., *In the Crisis*, July 27, 1833.

The whole of the " productive classes " were to take a month
"off." This "holiday" was to be organized by local committees
all over England, who were to see that holiday-makers behaved
with proper respect to economy and sobriety.   " The working
classes cannot lay in provisions for a month ; this is not
wanted, but every man must do his best to be provided with
food for the first week of the holiday.   Provisions for the
remaining three weeks can be easily procured.   As for wearing
apparel, since the holiday will take place in the summer, there
can be no great difficulty in being provided with sufficient
covering for one month."[1] During the first week, the local
committees were to act ; " they will be enabled to inquire
into the funds of their respective cities, towns, villages and
parishes, and to adopt means of having those funds, originally
destined for their benefit, now applied to that purpose."
Finally, " When all the details of the above plans are put into
execution, the committee of each parish and district shall
select its wise men to be sent to the *National Congress.* A
parish or district having a population of 8,000 shall send two
wise and cunning men to Congress, a population of 15,000
four, a population of 25,000 eight, and London fifty wise and
cunning men.   The advice of the different committees to be
taken as to the most convenient place for conference.   It
should be a central position and the mansion of some great
liberal lord, with its outhouses and appurtenances.   The only
difficulty of choice will be to fix upon a central one, for they
are all sufficiently vast to afford lodging to the members of
the Congress, their lands will afford nourishment, and their
parks a beautiful place for meeting.   It may be relied upon
that the possessor of the mansion honoured by the people's
choice will make those splendid preparations for the representatives of the people that are usually made for the reception of
a common sovereign."[2] Then, the Congress was to reform
society.   The   agenda   for   the   Congress   needed   too   much
discussion and explanation to find a place at the end of a
pamphlet, so Benbow produced a weekly paper, the *Tribune
of the People,* in order to elaborate the proceedings at length.

[1] Op. cit. p. 11.   [2] Ib. p. 13.

The first number was published on June 17, 1832, and does not appear to have had many successors. This is unfortunate, for the early issues contain the imperfectly redeemed promise of a series of articles exposing Owen.[1]

Although Hetherington was nominally the editor of *The Poor Man's Guardian*, much of the actual work was done by a young man named James O'Brien, who wrote elsewhere over the *nom de plume* " Bronterre," and subsequently came to be known as James Bronterre O'Brien. He was born in 1805, and came to London to study law twenty-four years later. Here he fell in with Cobbett and Hunt, and soon Lincoln's Inn knew him no more. In his own words, written in 1837 : " About eight years ago, I came to London to study law and Radical reform. My friends sent me to study law ; I took to Radical reform on my own account. I was a very short time engaged in both studies, when I found the law was all fiction and rascality, and that Radical reform was all truth and matter of dire necessity. Having a natural love of truth, and as natural a hatred of falsehood, I soon got sick of law, and gave all my soul to Radical reform. . . . I feel as though every drop of blood in my veins was Radical blood, and as if the very food I swallowed undergoes at the moment of writing a process of Radicalization."[2]

While he was working on *The Poor Man's Guardian*, Bronterre O'Brien also contributed largely to the innumerable and ephemeral journals which voiced the democratic opinion of the time. He was one of the few among the Chartists who had had the advantage of a good education, and his intellectual powers were among the greatest assets of the movement. As an orator, Bronterre O'Brien seems to have been effective,

---

[1] Benbow was also the author of *The Crimes of the Clergy* (1823), a compilation of crimes committed by Protestant priests in the United Kingdom during two centuries, and a pamphlet, *A Scourge for the Laureate* (1825), an attack upon Southey in reply to a letter by him in the *Times* of December 13, 1824, attacking Byron. In the preface to the first of these works, Benbow describes himself as a Christian. It appears that he had been present at Peterloo.

[2] *Bronterre's National Reformer*, January 7, 1831.

but not overwhelmingly so ; he lacked the irresistible fury
of Feargus O'Connor, or the easy style of Henry Vincent.   On
this point it is worth while remembering that " down to about
this period, with the single exception of the time of the Consolidated Trades Union, even the more enlightened of the working
class had been but little accustomed to public speaking.
The platform had been almost exclusively occupied by the
upper and middle classes, and it could hardly be expected that
the working men, deprived in a great measure of educational
advantages, would become adept speakers in a day."[1]   This
to a certain extent accounts for the success of educated sympathizers among the Chartists.

Bronterre O'Brien appears to have spent the interval between
the closing down of *The Poor Man's Guardian* and the appearance of the Charter by translating Buonarotti's *History of
Babeuf's Conspiracy*, and by gathering material, here and in
France, for a *Life of Robespierre*, of which the first volume,
published in 1837, showed that his object was to clear the
memory of the Jacobin from the calumnies of such writers as
Montgaillard, Mountjoye, and Desodoards.   In January, 1837,
he started a weekly paper, *Bronterre's National Reformer*.
This only ran for eleven weeks, but is nevertheless of interest
as showing the revolutionary cast of O'Brien's views.   The
object of the journal is " To promote a radical reformation in
Government, Law, Property, Religion, and Morals," practically
the whole paper was the work of the editor, who signed his
articles, even when they only extended to a single paragraph,
with the pen-name " Bronterre."   Long letters to the editor,
signed " Philo Bronterre," appeared in every number, including
the first, obviously the work of O'Brien himself.   The *National
Reformer* anathematized vigorously, interjecting short articles
annexed from other papers, on such diverse subjects as the
History of Influenza in Europe, and the Amazing Strength of
the Whale.   The new Poor Law was of course strenuously
assailed.   The Petition of the Working Men's Association was
printed in full in the issue of February 11, and approved in

---

[1] Gammage, *History of the Chartist Movement*, p. 17.

the leading article. After that, for the remaining month of its life, the new programme received the lion's share of the journal's attention. This was symptomatic of the future concentration of O'Brien's energies on the Chartists' demands. If in later years Chartism came to be popularly identified with Socialism, the reason is to be found in the intellectual leadership of Bronterre O'Brien. All the theories and most of the shibboleths bound up with Marxian Socialism are to be found in his pronouncements. The characteristic Marxian denunciation of the rôle of the middle class is O'Brien's. He asks : " Does the artisan or labourer receive a farthing of wages, save through the middle class ? Can the landlord receive a farthing of rent, save through the middle class ? Does not the Government receive almost all the taxes through the middle class ? "[1] Place, commenting on an article written to the greater glory of O'Connor by O'Brien early in 1839, calls it " a rhodomontade " and its author a " three-parts insane and savage man." He also adds in a footnote that when these two Irishmen quarrelled, a little later, they " abused each other to an extent as well as to time and in as bad language as perhaps never before had been done by any two men since newspapers were first published."[2]

We can perhaps best realize this period, as it appeared to the Radical working man of the time, by presenting to ourselves a picture of a crowd dominated by two great giants, Wellington and Owen, the Ahriman and Ormuzd of a long-lived generation. The Duke represented force, corrupt monarchy, flogging in the Army, opposition to reform of whatever character. Owen typified the energies which, if rightly used, could make the depressing world of William IV blossom as the rose. Lovett was one of the sanest of men, but even he could not completely resist the vision. Perhaps the extreme limit of his adherence to Owenism is indicated in a speech delivered at the Co-operative Congress held in London on April 23, 1832, Owen being in the chair. Lovett concluded this oration by

[1] *Northern Star*, April 17, 1841.
[2] Place MSS. 27,821, fo. 22.

declaiming that " the system which they sought to establish was the reverse of the competitive—it was all for each, and each for all ; and if carried into execution would sweep away all this world's cares and troubles, and make it bloom like a terrestrial paradise. (Continued cheers.)"[1]

[1] *The Crisis*, Vol. I, p. 12.

CHAPTER III

THE PEOPLE'S CHARTER

FOR a year or two after the passing of the Reform Act, a distinct working-class reaction took place against political intervention. In December, 1833, Owen formed the Society for National Regeneration,[1] which became the focus of the energies of the more intelligent manufacturers and factory reformers. This on one side, and the sudden growth of the Grand National Consolidated Trades Union on the other, gave a strong impetus to trade union organization, at the expense of political organization. The monstrous sentence of seven years' transportation was inflicted in March, 1834, upon six Dorchester farm labourers for simply belonging to a trade union. In spite of the effort of many of the Radical M.P.'s and the activity of the London Dorchester Committee, the unfortunate men had to serve four years of their sentence. After a short series of strikes, the Grand National ceased to exist by the end of 1834. The following year was filled with the agitation for the repeal of the newspaper stamp. As the result of this the tax was reduced from fourpence to one penny. *The Poor Man's Guardian* came to an end—after 750 persons, it is said, had been prosecuted for selling it, and a court had finally decided that it was not a newspaper at all, " within the meaning of the Act."

The Place Manuscripts, to which frequent references have already been made, were not the only legacy left by the indefatigable tailor of Charing Cross to future historians of his days. In a warehouse in Hendon, a stone's throw from what is facetiously called the " Flying Ground," the British Museum

[1] Webb, *History of Trade Unionism*, p. 143.

74

has caused to be stacked the files of such provincial and other papers as human investigation is unlikely to require for its purposes. Among these impressive and saddening monuments to journalistic effort lies what the authorities call the Place Collection. Here are 180 large volumes of papers, mainly printed, newspaper cuttings, manifestos, etc., gathered together and preserved by the energy of Francis Place. A set of twenty-nine volumes tells the story of the Chartist movement from 1836 to 1847. The first of the volumes of this set contains a long introduction in Place's handwriting, in which he summarizes—so far as the most prolix of men could summarize—the " Proceedings, principally of working men, to procure a reform in the House of Commons." In the following pages we shall follow Place's own account, but not in his words, which are too many.

Dr. John Roberts Black, of Kentucky, being desirous of helping the British working man, formed a committee, of which he acted as chairman, to pay the fines imposed on Hetherington and Cleave for printing and selling unstamped periodicals, especially *Hetherington's Twopenny Dispatch*, and *Cleave's Police Gazette*. This committee, having achieved its original object, decided to keep going and to wage an agitation for the complete repeal of the " taxes on knowledge." He therefore made the committee the nucleus (" under my direction," as Place takes care to explain in a marginal note) of a body first called the Association of Working Men to procure a cheap and honest press. The ostensible purpose of the Association was the instruction of working men in the three r's and a little more. The purpose which lay nearer the hearts of Place and Black, however, was the political education of their students. The notion was being spread by the working-class agitators of the day that " every kind of property belonged solely to the working people . . . and that the land belonged to them in common." Place regarded this doctrine as pernicious. So also did he consider the existing state of society. The agitators, however, attempted to unite their forces and adopt a simple programme. On June 10, 1836, five or six persons met in London, and called themselves a " General

Meeting of the Central Committee of the Metropolitan Radical Unions " ; as Place acidly explains in a footnote, " there were no such unions in existence at this time." These persons decided to form the Working Men's Universal Suffrage Club. Feargus O'Connor was appointed treasurer, and John Russell, secretary. Various other persons (notoriety hunters, says Place) soon joined O'Connor. Augustus Harding Beaumont was one of the most prominent of these ; he was the editor of the weekly *Radical*, had been through the Belgian revolution of 1830 and had written a book about it, and was nearly insane. Daniel O'Connell, M.P., also gave the new body his blessing. Place was asked to join, but refused tactfully. The working classes, however, refrained from welcoming the Club. The subscription, to tell the truth, was the reason. A working man could not be expected to pay £1 yearly, in addition to an entrance fee of five shillings. After the end of June, consequently, no more was heard of the Club.

Place, however, seems to have promptly picked up the pieces of this unsuccessful venture and united them with his Association, which, after August, developed into a propagandist body and called itself the Working Men's Association for Benefiting Politically, Socially and Morally the Useful Classes. The Association, probably in ignorance of its originator, unanimously elected Place an honorary member, and in equal ignorance of his views, conferred the same honour upon Feargus O'Connor and Robert Owen.

The Working Men's Association was formally established on June 26, 1836, when a prospectus and rules were submitted and agreed to. The prospectus began as follows :

" Among the causes that most contribute to the perpetuation of abuses and corruptions in every department of the State, and the indifference manifested towards the interest of the millions, none have been more pregnant with evil than the divisions and dissensions among the working classes themselves." [1] The prospectus continues in this strain throughout, and the objects are to the same effect. The Association, it would appear was to concentrate on the industrial salvation of the

[1] British Museum, Additional MSS. 37,773.

working classes. Members were to belong to the " industrious classes " ; others might be elected, but they were to be mere honorary members not of the working classes. The original list of members contained thirty-three names. William Lovett was the first secretary, Henry Hetherington the first treasurer.

By October 18 the Association had decided—or been persuaded by Lovett to decide—that they had " no confidence in either Whig or Tory government, believing both parties to be alike the enemies of just legislation and obstacles in the way of establishing peace and happiness in this country." They had not gone so far as to demand the establishment of a Labour Party, in spite of their distrust of the powers that were. All that was demanded was " Universal Suffrage, the Protection of the Ballot, Annual Parliaments, Equal Representation, and No Property Qualification for Members."[1] The same declaration objurgates the " men under the guise of reformers . . . etc. . . . And who, to complete the catalogue of their iniquity, have passed, supported, and landed the infamous Poor Law Bills."

On November 15 Feargus O'Connor was elected an honorary member ; three weeks later, Robert Owen was also elected

At the end of February 28, the W.M.A. held a meeting at the Crown and Anchor Tavern, in order to submit a petition for presentation to Parliament demanding Equal Representation (200 electoral districts of equal size), Universal Suffrage (males over the age of twenty-one, residential qualification six months), Annual Parliaments (general election every June 24), No Property Qualification (but 200 supporters required to nominate), Vote by Ballot (to take place in the Church buildings), and Payment of Members (£400 a year). This petition was submitted to a public meeting at the " Crown and Anchor," in the Strand, on February 28, 1837, and approved. This was the " nucleus of the far-famed *People's Charter*, which may be said to have had its origin at this meeting."[2]

The petition also contained, by way of preamble to the demands, a number of abstract propositions. In these, as

[1] Fo. 17.   [2] *William Lovett : an Autobiography*, p. 102.

may be expected, natural rights are assumed without qualification. Thus we are told : " That any constitution or code of laws formed in violation of men's political or social rights are not rendered sacred by time nor sanctified by custom."[1]

On May 31, 1837, a meeting was convened by the Working Men's Association at the British Coffee House in Cockspur Street. This was attended by several M.P.'s,[2] who had been invited in order that the Association might see to what extent they might be relied on to give parliamentary support to the petition. J. A. Roebuck (1801–79), the philosophic Radical M.P. for Bath, was to present the petition to the House. These members, however, unanimously declared that they could not support all the principles laid down in the petition, on various grounds. Lovett appears to have protested with some warmth that the " gentlemen thought more of their *seats* in Parliament than they did of their *principles*," whereupon Daniel O'Connell " began a warm and very eloquent philippic." Peace, however, was restored, and the meeting adjourned for a week. O'Connell then brought forward a series of motions, all of which were agreed to, and then the following resolution was carried :

" That a committee of twelve persons be appointed to draw up a Bill or Bills in a legal form embodying the principles agreed to, and that they be submitted to another meeting of the Liberal members of Parliament and the Working Men's Association."

The committee appointed on the strength of this resolution consisted of :

O'Connell, Roebuck, Leader, Hindley, Thompson, and Crawford (M.P.'s).

Hetherington, Cleave, Watson, Lovett, Vincent, and Moore (W.M.A.).

The death of William IV immediately after this meeting,

---

[1] A copy of this petition is in the British Museum, with the inscription " The Prayer of this Petition was the origin of the People's Charter. W. L." (Lovett). 1838. A. 55(10).

[2] Joseph Hume, Daniel O'Connell, Dr. Bowring, J. T. Leader, Col. Thompson, B. Hawes, W. S. Crawford, and Charles Hindley.

and the consequent stir of a general election, postponed the operations of the committee.

The election dealt hardly with the members of Parliament who had gone as far as we have just described. Roebuck and Thompson lost their seats, while Daniel O'Connell antagonized the W.M.A. by furiously attacking trade unionism. When the committee was at last to meet Roebuck was suddenly drawn away by his interest in the Canadian troubles of 1837-8. Finally it fell to Lovett alone to draw up the Bill. He made an effort, and took the result to Roebuck, who suggested that Lovett should show it to Francis Place, who made several suggestions, which were immediately adopted. Then the committee of twelve met, and various alterations were made at the instance of Hume and Roebuck. The first draft contained a provision for woman suffrage, " but as several members thought its adoption in the Bill might retard the suffrage of men, it was unfortunately left out."[1] That is Lovett's account. An MS. statement by Francis Place as to the origins of the Charter[2] does not even mention Lovett and is even more explicit.

" You will recollect," he tells the future historian, " that three or four years ago there were a number of weekly newspapers conducted by A. Beaumont, O'Brien, John Bell, O'Connor, Bernard, and several others, the purpose of which was (to) excite insurrections against property, which, under the name of capital, they denounced as the principal cause of low wages and the depression of the people, and the poor law as the production of the higher and middle classes, the ' plundering ' classes, for the purpose of robbing and keeping in ignorance the productive class, who alone were entitled to all the produce and all the commodities in the country. . . . There was foolish Owenism, too, operating to some extent and great mischief was done. As, however, the doctrines of each of these men differed in some particulars, so the people were formed into many different squads, but all believing or hoping that a change in their favour was about to take place. . . . But some among

---

[1] *Life and Struggles of William Lovett*, p. 170.
[2] P. 160, 27,835, dated August 2, 1839.

the Working Men's Association were displeased with this state of things and persuaded that it would be much better that a plan should be adopted in which all might concur, and by concurring call the people off from these absurdities, and they proposed Annual Parliaments, Voting by Ballot, Universal Suffrage, etc. The proposal was laid before the Society and unanimously adopted. A correspondence was opened with several members of the House of Commons, and it was agreed to call a public meeting for the purpose of adopting a plan to obtain Annual Parliaments, etc., etc. The meeting was held at the British Coffee House. Several M.P.'s attended it. The meeting, after some time spent in speech making, was adjourned for a week, when about a dozen M.P.'s attended, and a committee of six M.P.'s and six Working Men was appointed to draw up a Bill for Annual Parliaments, etc., each of the twelve signing his name to the resolutions. The M.P.'s, however, never gave themselves any further trouble in the matter; time went on, nothing was done and the men became dissatisfied. After a time they came to me, and I agreed to draw up the outlines of a Bill for them : (1) because if it was left to them it was probable that it would not be a creditable production ; (2) because Roebuck, who had undertaken to draw it, was in very bad health, and occupied with parliamentary business to an extent which induced him to promise that if I would draw the Bill he would look over the draft and perfect it ; (3) a genuine promise being made to me that the Working Men's Association would give up the writers before alluded to and would take no further cognizance of the poor law."

How are these two accounts to be reconciled ? Both Lovett and Place were men of sterling honesty. An explanation is suggested by two documents in the Place Collection. When Lovett was starting his National Association in 1841, he sent the rules in proof to Place for his advice. The Collection contains the rules in proof, with all Place's suggested emendations marked on it, and a copy of the rules as finally printed. By comparing the two we see that Lovett adopted virtually none of Place's suggestions. This leads one to suppose that in the authorship of *The People's Charter* Place was responsible for less than he, in perfectly good faith, claimed as his own work.[1]

On the title page of the thirty-six-page pamphlet which bore the name of *The People's Charter*, we find in the place of the author's name, " Prepared by a Committee of Twelve Persons—Six Members of Parliament and Six Members of the London Working Men's Association—and addressed to the People of the United Kingdom." The names of the M.P.'s are not divulged ; while the short introduction is followed by the signatures of thirteen working men, the Committee of the Association, with Hetherington as treasurer, and Lovett as secretary. There is a frontispiece showing elaborately how voting in secret is to be conducted. The introduction is partly historical, otherwise it is an expansion of the thesis that " self-government by representation is the only just foundation of political power—the only true basis of Constitutional Rights—the only legitimate parent of good laws." The preamble repeats this in different words.

The practical proposals of the Charter then follow. First come the qualifications for an elector. He must be male, a British subject, " twenty-one years " (presumably not less than that age), not declared insane by a jury, unconvicted of felony, bribery at elections, personations, or forgery of election certificates. The next clause deals with electoral districts, of which there are to be 300 in the United Kingdom, each containing " as nearly as may be," an equal number of inhabitants, according to the figures of the last census. Each electoral district is to return one member, and the Home Secretary to be responsible for the delimitation of the districts after the passing of the Charter into law, and after every subsequent decennial census. The expenses of these operations to be paid out of the public treasury. The next clause deals with registration and returning officers. These are to be elected every three years at the same time and in the same manner as the member of Parliament for the district. He is to appoint a deputy, to receive nomination, to proclaim the state of the

[1] Lovett is described on his tombstone as " the author of the People's Charter."

ballot, to keep the list of voters, and decide whether a man is eligible to vote or not.   He is to be paid £500 per annum out of the public treasury, and may be dismissed by a committee of the House of Commons, numbering seven, on proof of incapacity or corruption.   The first election is to be conducted by returning officers appointed temporarily *ad hoc* by the Home Secretary.   The deputy returning officers will preside at each balloting place, and will make local arrangements and be responsible for the conduct of each voting station.   He is to be paid three guineas for his day's work.   Voting is to begin at 6 a.m. and end at 4 p.m. on the same day.   Subsequent clauses explain the method of registration through the parish clerks.   To avoid frivolous candidatures, a hundred electors are required to nominate.   They are to present their requisitions to the local returning officer, between the 1st and 10th of May in each year, and he is to exhibit the names of the candidates so nominated not later than May 13.   A similar arrangement is suggested in the event of seats falling vacant by the death of their holders, etc.   If there is more than one candidate, the returning officer " shall, at any time between the 10th and 31st of May (Sundays excepted), appoint such times and places (not exceeding) as he shall think most convenient to the electors of the district for the candidates to appear before him at midday, then and there to explain their views, and solicit the suffrages of the electors."   The returning officer is to make the arrangements for these meetings, and " for the purpose of keeping good order and public decorum, the returning officer shall either take the chair at such meetings himself, or appoint a deputy for that purpose."   The election day is to be the first Monday in June.   Further regulations prescribe the exact course of action to be taken by the returning officer and his subordinates.   The House of Commons is to meet on the third Monday in June of each year, and is to be prorogued on the first Monday of the following June.   A register of the daily attendance of each member is to be kept, and published at the end of each session.   Members are to be paid £500 a year. The last section of the Charter is a list of penalties for register- ing in more than one district, forging certificates of residence,

personating voters, bribery canvassing (one month's imprisonment for the first offence, two months for the second), etc.

We may nowadays laugh at the state of mind which could
contemplate with equanimity, indeed with pleasure, the
prospect of an annual general election, involving electioneering
excitements over a period of about five weeks. We may criti-
cize the Chartists for that palpable lack of subtlety in political
thought which hindered them from foreseeing those difficulties
in the system of direct representation for which the advocates
of Proportional Representation profess to have found a remedy.
We may wax cynical over their naïve belief that uneducated
humanity would immediately seize the new machinery of
government for the amelioration of its own lot. The fact
remains that the external symbols of democracy had lost
none of their exaggerated importance since 1776, but that
rather the French Revolution had given democratic ideas a
new impetus.

This pamphlet, we may add, was widely read, and passed
through several editions, being slightly amended in view of
various suggestions made by its readers. In the preface to
the third edition, we find this significant paragraph :

" Among the suggestions we received for improving this
Charter is one for embracing women among the possessors
of the franchise. Against this reasonable proposition we have
no just arguments to adduce, but only to express our fears of
entertaining it, lest the false estimate man entertains for this
half of the human family may cause his ignorance and prejudice
to be enlisted to retard the progress of his own freedom. And,
therefore, we deem it far better to lay down just principles,
and look forward to the rational improvement of society, than
to entertain propositions which may retard the measure we
wish to promote."

We have heard all this repeated very recently.

It is important to remember, nevertheless, that the ideas and
proposals contained in the Charter was but the crystallization
of a body of thought held in solution by two generations of
Radicals. The word Charter itself was probably suggested by
unconscious memory rather than by inspiration. About the

year 1832 there flourished an anonymous pamphleteer who actually brought out a booklet, entitled *The People's Charter*, in which every one of the Six Points was anticipated. It would be interesting, were it possible, to have the identity of the writer established. He wrote a fair-sized book, *The Rights of Nations* (1832), which began as an attack on monarchy, but developed into a political programme in which opposition to aristocracy and religion were the principal factors. The author had a touching faith in the power of the facial angle to indicate the level of intelligence, and published an amusing array of portraits on this assumption, showing that the profile of Ferdinand VII had a facial angle half-way between that of an orang-outang and that of Jeremy Bentham. *The People's Charter* was virtually a condensation of this book, the first half being anti-monarchical, and the second, the " Principles of Representative Government," expressed as a number of postulates, with comments and illustrations. In the same year, the author brought out *The Reformer's Catechism*, " in which the principles of *The Rights of Nations* are reduced to question and answer, adapted to the capacities of youth, and rendered a substitute for the mind-destroying trash too generally taught at an early age." The memorizing of a catechism running to 139 pages, consisting mostly of either statistical or theoretical affirmations, it is feared, would frustrate this amiable desire to preserve the youthful mind from unnecessary damage. There were several catechisms, generally shorter than the one just mentioned, on the market during the last years of the Reform agitation. We find in them all, generally speaking, partial anticipations of the Chartist programme, and occasional bursts of humour. Quotations from Byron are a characteristic feature of these publications. The more revolutionary Shelley does not appear to have struck the Radical imagination to any appreciable extent.

References have already been made to Feargus O'Connor, to whom a full-length introduction is now advisable. This character, who plays the most conspicuous part in the Chartist drama, had most of the qualities of a great demagogue, and all the defects of the lower-grade politician. Like so many of those who have swayed great masses of working men, he came of another class. His father, Roger O'Connor (1762–1834), had been an active member of the United Irishmen, and was not completely sane. A brother of his father, Arthur O'Connor (1763–1852), had also belonged to the United Irishmen, and had been tried with O'Coigley in 1798. On his liberation in 1803 he went to France as the authorized agent in that country of the Irish revolutionists, and was made a general by Napoleon in the following year, although neither before nor after his promotion did he see active service. In 1818 he was naturalized in France, and remained there until his death. Feargus O'Connor therefore could always enjoy the feeling that he came of a family of revolutionaries ; this, when communicated, added to his prestige and was a great asset, especially when counselling moderation. He was born in 1794, and, naturally enough considering his heredity and environment, attached himself to the " Liberator," Daniel O'Connell. His youth was divided between farming and skirmishing. When the Reform agitation entered Ireland, O'Connor enlisted in its support in his native county, Cork, and was rewarded by being returned to Parliament for the county at the General Election of 1832. His energies were now distributed between Ireland and Radicalism, both causes being attended to with a keen eye to possible leadership. In 1835 he quarrelled with O'Connell, and shortly afterwards was unseated on account of some question of property qualification. When Cobbett died in the same year, O'Connor contested the vacant seat, having decided that, on the whole, an English spring-board promised the more striking flight. His candidature merely succeeded in splitting the vote of Cobbett's son, and so allowed Oldham to go over to the Tory party. After this adventure O'Connor spent nearly two years in touring the country and addressing meetings. He had a fine commanding presence ; he stood more than six feet high, and was broad in proportion. He had a thunderous voice and gigantic physical strength, both of which he could display to great advantage. The need for factory legislation, Radical principles in general, and virulent abuse of the new Poor Law were the raw material of his oratory. O'Connor possessed in an extraordinarily developed degree, sharpened by vast practice, the gifts of the mob-orator. Although a poor humorist, he could raise prodigious laughter on the least attractive basis. His speeches read poorly, for the intellectual element is very thinly diffused in them, but it is obvious that given the right delivery, and a suitably uncritical audience, they would have enormous effect. It was not long before O'Connor realized that the English working class was to be his master and his servant, and he therefore chose a deliberately ostentatious manner to break with middle-class reformers.

On April 20, 1837, a meeting was held at the Crown and Anchor Tavern to raise a subscription to erect a monument to the " Scottish Reform Martyrs " of 1794–5, Muir, Margarot, Skirving, Palmer, and Gerrald. Virtually all the speakers were Whig M.P.'s, among them Joseph Hume, Sir William Molesworth, and Colonel Thompson. Things went fervently and unanimously until Feargus O'Connor rose to speak. Francis Place has preserved for us three contemporary newspaper reports of the riotous subsequent proceedings. In the intervals during which speech was possible O'Connor moved a long amendment to the original resolution, the gist of which was that " this meeting recognize universal suffrage as the only basis of a free constitution."[1] This, after a speech by Henry Vincent applauding, on the part of the W.M.A., the monument proposal, could not be regarded as anything but an effort to break up the meeting, in the name of democracy.

In the same year he quarrelled with the leaders of the W.M.A., and attempted to wreck the society by starting the London Democratic Association as a rival body. He also founded *The Northern Star*, basing its fortunes on his personal popularity in the factory districts. The following account is given of its start : " J. Hobson, Mr. Hill, and others in Yorkshire, seeing the want of a newspaper, as an organ for the rising movement, had succeeded in raising a few hundreds of pounds,[2] by shares, to establish one. O'Connor persuaded them that they would not be able to get the necessary amount, and that the mixed

---

[1] Place MSS. 27,816, fo. 430–440.
[2] According to Gammage, £800 was the amount.

authority of a committee would hamper the editor, and make the paper inefficient. He proposed that the shareholders should lend him the money raised, for which he would guarantee interest, and that he would find the rest of the capital, and commence the paper at once ; and that Hobson should be the publisher and Hill the editor. . . . There is every reason to believe that at that time he had no capital, and that the money of the shareholders was the only money ever invested in the paper. Fortunately for him it soon rose to a very large circulation, reaching at least to some 60,000 a week."[1] For that matter, all O'Connor's financial operations are wrapped in mystery, owing to his non-possession of any arithmetical sense, rather than to frequently-alleged but never-substantiated dishonesties. The headquarters of the paper was in Leeds, and its sale, considering the price was $4\frac{1}{2}d.$, is truly remarkable. The editor was the Rev. William Hill, a Unitarian minister and a writer of some ability. *The Northern Star* gave the utmost publicity to O'Connor's speeches and, in fact, to everything that was said on the Radical side, provided, of course, that it emanated from quarters which were approved of by the dictatorial orator. Thus, when the Charter was actually published, O'Connor neglected to pay it any attention for some months. This course was probably dictated by his dislike of the W.M.A., which called him " the great I AM of politics "[2] in a reproachful letter, which he published in his own paper, in accordance with his usual custom. Little by little, however, O'Connor allowed himself to be converted to Chartism, owing to the virtual identity of its " Six Points " with his own tenets, and for the purely physical reason that he was unable to write the whole paper himself and had therefore to allow his contributors a certain scope. Oastler was one of these, and wrote up the grievances of the factory-workers in a fiercely indignant series of signed articles. Bronterre O'Brien became a sort of London correspondent, sending every week a curious, spluttering mixture of statistics and socialism, diluted with abuse of the Gov-

[1] Quoted by Lovett from the *Temperance Weekly Record* in his autobiography, p. 173.
[2] *Northern Star*, February 24, 1838.

ernment, with occasional excursions into the merely topical.

The year 1835 contained enough to infuriate a milder team of contributors than those associated with O'Connor. Prices had suddenly leaped upwards ; employment had as suddenly become scarce, especially in the North. O'Connor began to look about him for a programme, and decided to give his backing to Radicalism. He began the 1838 campaign by declaring for rejecting secret voting, and continued by accepting a panacea.

" In our last we threw away the scabbard, the Ballot ;[1] we now draw the sword, which is *Universal Suffrage.* At no period of the history of this country was there a greater necessity for a strong manifestation of popular moral force than at the present moment. For now more than five years of the reformed era have we been looking in vain to the promised produce of that tree. . . ." The article ends : " Laws, made by all, would be respected by all. . . . Universal Suffrage would, at once, change the whole character of society from a state of watchfulness, doubt, and suspicion, to that of brotherly love, reciprocal interest, and universal confidence."

By the time the People's Charter came to be published, O'Connor's enthusiasm for Universal Suffrage was barely controllable. In the week in which the Charter was issued, he came out with the following :

" Away, then, with the whole system at once : the wound is too deep to be healed by partial remedies ; the nation's heart's blood is flowing too rapidly to be stopped by ordinary stypticks. Talk not to us of your Eleven Hours Bill ; the demand will regulate the supply, and if we have now two hundredfold the producing power which we recently had, either the producers must work in proportion, or else those who talk of over-population must create a sufficient population to require the increased produce. Give us, then, the only remedy for all our social and political maladies ; make every man in his artificial state as he might be in his natural state, his own

---

[1] *Northern Star*, February 17, 1838. The point of the leading article of the previous week was that the Secret Ballot would be an obnoxious innovation in the actual state of the franchise law.

to the " physical force " Chartists, with Bronterre O'Brien
and Feargus O'Connor, and a few specimens of his eloquence
given us by Gammage certainly somewhat discredit his pacific
claims. Thus, at a meeting held in Newcastle on January 1,
1838, four months before the publication of the Charter, that
is to say before Chartism could be described as a movement at
all, Stephens declared that he " was a revolutionist by fire,
he was a revolutionist by blood, to the knife, to the death."[1]
We may concede that Stephens did " protest too much " without ceasing to believe that he anticipated that moral suasion
would be insufficient to bring his views into operation. Another
quotation supplied by Gammage represents Stephens as saying :
" If the rights of the poor are trampled under foot, then down
with the throne, down with the aristocracy, down with all
rank, all title, and all dignity." The extraordinary thing is
that in spite of having expressed such sentiments, Stephens
continued to describe himself as a Tory, and to deny that he
was a democrat. In point of fact he always denied that he
was a Chartist himself, even though his energies were so largely
spent on the spread of Chartist principles.

While we are enumerating the various towers of strength at
the disposal of the physical force party, it should not be supposed
that the W.M.A. was deficient in oratorical weight. Hetherington was a fine, convincing speaker, and Lovett could hold
his own in argument. The best orator of the Association,
however, was Henry Vincent, one of the six working men on
the committee from which the Charter emanated. He was
born in London in 1813, was a journeyman printer by profession, and had spent his boyhood in Hull. The Revolution of
1830 had roused his interest in politics, and Vincent soon found
himself a Radical ; he came to London about 1835, and made
friends with the Lovett-Watson group within a year or so. A
description of him, written a few years later, may be quoted :
" In figure Vincent is rather below the average height ; he is
firmly and handsomely built, and dresses with neatness and
good taste. His complexion is clear, fresh, and ruddy ; his
hair light and flowing ; and his eyes, keen and animated, are

[1] Gammage, *History of the Chartist Movement*, p. 56.

of a dark blue. His head is large, and well developed in the intellectual regions ; his features are finely cast and expressive of much feeling, benevolence, and good humour. In his moral character we believe Vincent to be unimpeachable."[1] At the age of twenty-five, he was already the "Demosthenes of Chartism." It may be added that Vincent was a Christian, had hankerings after respectability, and shared Lovett's feminist opinions. Vincent, Hetherington and Cleave became the missionaries of the W.M.A., journeying over England to propagate universal suffrage.

Independently of either the W.M.A. or of O'Connor, Birmingham was awakening to life. Thomas Attwood, one of its M.P.'s, continued the battle for reform. A piece of exaggerated verbosity gained the attention of the young Benjamin Disraeli and so, indirectly, of the country. It became generally understood among the Radical reformers that much was to be expected of Birmingham, and the movement gained in strength in consequence. On January 18, 1836, Attwood addressed a meeting in the Birmingham Town Hall, urging the completion of the measures of Corporation Reform brought forward during the previous years, " a substantial but judicious and safe Reform of the House of Lords," and the Reform of the Irish Church. In the course of his address he threatened he would raise twenty million men and bring them down upon his opponents. Three days later Disraeli published his third *Letter of Runnymede*, the exuberant verbiage of which must have done much to advertise Attwood. The first paragraph is worth quoting—it is so quintessentially Disraelian : " Sir,— You may be surprised at this letter being addressed to you ; you may be more surprised when I inform you that this address is not occasioned by any conviction of your political importance. I deem you a harmless, and I do not believe you to be an ill-meaning, individual. You are a provincial banker labouring under a financial monomania. But amidst the seditious fanfaronnade which your unhappy distemper occasions you periodically to vomit forth, there are fragments of good feelings

[1] *Cheltenham Free Press*, November 5, 1842, quoted from *Leeds Times*,

which show you are not utterly denationalized in spite of being
' the friend of all mankind,' and contrast with the philanthropic
verbiage of your revolutionary rhetoric, like the odds and ends
of ancient art which occasionally jut forth from the modern
rubbish of an edifice in a classic land—symptoms of better
days, and evidences of happier intellect."

After which Disraeli proceeds to belabour the " mystical
yet expeditious means by which 20,000,000 men are brought
into the field by a modern demagogue," for the total number
of adult men in the country was but 4,000,000.

Attwood, however, had revised the Birmingham Political
Union, and by the time Victoria had become Queen it had
regained its old qualities of royalist Radicalism, with, of course,
the distinctive Attwood views on currency.   In 1837, a month
before her accession, the Princess Victoria was presented by
Attwood and Scholefield with an expression of loyalty and
admiration on the part of the Radical Reformers of Birmingham.   In the course of the same year Lord Melbourne received
three separate memorials on the currency question from the
B.P.U.[1]   It is said that such was his popularity in Birmingham
about this time that on the day of the proclamation of the
Queen in that city, " a most extraordinary and unprecedented
compliment was paid by the people to Thomas Attwood.   As
soon as they caught sight of him walking in the procession, the
young and interesting Queen was entirely forgotten, and the
whole affair was turned into a gigantic demonstration in honour
of him, to the infinite disgust of the Tories, who were compelled to walk about for three hours listening to deafening
shouts of ' Attwood for ever!' "

" Birmingham soon became the centre from which all political proceedings emanated, but the very same causes which
gave it this influence divided its power and at length put it
at least into a state of abeyance.   Mr. Feargus O'Connor . . .
had become the working people's orator ; he was indefatigable
in travelling from place to place, and everywhere he went
great crowds assembled and to them he said whatever seemed
to him useful for his own purpose, with very little sense and

[1] Wakefield, *Life of Thomas Attwood*, p. 305.

even less judgment, but with a volubility, a clear good voice and a manner which was sure to carry his much less informed hearers along with him. In this business he was mainly assisted by A. H. Beaumont, Dr. Taylor, Oastler, Stephens, Vincent, Harney, and several others, all of them ill-informed, outrageous, mischievous persons. Thus was Mr. Attwood and his especial friends pushed into the background. These men (O'Connor, etc.), by their earnestness, their confident way of predicting events, and especially their repeated assurances of a speedy overthrow of all our social institutions and the establishing in their places a much more rational and consequently just system which should give to each of the producing, ' the only useful class,' all the wealth in the country, the complete control for the future, with treble wages and never-failing employment, yet not exceeding eight hours a day, by these means they became the acknowledged leaders of the masses of the working people in many thickly populated places, at least of all those who were at all willing to interfere in public matters, and these, who must have been nearly the whole of them, were more at their command than they or their fellows had ever before been to anything like the same comparative extent. This, in proportion as it excited the people, made their leaders crazy and they committed wonderfully foolish extravagances."[1]

In Birmingham a virtual contest took place for the leadership of the local Political Union between Attwood and O'Connor. Both men talked largely, attempting to outdo each other in violence. In the end both O'Connor and Attwood were discredited. The rhetoric of the Irishman frightened the Council of the B.P.U., who could hardly bring themselves to believe O'Connor's statement that he never invoked any force more physical than public opinion.[2] Attwood was growing disinclined to take a strenuous part in politics, and so the Birmingham movement lost both leaders. In May, 1839, we find Attwood complaining that he had " set the whole machinery in

[1] Place Collection at the British Museum (Hendon), set 56, Vol. 2, preface to newspaper cuttings.
[2] *Northern Star*, November 17, 1838.

motion," but that his followers refused to follow.[1] Whatever
Birmingham thought of its leaders, it at any rate listened to
them.   At an open-air meeting held on August 6, 1838, 200,000
persons are said to have been present.[2]

We see, therefore, that no sooner was the Charter published
than three bodies of opinion, differing in several important
respects, were ready to take it up.   These were first the members of the W.M.A., led by Lovett, Hetherington, Cleave,
Watson, and Vincent, who took care not to adulterate the
pure doctrine of the Charter by any admixture of other social
reforms.   This party was composed largely of atheists ; its
leaders had all been concerned previously in the agitation for
an unstamped press ; they were deliberately plebeian, believed
in peaceful methods, and were centred in London.   The second
party was led by Attwood, Scholefield, and Muntz ; its members belonged to the Birmingham Political Union, and were
more or less committed to Attwood's monetary reform proposals, and were extremely loyal to the Queen, and generally
constitutional.   Finally, in the north were the readers of *The
Northern Star*, the followers of O'Connor, Oastler, and Stephens,
who held views on factory legislation and the Poor Laws, and
did not bind themselves to the letter of the Charter.   These
believed in the use of physical force, and were represented in
London by the Democratic Association, led by Harney.   One
additional line of demarcation might be furnished by the attitude of these three parties towards the repeal of the Corn Laws,
but we omit this, believing that this was accidental rather
than essential.   Around the three parties veered the uncertain
figure of Bronterre O'Brien.

" Before consenting to draft the Charter, Place made the
leaders of the W.M.A. promise that they would prevent speeches
against the New Poor Law or for Socialism from being delivered on their platform."[3]   The promise was frequently
broken ; naturally enough, the frequency of its infraction varied

[1] Wakefield, *Life of Attwood*, pp. 344, 345.
[2] Ib. p. 327.
[3] Quoted by Wallas in *Life of Francis Place*, from MSS. 27,835
(160, *b*).

directly with distance from London. Outside London the
W.M.A. had little influence, and the self-denying ordinances of
its leading members could not be expected to have any binding
effect upon the Radical propagandists of the North. The Rev.
J. R. Stephens, for example, hated the New Poor Law with a
bitterness that this century, even at war, cannot parallel. In
Northumberland and Durham he was the most prominent
and the most strenuous supporter of the Charter. Was it to be
expected of him that he should renounce an end for the sake
of a new means to it ? Obviously not. The singleness of
purpose, therefore, for which Place strove was never completely
realized. In so far as it was realized, it is perhaps open to
argument that the extravagant hopes to which the Charter
gave birth, and the utopianism of so many of its less-educated
supporters, were due to this deliberate attempt to isolate and
to strive for one thing only. Its very segregation from other
political tasks accentuated its value.

The shadow of the Physical Force party was visible very
soon after the publication of the Charter. *The Northern Star*
published[1] a series of extracts from speeches by O'Connell in
which force was invoked. Those quoted were concluded with
a few words on the subject of Feargus O'Connor. " I declare
the man who attempts to marshal physical force to be a
coward and a traitor. In every instance where it has been
resorted to, the dupes always consider the last shot and murder
as the completion of their object, whereas it is the commence-
ment of their misery. Moral power is the deliberative reasoning
quality in man's mind, which teaches him how to bear, and
when forbearance becomes a crime. Never will I acknowledge
that you have used your full moral power till every man works
as I have done, and has the vanity to consider that himself,
and himself alone, has gained the point ; and then, should
moral power fail, I will lead you on to death or glory."

Three months later, the irrepressible Harney was beginning
to foam at the mouth in a somewhat dangerous manner.[2]
The breach between O'Connor and the B.P.U. was ostensibly

[1] *Northern Star*, August 25, 1838.
[2] Ib., November 17, 1838.

closed. It had been complicated by what seemed an alliance between the B.P.U. and the hated O'Connell. Feargus O'Connor published a recantation, written more in sorrow than in anger.[1] He pleaded his past services to the Radical cause. " I led you for three years under the fire of the press, the scorn of the respectables, and the denunciation of the interested. . . . I have been arraigned as a physical-force man, when I can confidently appeal to all who have heard me that in my speeches and writings I have been the first to portray the horrors of confusion and civil war. I have never said to the people so much as arm yourselves. . . ." But the very number of *The Northern Star* in which this appeared had another article, also signed by O'Connor, headed " Physical Force," with a disconcertingly different moral. The possession of weapons by a few, he said, was bad, but " the arming of the whole community capable of bearing arms would be the finest means of preserving peace abroad, and harmony and satisfaction at home. . . . By reference and speeches and writing it will be found that I have never so much as said ' arm.' But now I say, ' arm ' ; and I having said it, the fulfilment shall rest with the whole people. ' Arm ' ; but in nowise use those arms—offensively nor defensively—as individuals. . . . They must in nowise be used against the constitution, even in your united strength."

The behaviour of Attwood is also curiously inconsistent. At a meeting got up by the Birmingham Political Union on January 8, 1839, he and Joshua Scholefield recommended the use of physical force.[2] On the 14th of the same month, at a meeting of the Council of the B.P.U., with himself in the chair, Attwood denounced physical force and rhetorically held forth on the certainty of its leading to " an iron despotism."[3]

As the result of these agitations Political Unions were revived all over the country, differing widely in promise, though agreeing on their principles. The Manchester Political Union (formed in 1838) was perhaps an extreme example of the strictly constitutional Chartist organization. Peace and goodwill fairly saturated its objects and rules. There were seven objects in

---

[1] *Northern Star*, December 15, 1838.
[2] Place MSS. 27,821, fo. 10.   [3] Do. fo. 19.

its *Regulations*, etc., and every one of them laid stress on legality. Seven duties were prescribed for the members of the Manchester Political Union, and these are worded in an equally law-abiding spirit. The last two of these are counsels :

" To bear in mind that the strength of our Society consists in the *Peace, Order, Unity* and *Legality* of our proceedings, and to consider all persons as enemies who shall in any way invite or promote violence, discord, or division, or any illegal or doubtful measures.

" Never to forget that, but for the exercise of the above qualities, we shall produce the peaceful display of an immense organized moral power which cannot be despised or disregarded; but that, if we do not keep clear of the *innumerable and intricate Laws* which surround us, the *Lawyer* and the *Soldier* will probably break in upon us, and render all our exertions vain."

The eight duties of the members of the Political Council are in a similar strain.[1]

The Charter had been suggested, and drafted as a compromise, a common basis for Radical action. Launched upon the world at a period of great excitement, it was itself a cause of quarrels and divisions, though not at first acute. We may realize how bitter the feelings of reformers were in those days from the introduction to an article.

" At a time when the rights of industry have received a dangerous, not to say mortal stab, in the persons of the five Glasgow cotton spinners—at a time when O'Connell has avowedly joined the middle-class conspiracy to put down Trades' Combinations—at a time when the artisans of Dublin are threatened with a new police, which is to be so vigilant and effective that ' not two working-men can walk and talk together in the streets without its being know what they are about ! '—at a time when the producers of the nation's wealth are told that they must not meet to consult on the interests of their respective trades, except in the presence of a constable or other constituted spy of the ruling classes—at a time when, in consequence of these nefarious proceedings, every workman in the United Kingdom is threatened with the utter extinction

---

[1] Manchester Political Union, 1838, Regulations, etc.

of his social rights as well as of his civil, and when he is thrown
back as it were on the laws of nature for self-preservation—at
a time when, to facilitate the execution of this foul and fiendish
plot against the interests of labour, the New Poor Law Act is
being forced down the people's throats at the point of the
bayonet (Bradford and Huddersfield, to wit)—at a time of
horrors like these, when every moment that the producers can
steal from their tasks and meals ought to be religously con-
secrated to plans of mutual defence against the enemy—at
such a time, gentlemen, it does verily vex me to have to withdraw their attention for even one hour from the immediate
perils which encompass them."[1]

Into this sentence Bronterre O'Brien, before going on to
write about Canada, compresses all the grievances which the
Reformers of 1838 were attempting to remove. The passage
quoted, however, merely summarizes things as they were at
the beginning of the year. Yet compared with the immediately
preceding years, 1838 was a hubbub of movements and excitements. Opposition to the New Poor Law and the " Bastilles "
animated even the least political members of the working classes.
Neither the King who had just died nor the young Queen who
had succeeded him enjoyed the confidence or even the respect
of the people. Radical organizations suddenly began to come
into existence all over the country. An eruption of manifestos
from all Radical quarters caused attention to be concentrated
in the possibility of immediate political action. Monster
meetings were held in every part of England, Wales, and the
southern half of Scotland. *The Northern Star*, begun late
in 1837, boomed prodigiously. Petitions to Parliament,
calling for the prompt repeal of the New Poor Law, were
presented in large numbers. The Charter was published.

Two events of the year, not of great importance in themselves, attracted an enormous amount of attention and were
the centres of crystallization of much Radical sentiment. The
Dorsetshire labourers, who had been so unjustly deported in
1834, were allowed to return in 1836, but did not actually
arrive until 1838. The tumultuous reception offered them

[1] *Northern Star*, January 31, 1838.

gave a new impetus to the trade-union spirit and to forces working in opposition to aristocratic government. The other incident was the adventure of an ex-brewer named Thom, or Tom, of Canterbury, who went mad and proclaimed himself to be Sir William Courtenay, Knight of Malta, King of Jerusalem, and the Messiah. In the last capacity he preached various doctrines, one of which was the destruction of the Poor Law. Here was something the Kentish labourers understood only too well. An armed force came to the help of Thom. A march was made upon Canterbury, shots were fired, the garrison replied, and finally, Thom and many of his followers were killed, and the remainder captured. The significance of the affair, which caused an enormous sensation at the time, lies in the fact, now made obvious, that the peasantry and the working classes were ready to risk their very lives on the chance of getting rid of the Poor Law, even under lunatic leadership, if no better were forthcoming.

But we have now arrived at the end of a period, and the beginning of an episode.

CHAPTER IV

THE CONVENTION

THE Chartist campaign had begun with a tussle for leader-ship. The various Radical parties had agreed to sink their political differences, and fought for precedence by exaggerating their personal disagreements. An exchange of tactical moves took place between the W.M.A. and the B.P.U. The latter, in effect, accepted the People's Charter on condition that the former accepted the Birmingham Political Union's Petition, and the policy which this implied. In this way each organization succeeded in making impossible the hegemony of the other.

The petition was a document drawn up by R. K. Douglas, editor of the *Birmingham Journal*;[1] it was published only eleven days after the appearance of the Charter. This some-what windy screed began on a note of national self-congratu-lation : " We your petitioners dwell in a land whose merchants are noted for enterprise, whose manufacturers are very skilful, and whose workmen are proverbial for their industry. The land itself is goodly, the soil rich, and the temperature whole-some. . . . For three-and-twenty years we have enjoyed a profound peace." Then follows the other side of the picture. " Yet with all these elements of national prosperity, and with every disposition and capacity to take advantage of them, we find ourselves overwhelmed with public and private suffering. We are bowed down under a load of taxes . . . our traders are trembling on the verge of bankruptcy ; our workmen are starving, capital brings no profit, and labour no remuneration . . ." etc. Then comes the remedy, arrived at by a process

---

[1] Lovett, *Life and Struggles*, p. 201.

of deduction. "We have looked on every side, we have searched diligently in order to find out the causes of distress so sore and so long continued. We can discover none in nature, or in Providence. Heaven has dealt graciously by the people ; but the foolishness of our rulers has made the goodness of God of none effect." And so on, in a tone of deepest disappointment. The Reform Act of 1832 is then described, it " has effected a transfer of power from one domineering faction to another, and left the people as helpless as before. Our slavery has been exchanged for an apprenticeship to liberty, which has aggravated the painful feeling of our social degradation by adding to it the sickening of still deferred hope." Then the tone becomes severe. "We come before your Honourable House to tell you, with all humility, that this state of things must not be permitted to continue . . . and that if by God's help and all lawful and constitutional appliances, an end can be put to it, we are fully resolved that it shall speedily come to an end. We tell your Honourable House that the capital of the master must no longer be deprived of its due reward ; that the laws which make food dear, and those which by making money scarce, make labour cheap, must be abolished ; that taxation must be made to fall upon property, not on industry ; that the good of the many, as it is the only legitimate end, so must it be the sole study of the Government. As a preliminary essential to these other requisite changes, as a means by which alone the interests of the people can be effectually vindicated and secured, we demand that those interests be confided to the keeping of the people. When the state calls for defenders, when it calls for money, no consideration of poverty or ignorance can be pleaded in refusal or delay of the call. . . . We perform the duties of freemen ; we must have the privileges of freemen." Then, at last, come the demands, each of them annotated and explained by corollary propositions. With these we are familiar. It should be pointed out that in this petition only five of the six points of the Charter are mentioned. Equal electoral districts are not demanded ; we find this omission in a great many Chartist documents. It is the only point of which the entire feasibility is open to doubt, and the Chartists themselves probably felt that five-sixths of their programme mentioned in the petition would yield at least ninety-nine hundredths of their expectations.

The next things on the programme were the collection of signatures to the Petition, and the arrangement of its presentation to Parliament, and decision as to subsequent action, should any be required. In order to obtain the signatures, the Petition was brought forward at Chartist meetings all over the country after its publication. It figured conspicuously at the great meeting in Birmingham on August 6, which has already been mentioned. The enormous size of this gathering and its apparent assent to the physical force sentiments and currency theories enunciated by several speakers seriously alarmed the W.M.A. It was at once decided to hold a monster meeting in London, by way of counterblast. About the same time the idea of holding a Convention appears to have been accepted. It was intended that the various Chartist organizations, the Working Men's Associations and Political Unions, should elect forty-nine delegates (an assembly of fifty might constitute a meeting and be illegal), who should meet in London, superintend the final stages of the Petition, present it to Parliament, and decide on further action. The Convention was to raise a fund for its own subsistence, and for the purposes of the campaign. This was to be known as National Rent. Each delegate was to be responsible for the National Rent of his own constituencies, and was to be paid at the rate of ten shillings a day for his attendance. The allocation of seats in the Convention appears to have been left to chance. The B.P.U. elected eight delegates, the W.M.A., with a membership of only 400, elected seven. The Birmingham delegates, on the whole, were middle-class men. They included the two Muntz brothers (one of whom became Attwood's successor in the House), R. K. Douglas, Clutton Salt, John Collins (a Sunday-school teacher), and J. George Edmonds, who was afterwards Town Clerk of Birmingham.

The meeting, to which the W.M.A. had attached the hope of the downfall of O'Connor, was held on September 17, in Palace Yard, Westminster. But how was O'Connor to be kept out?

After all there was a nominal truce between the various sections, and O'Connor was undeniably among the leaders.   The speakers were consequently heterogeneous as to views and expression. J. T. Leader, M.P., was in the chair.   Lovett and Hetherington, Ebenezer Elliott, Cleave, Douglas, Colonel Thompson, and O'Connor were among the speakers.   Elliott and O'Connor metaphorically foamed at the mouth, and the meeting took on itself a hue not expected by its organizers.   O'Connor, claiming to represent " forty or fifty towns in Scotland and England," thrust himself forward as a figurehead.   From the point of view of numbers, the meeting was not to be compared with the Birmingham demonstration.   Only 30,000 are said to have been present, although their earnestness was such as to enable proceedings to last five hours.[1]   On the following day the Anti-Corn Law League was established.   The mere fact that it, too, was to call for working-class support, for purposes similar to those for which the People's Charter had come into existence, made Chartism and Free Trade into rival movements.

As the year 1838 drew to an end, the leaders maintained their ostensible truce and their unspoken feud.   At the end of December, the Rev. J. R. Stephens was arrested for seditious language.   He was speaking of the factory system, not of the Charter, but the Chartists felt his arrest to be very personal to them.   Early in the year The Northern Star had described him as " our pride ; our boast ; our glory ; and our Radical."[2] The movement now felt that it had incurred the anger of the Government ; it was truly revolutionary ; in the modern phrase, it had touched reality.   In January, 1839, Lowery, Harney and Dr. Taylor were chosen delegates to the General Convention at a big meeting at Newcastle-on-Tyne.   Harney, addressing the crowd, assured them, as the representative of the London Democratic Association, that that body had little faith in the coming Convention.   " There were too many men in the Convention who felt no other interest in the movement than their own popularity."[3]   This was virtually a hint that

[1] Gammage, p. 47.   [2] Northern Star, February 10, 1838.
[3] Place MSS. 27,821, fo. 5.

Newcastle need expect no unanimity and that Harney's party (i.e., O'Connor's) did not mind how uncomfortable they made it for their opponents.

It is difficult in these days to realize what hopes were entertained by the organizers of the National Convention of its ultimate effects. There was magic in the very word convention ; its connotation was revolutionary and legislative, although its actual meaning was no more than conference. But in 1839 the very right of public meeting and the liberty to carry on Radical agitations had not yet been completely established, and the thrill of committing an action in defiance of existing governments could be easily earned at the price of attending a Chartist meeting. Some of the Chartists understood the psychological attraction of this aspect of their movement and skilfully exploited it by means of midnight meetings, torchlight processions, and all the paraphernalia of insurrection, inspired and made real by the utterances of the " physical force " party. Thus Dr. John Taylor was able so far to lose his sense of proportion as to declare this debating society " the most extraordinary experiment in politics which was ever presented in the history of any country," and to compare it with other assemblies with which it had nothing in common save its title. Thus Conventions have been more than once held in England, and on several occasions have performed all the functions of Government. Such was the Convention which declared the Throne vacant on the abdication of James, and presented the crown to William ; and another was the Convention which recalled Charles II ; but there was this difference between their position and that of the late Convention, viz., that in their case there existed no other Parliament, while in ours both Lords, and Commons were in full and mischievous operation. From which it would appear that the good doctor actually believed that the National Convention possessed a degree of legislative authority equal to that of the other bodies, although it had not the same power. *The Northern Star* went even farther, contrasting the impotence of Parliament with the omnipotence of the Convention. " The Convention has met ; and never did the eye of freeborn man light upon a more heavenly spectacle. . . . The first sight of the Convention has amply repaid us for years of toil."[1] Even that cooler organ, *The Charter*, declared that, " The aptitude for business—the acuteness—the knowledge—the comprehensiveness of purpose—the singleness of mind—and, above all, the deep and genuine sympathy evinced for the people by the delegates who compose the Convention, would do honour to any body of men, however high the artificial distinctions of society may have placed them, and reflect credit on any constituency by whom they had been selected for the trust confided to them."[2]

The impetus given by the interest in the Convention to the growth of Chartism is indicated by the sudden appearance of several journals. Place says that early in 1839 nine such papers were running. On January 27 the W.M.A. started its own weekly paper *The Charter*, edited by Carpenter. On February 2 a rival called *The Chartist* made its first appearance. Place tells us that Carpenter obtained the backing of the W.M.A. by making false representations, and criticizes the make-up of the paper rather harshly. From a bundle of letters in the first volume of *The Charter* in the Place collection it is, however, to be concluded that he subsidized the unworthy organ with considerable generosity in the evil days which befell it early in 1840. There was no permanent chairman, partly because no single delegate could claim to have the confidence of all the others, partly because a permanent chairman meant a permanent body, which was possibly illegal. For this reason the Convention always solemnly adjourned from day to day, and the members took it in turns to occupy the chair. The number of delegates was originally fixed at forty-nine, in view of the Act (one of the Six Acts) which made fifty the minimum size of a prohibitable seditious meeting. Although fifty-three delegates were elected,[3] in point of fact as many as forty-nine

---

[1] *Northern Star*, February 9, 1839.

[2] *The Charter*, February 17, 1839.

[3] *Northern Star*, March 16 and October 26, 1839, contains the official list. Accounts differ as to the exact number. Lovett's figure and that given by the official list agree with the number we have given.

were never gathered together at any one time. The methods of their election appear to have been various ; and as far as one can gather from the incomplete and inconsistent accounts of what happened, the utmost elasticity seems to have prevailed. Thus, some constituencies elected more than one delegate ; other constituencies, to save expense (so Gammage assures us), combined for the purpose of electing a joint representative. The Chartist plan of equal constituencies and secret voting appears to have been abandoned entirely. The actual election was carried out by the acclamation of a huge crowd, perhaps the most undemocratic method of selection conceivable. The delegates were a curiously mixed body. Besides the leaders of the movement, who, naturally, were elected *en masse*, there were three magistrates, six editors, one Church of England clergyman, one Nonconformist minister, and two doctors. There was a publican, and several working men. The rest were almost all small tradesmen. Several were not appointed until the Convention was actually sitting.[1] According to Place, twenty-nine of the delegates did not work for wages, while the remaining twenty-four did so work.

An examination made by Place of Lovett's monthly report on the attendances for March shows that twenty-nine of the fifty-three delegates were middle-class men and twenty-four working-class men. Thirteen never attended at all and six deserted. Of these nineteen useless members, only five were working-class men.

The Convention met on Monday, February 4, 1839, at the British Coffee House in Cockspur Street, London. Craig, an Ayrshire delegate, took the chair. Proceedings began apparently by an announcement from the chairman that 500,486 signatures had been obtained for the Petition, and that £967 of " National Rent " had been collected. There are three separate accounts of the proceedings of the Convention. One is that of Francis Place,[2] who was not a delegate. The second was that of Dr. John Taylor, who represented Renfrewshire,

---

[1] Place MSS. 27,821, fo. 143.
[2] Ib. MSS. 27,821.

Dumbartonshire, Alva, Tillicoultry, Northumberland, Westmorland and Cumberland at the Convention, and reported its doings subsequently for *The Northern Star.* The third and best is the report in *The Charter.* The first day's proceedings were short ; it is sufficient to quote from the official minutes.

The Rev. Arthur Wade,[1] LL.D., opened the proceedings by a solemn prayer.

On the motion of Messrs. Collins and Moir, Wm. Lovett was elected secretary for the day. It was resolved that any person, whose election is known to two of the delegates present, be considered provisionally a member of the Convention ; but that such person be required to bring a petition and money within a month, to constitute him a permanent member.

It was resolved that the individual expenses of the delegates be a question between them and their constituents.

That Messrs. O'Brien, Vincent and Lovett be appointed a committee to look out for a proper place to meet in, and that they report to-morrow.

Another committee was appointed to draw up rules, etc., and a further committee to draw up an address to the people of Great Britain.

The second day's business consisted of some formal matters, and the adoption of a report recommending that the Hall at Doctor Johnson's Tavern, Bolt Court, Fleet Street, should be the scene of subsequent meetings. It was also resolved " that the delegates present form themselves into sub-committees for the purpose of waiting upon every Member of Parliament, to induce them to support the National Petition and the People's Charter, and that such committees make a written report to the Convention." We find that some members protested against this resolution, declaring that they would not degrade themselves by recognizing the House of Commons in any way. Harney wrote to his " constituents " in March saying : " I have refused to visit members of Parliament to solicit their support of the people's Charter, and why ? Because it is a miserable farce—because it is an absurd waste of time, and, moreover, de-

[1] The delegate for Nottingham.

grading to the characters of free-chosen representatives of the people. Think ye, Englishmen, that these usurpers can be convinced or converted by mere words ? No ; they uphold their usurpation by brute force, and only will they be compelled to listen to our petitions—only will they grant our demands, by force, or the fear of force."[1]

The subsequent days' proceedings of the Convention were devoted to the preparation of a huge Petition to be presented to Parliament—a course of action, it will be noted, hardly compatible with much of the revolutionary verbiage which had preceded the formation of the body. Indeed, in answer to a question in the House of Commons, Lord John Russell, the Home Secretary, stated that the National Convention was " a body for the sole purpose of preparing and presenting petitions to Parliament."[2] The collection of funds was another of its functions. Much of the business of the Convention was of an indescribably petty nature. A committee is appointed to select a doorkeeper. Its report is considered and the delegates who were to reform the universe give a lengthy assent to the employment, at thirty shillings a week, of Mark Crabtree, as doorkeeper and messenger. Yet the delegates kept up their enthusiasm, addressing meetings when they were not addressing one another, still dreaming of the golden days to come when universal suffrage was an established fact—say in three months' time. O'Connor still has the same conceit of himself and his colleagues, writing in his *Northern Star* leader.[3] " The eyes of the whole world are now of necessity directed to the People's Parliament, and it is worthy of universal contemplation." O'Connor, in fact, probably did a great deal to keep up the delusion of the importance of the Convention by harping on the possibilities of its illegal activities. At a public meeting, for example, at which he was the last speaker, he concluded the process, ably started by the previous speakers, of raising the audience to a frenzy of enthusiasm in the following words.[4] " Suppose then, that on the morrow the Convention, in the

---

[1] *Northern Star*, March 30, 1839.
[2] Hansard, February 11, 1839, pp. 219–220.
[3] February 16, 1839.   [4] Do.

discharge of their sacred duty ,were to be illegally arrested—for if they should be arrested it would be illegally—what would they (the meeting) do ? " Here the whole meeting, numbering about 3,000, yelled as one man, " We'd rise ! " and cheered ecstatically. O'Connor, with enormous demagogic skill, declared that he was " hard of hearing," and asked the audience to repeat its promise. And the meeting concluded with deafening cheers and the deep-throated assertion that " We'd rise, we'd fight ! "

So the Convention proceeded, but by degrees even its warmest admirers began to show signs of the qualities which lie between enthusiasm and boredom. *The Northern Star* reporter soon finds it advisable to condense. Much of the discussion to which he listened seems to have impressed him as merely peevish. " A long and desultory conversation ensued, occupying nearly, or fully, two hours."[1] Much time was occupied in the endeavour to induce the people of Ireland to take a share in the doings of the Convention, to which they had elected no delegates. Speeches were made about Ireland and her problems, and a manifesto was drafted and discussed. All this took up a great many days. The Convention, hoping against hope, took legal advice as to its own legality. The solicitor consulted gave as his opinion that there was nothing illegal about the Convention so long as it remained free from the responsibility, direct or indirect, of illegality.

The tendency towards the advocacy of physical force gradually grew. On April 9 Richardson moved the appointment of a committee to draw up a case to be submitted to the Convention relative to the power of the people to arm themselves.[2] He named thirty-one authorities " all of whom spoke in universal terms as to the fact that the possession of arms was the best proof of men being free, and the best security for their remaining so." Lovett cautiously supported this motion, which was all too mild for the majority. Dr. Fletcher moved as an amendment, " That we should not take any legal advice on the subject ; but that this Convention is fully convinced

[1] *Northern Star*, February 23, 1839.
[2] Ib., April 13, 1839.

that all constitutional authorities are agreed in the undoubted right of the people to possess arms." This was carried after a warm debate. Richardson's motion had but four supporters, the " previous question " found six, while Fletcher's amendment had nineteen.

When the petition sheets came to be examined after about a month's session it was found that several populous parts of this country had apparently not been touched by the Chartist propagandists, and missionaries were accordingly sent out, and the presentation of the Petition was deferred. In the meantime the delegates talked. The Secretary of the Convention himself observes, with a sigh : " In fact the love of talk was as characteristic of our little house as the big one at Westminster."[1] As was only to be expected, severe skirmishes took place between the advocates of " physical force " and the constitutional Chartists. G. J. Harney was doing his best to outdo the object of his emulation by flourishing daggers about at the meetings he addressed, by wearing a red cap, and by apostrophizings such as this :

" Hail ! spirit of *Marat* ! Hail ! glorious apostle of equality ! ! Hail ! immortal martyr of Liberty ! ! ! All Hail ! thou whose imperishable title I have assumed ; and oh ! may the God of Freedom strengthen me to brave, like thee, the persecution of tyrants and traitors, or (if so deemed) to meet, like thee, a martyr's death."[2] Thus G. J. Harney, forced by the apathy of the authorities to ever more extreme flights of rodomontade.

The Convention itself endeavoured to put a stop to these histrionics. Harney attempted to get three resolutions passed as follows :

That if the Convention did its duty, the Charter would be the law of the land in less than a month.

That no delay should take place in the presentation of the National Petition.

That every act of injustice and oppression should be immediately met by resistance.

[1] *Life and Struggles of William Lovett*, p. 204.
[2] *The London Democrat*, No. 1, April 7, 1839.

These resolutions meant, of course, the endorsement of " physical force " by the Convention.

James Whittle, the editor of *The Champion*, a paper upholding the Cobbett tradition, brought forward a resolution that Harney and two other members of the Convention who shared his views should apologize for and disclaim the three resolutions quoted above. They refused, whereupon Whittle threatened a resolution expelling them from the Convention. They then climbed down and apologized as required. But that was not the end of the mischief. At a public meeting held on March 16, Bronterre O'Brien announced that 1,200,000 signatures to the Petition had already been obtained,[1] and hinted at " an equal number of pikes." Harney predicted universal suffrage and death within the year. In consequence of these and similarly-intentioned declarations,[2] three of the Birmingham delegates resigned—Salt, Douglas, and Hadley. J. P. Cobbett, the son of William Cobbett, and Dr. Wade had already unostentatiously stepped out. Matthew followed shortly in their footsteps.[3]

Not only did these members resign, but the others soon became particularly casual in their attendance. On April 23 O'Connor moved that " No Member of the Convention should, from this day forth, be sent on the business of agitating, or as a missionary, until after the presentation of the National Petition."[4] He stated that thirteen members never attended at all, and named as such, or as members who had only turned up once or twice, Bunce, Wroe, Vincent, Good, Lovelace, Richards, Cobbett, Osborne, and Whittle. In order to combine propaganda with attention to the business of the Convention, he suggested that it might become a peripatetic affair, sitting one week in one large town, and the next week in another. This suggestion was warmly received. It was decided that the Convention should stay in London until May 6, and then, the Petition having been presented, a move would be made to Birmingham. Attwood and Fielden were the members of Parliament who were selected for the purpose of

[1] *The London Democrat*, March 23, 1839.   [2] Ib., April 6, 1839.
[3] Ib., April 27, 1839.   [4] *Northern Star*, April 27, 1839.

presenting the Petition to the House. Both were willing and prepared to do the Convention this service, but they wished to have, before the actual presentation of the document, a resolution condemning the incendiary language of some of the delegates, and also a letter saying that in future the Convention would be " governed in its exertions to procure the People's Charter by the principles of peace, law, and order."[1] This request met with the unmitigated disapproval of several delegates who induced the remainder to pass a resolution declaring that the right to petition was a constitutional privilege of British subjects, that the Convention was determined to make use of this privilege without qualification, that if Attwood and Fielden would not present the petition, then some other M.P. would be found for the purpose, and if such an M.P. could not be found " this Convention will declare the right of Petition a farce." Finally, however, Attwood and Fielden consented to present the Petition. This " beautiful and majestic roll "[2] was three miles long, with 1,200,000 signatures.

On May 7, 1839, it was put into a van, decorated with flags and explanatory inscriptions, and trundled off to Fielden's House in Panton Square, followed by the delegates in procession. Fielden was out when the Petition arrived, but Attwood received the Convention and chatted with its members. He was asked to move, as soon as possible after the presentation of the Petition, for leave to bring in a Bill for the enactment of the principles of the Charter. This Attwood refused to do on the grounds that while he believed in five points of the Charter, universal suffrage, annual parliaments, vote by ballot, no property qualification, and payment of members, he could not approve of the sixth, i.e., equal constituencies, which would give Ireland 200 M.P.'s, against only 400 for the rest of the United Kingdom. Finally the Petition was left in the passage of the house, and the delegates went away until the time should come to take it to Westminster.[3] The National Petition of the Chartists was not presented to the House of Commons by

---

[1] *The Charter*, May 5, 1839. [2] *The Northern Star*, May 11, 1839.
[3] *The Charter*, May 12, 1839.

Attwood until Friday, June 14.' He introduced it in a brief speech, describing its history, from its adoption in Birmingham on August 6, 1838.' "Having been so adopted, it was then forwarded to Glasgow, where, in a short time, it received no less a number than the signatures of 90,000 honest, industrious men." Attwood "held in his hand" a list of 214 towns and villages where the Petition had been signed ; it now contained 1,280,000 signatures.' Attwood thoroughly realized that the motive force behind the Petition was economic, and he attempted to impress the House with the depressed condition of the working classes. "The first thing sought for by these honest men, every one of whom produced by his labour four times more to the country than they asked for in exchange, was a fair subsistence, and yet their country refused them one-fourth of the value of their labours. Not only did the country do that, but some of them had only three days' wages in the week, and hundreds of them were paying 400 per cent. increase on debts and taxes." He concluded by emphatically disassociating himself from the physical force party, and by moving that the Petition be now brought up. This caused some laughter owing to the bulk of what Sir G. H. Smyth called "that ridiculous piece of machinery." However, Attwood managed to unroll sufficient to enable him to place one end of it on the Clerk's table, and the House passed on to other business.[1] Hansard, from whom the above account of the presentation of the Petition has been condensed, makes no mention of the contemptuous laughter with which the House, according to *The Northern Star*,[2] greeted Attwood's speech. It was not possible to move a resolution relative to the Petition until July 12.

Before the members of the Convention left London, they passed a series of resolutions suggesting what they described as "ulterior measures," to be put to meetings held all over the country before July 1. The fate of these resolutions would give the reassembled Convention an estimate of the strength of the report upon which it could count. The meetings in

[1] Hansard, June 14, 1839, vols. 222–227.
[2] June 22, 1839.

was to be made the basis of the simultaneous meetings and contained a number of questions to be put to the crowds at these gatherings. The most prominent questions were :

Are they prepared, in the event of the Petition and Charter being rejected, to make a run upon the banks, and convert their paper into gold ?

Will they refuse the payment of all rents, rates, and taxes ?

Will they keep a sacred month ?

Will they cease reading all papers opposed to them ?

Will they support Chartist candidates at the next General Election ?

Are they armed ?

O'Connor induced the others to delete the questions about payment of rents, rates, and taxes, and the reading of hostile newspapers.

The next day or two brought reports of arrests at Westbury where the Yeomanry had dispersed a meeting with great violence. Such reports had already been received from other places, and we find, in reading the proceedings of the Birmingham Convention, a growing intensity of bitter determination on the part of the delegates. They had not yet all become avowed disciples of the Physical Force leaders but they had all but ceased to speak of moral force. When the dates of the Scottish simultaneous meetings had been fixed (June 10 and 19), Carpenter declared that " For himself he should go on the mission, if appointed, with the full persuasion that he should never come back." (Hear, hear.) "And every delegate should go out with the same feeling." (Hear, hear.)[1]

It had been originally intended that the " simultaneous meetings " should all be held on the same day, as the police would have been weakened by having their attention distributed over so many points at once. As usual, *The Northern Star* spoke with two voices on the matter of physical force. In a leading article it counselled, " Let no arms of any description be paraded. . . . Let even your words be carefully chosen and rightly guarded. . . . If any foolish old applewoman of a magistrate, upon the affidavit of any fish-wife

---

[1] *Northern Star*, May 18, 1839.

I

as foolish as himself, choose to consider the meeting as unlawful and read the Riot Act, let every one go peacefully home. . . . But if, as is not unlikely, the peace be broken by its professed conservators ; if the people, having given no provocation, be wantonly attacked ; if British blood be shed by lawless violence, why then—then we give the people no advice at all. We merely repeat our last week's quotation : ' When it is their cue to fight, they'll know it without a prompter ! ' "[1] In the very next column to that in which these words were contained, appeared an illustration of a " New Chartist Weapon," with a statement to the effect that they have been manufactured in Winlaton in large numbers. The weapon was the old-fashioned caltrop, said to have been used with considerable effect against the English cavalry at Bannockburn.

The last of the Convention before its adjournment was the passing of three resolutions moved by O'Brien, on the subject of bearing arms.

1st. That peace, law, and order, shall continue to be the motto of this Convention, so long as our oppressors shall act in the spirit of peace, law, and order, towards the people, but should our enemies substitute war for peace, or attempt to suppress our lawful and orderly agitation by lawless violence, we shall deem it to be the sacred duty of the people to meet force with force, and repel assassination by justifiable homicide.

2nd. That in accordance with the foregoing resolution, the Convention do employ only legal and peaceable means in the prosecution of the great and righteous objects of the present movement. Being also desirous that no handle should be afforded to the enemy for traducing our motives, or employing armed force against the people, we hereby recommend the Chartists who may attend the approaching simultaneous meetings to avoid carrying staves, pikes, pistols, or any other offensive weapons about their person. We recommend them to proceed to the ground sober, orderly, and unarmed. As also to treat as enemies of the cause any person or persons who may exhibit such weapons, or who by any other act of folly or wickedness should provoke a breach of the peace.'

[1] *Northern Star*, May 18, 1839.

3rd. That the marshals and other officers who may have charge of the arrangements for the simultaneous meetings are particularly requested to use every means in their power to give effect to the recommendation embodied in the preceding resolution. We also recommend that the aforesaid officers do in all cases consult with the local authorities before the meeting takes place.

4th. That in case our oppressors in the middle and upper ranks should instigate the authorities to oppress the people with armed force, in contravention of the existing laws of the realm, the said oppressors in the upper and middle ranks shall be held responsible in person and property for any detriment that may result to the people from such atrocious instigation.

These resolutions mean two things. In the first place they were passed in Birmingham where the B.P.U. prevailed. This was of all the Radical bodies the most middle-class ; the tone of the resolution however indicates that no *rapprochement* or amicable relationship with the middle classes was even contemplated. In short, the Convention, largely composed, as we have shown, of middle-class delegates, deliberately adopted working-class sentiments, and by shaking off its own origin, became a movement intended to benefit a single class, rather than the nation as a whole. In the second place, these resolutions demonstrate the waning hopes of the pacifists among the delegates. We have already quoted Lovett's despairing comments on the situation, the tension of which was accentuated immediately after his imprisonment. The events that were to follow directly gave the movement no chance of ever regaining the paths of quietness ; force can only be met by force, persecution is a sword that cuts both ways.

Whit-Monday duly arrived and was the starting-point of an oratorical campaign. The result of this was a great deal of cheering and of moral encouragement for the Chartist leaders, but of an altogether exaggerated and misleading nature. Gammage gives a list of meetings as a " sample " of the scale on which the " simultaneous meetings " attracted attention, and he gives the numbers present at several of them. These, as is usual with this form of estimate, are probably greatly inflated ; it would seem that the meetings at Manchester, Liverpool, Newcastle, Carlisle, Sunderland, Bath, Blackwood (Glam.), Sheffield, Leigh (Lancs), and Glasgow attracted up to 1,351,000 hearers. This figure, as we have said, is certainly above the truth, yet, as meetings also took place in London, Hull, Preston, Northampton, Bradford, Penrith, Cockermouth, and other places mentioned by Gammage, and as we know that O'Connor and Harney separately toured the provinces and addressed crowds at many other great towns, it is probable that an even larger number than that stated applauded the Chartist speakers.

On May 30, 1839, O'Connell addressed a remonstrance to the Chartists of Birmingham, which embodied the middle class liberal objections to the campaign of the Six Points. He suggested that the Chartists were actually injuring their own cause by their " exclusiveness." They excluded the aristocracy and the middle classes, men aged from eighteen to twenty, idiots and lunatics. The suffrage they demanded was therefore not truly " universal." O'Connell then went on to suggest the substitution of the words " household suffrage " for the offending term. He proposed that there should be four classes of household voters : (1) Male householders ; (2) male heads of families, whether householders or " latchkey tenants " ; (3) male artisans who had served a term of apprenticeship ; (4) male teachers and apprentices. These proposals would in any case have been exasperating to men who had pinned their faith to a catchword ; O'Connell made them superlatively so by suggesting triennial instead of annual parliaments, and by telling the Chartists that their manners at public meetings were unpleasant. After this the " Liberator," as may be expected, became a byword. *The Northern Star* rose and rent him to pieces week by week. It is probable, however, that O'Connell succeeded in making an unrecorded impression. Without his Address would the Convention have adopted on July 22 its Address to the Middle Classes ? We venture to think that the tone of this document, with its placatory assurances and its avowed detestation of physical force methods, was inspired very considerably by the much-abused O'Connell.

DELEGATES TO THE NATIONAL CONVENTION OF THE INDUSTRIOUS CLASSES

William G. Burns . .	Forfarshire and Aberdeenshire.
Peter Bussey . . .	Yorks (W. Riding).
J. P. Cobbett . . .	Do. Do.
John Collins	Birmingham, Cheltenham, and Coventry.
John Cleave	London (except Marylebone) and Reading.
William Carpenter . .	Bolton-le-Moors.
William Cardo . . .	Marylebone.
Hugh Craig	Ayrshire.
Robert Kellie Douglas .	Birmingham.
Abram Duncan . . .	Dumfries, Maxwelltown.
John Deegan . . .	Hyde, Stalybridge, Glossop, Newmills.
John Frost	Newport, Pontypool, Caerleon.
Matthew Fletcher . .	Bury, Heywood, Prestwich, Ratcliffe and Ramsbottom.
James Fenney . . .	Wigan, Hindley and West Houghton.
William Gill	Sheffield and Rotherham.
John Goods	Brighton.
Henry Hetherington .	London (except Marylebone) and Stockport.
Robert Hartwell . .	Do. Do. Do.
George Julian Harney .	Northumberland, Norwich, and Derby.
Alexander Halley . .	Dumfermline, Kirkcaldy, Allva, Clackmannan, Stirlingshire and Falkville.
Benjamin Hadley . .	Birmingham.
Charles Jones . . .	Newtown, Welshpool and Llanidloes
Robert Knox . . .	Durham County.
William Lovett . . .	London (except Marylebone).
Robert Lowery . . .	Newcastle and Northumberland.
George Loveless . . .	Dorsetshire.
Patrick Matthew . .	Perthshire and Fife.
Richard Mealing . .	Bath, Trowbridge, Frome, Holt, Bradford (Wilts) and Westbury.
Richard Moore . . .	London (except Marylebone).
Richard Marsden . .	Preston and Chorley.
James Mills	Oldham.

James Moir	Glasgow and Lanarkshire.
Peter Murray M'Douall.	Ashton-under-Lyne.
Charles Hodgson Neesom	Bristol.
Feargus O'Connor . .	Yorks (W. Riding) and Bristol.
James Bronterre O'Brien	London (except Marylebone), Leigh Bristol, Norwich, Newport (I. of W), and Stockport.
John Pierce	Birmingham and Reading.
Lawrence Pitkeithly. .	Yorks (W. Riding).
John Rickards . . .	Potteries.
George Rogers . . .	London (except Marylebone).
Reginald John Richard- son	Manchester.
William Rider . . .	Yorks (W. Riding).
Thomas Raynor Smart	Loughborough and Leicester.
John Skevington . .	Loughborough and Derby.
William Stephen Villiers Sankey	Edinburgh and Midlothian.
Thomas Clutton Salt .	Birmingham.
John Taylor	Renfrewshire, Newcastle, Carlisle, Wigton, Alva and Tillicoultry.
James Taylor . . .	Rochdale and Middleton.
Benjamin A. Tight . .	Reading.
Henry Vincent . . .	Hull, Cheltenham and Bristol.
Arthus S. Wade . .	Nottingham, Sutton-in-Ashfield, and Mansfield.
Joseph Wood . . .	Bolton-le-Moors.
James Wroe	Manchester.
James Whittle . . .	Liverpool.

CHAPTER V

THE PERIOD OF REPRESSION

WITH the reassembling of the Convention in Birmingham
on July 1, the Chartist movement abruptly entered
into another phase.   To explain this apparently sudden transition, a retrospect is necessary.

The steadily growing intensity of economic distress had
been accompanied by an increasingly obvious restiveness.
In the North especially, and in South Wales, a sullen determination to use whatever methods might be needed to upset
the Government appeared to dominate labour.   Rumours
reached the Cabinet of preparations for armed revolt, drillings,
pikes, and so on.   Undoubtedly these anticipations were
dictated by fact as much as by panic.   We have no means of
knowing to what extent preparations for bloodshed were
actually made.   Appendix I[1] contains a review of the evidence
tending to show that extreme measures were in contemplation.
The direct evidence that armed Chartists were ever organized
on more than a local scale is very slight indeed.   The impression
gathered by the non-Chartist public of these preparations is
obviously enormously exaggerated.   Virtually every volume
of memoirs covering 1838–41 testifies to the prevailing fear
of a revolutionary outbreak.   A few specimens may be given.

On October 25, 1838, we find in Queen Victoria's diaries a
reference to Chartism in a fearful warning from Lord Melbourne.
" I am afraid that times of some trouble are approaching for
which Your Majesty must hold yourself prepared."[2]

John Bowes, the well-known Methodist preacher, writes on
July 1, 1839, to William Essler, a member of his own calling :

[1] *This appendix does not appear to have been written.—J.C.S.*
[2] *The Girlhood of Queen Victoria*, Vol. II, p. 61.

" I am sorry to learn that you have thrown yourself into the army of the bloodthirsty Chartists."[1]

In his autobiography, *These Eighty Years*, the Rev. H. Solly gives an account of his introduction to Chartism in Yeovil, in 1840, illustrating by his description the normal middle-class attitude to this phenomenon. He was taken by a local Chartist named Bainbridge (who afterwards rose to some prominence in the movement), of whose political views Solly was then ignorant, to the Mechanics' Institute of the town. There he found a dozen or so working men, some in their shirt-sleeves, seated round a table, discussing something or other. Suddenly a brawny man with a black beard thumped the table and began a speech by exclaiming, " Mr. Chairman ! Though I'm as good a Chartist as any of you. . . ." Solly's feelings are reflected in his own words : " I remember no more, and doubt if I heard anything more, for that was enough to fill me with intense alarm and disgust. It was clear to me that I had fallen among a band of those desperate and violent men, as I supposed them to be, who were engaged in their nefarious conspiracy, and as soon as I could I left the room, grievously distressed."[2] Yet the dread Chartists were in this case not physical-force men, but admirers of Lovett. Bainbridge, by the way, soon effected Solly's conversion.

Blackwood's Magazine contained an article, almost on the eve of the Reform Bill passing into law, the tone of which admirably illustrates the opinion and the fears of the wealthier classes as to the probable consequences of the measure. " It will be a general insurrection of the lower orders against the higher ; an effort of the populace to take the powers of sovereignty into their own hands, and divide among themselves all that is now enjoyed by their superiors. It will be followed by the consequences which attended similar efforts in the neighbouring kingdom. . . . The property of the Church will be the first victim. . . . The national debt will be the next object of attack ; the people will find it intolerable to pay the interest of burdens which they had no hand in imposing ; public

---

[1] *Autobiography of John Bowes*, p. 212.
[2] *These Eighty Years*, Vol. I, pp. 345-346.

creditors will be swept off, and the industry of the people relieved by destroying the accumulation of a thousand years (*sic*). The estates of the nobility will then become an eyesore to the purifiers of society ; land will be viewed as the people's farm ; the public miseries will be imputed to the extortions of those unjust stewards, and a division of the great properties will be the consequence. In the consternation occasioned by these violent changes, commercial industry will come to a stand—agricultural produce will be diminished—the employment of capital will be withdrawn—famine, distress, and want of employment will ensue—the people will revolt against their seducers—more violent remedies will be proposed—strong principles of democracy will be maintained. In the struggle of these desperate factions, blood will be profusely shed. Terror, that destroyer of all virtuous feeling, will rule triumphant. Another Danton, a second Robespierre, will arise, another Reign of Terror will expiate the sins of a new revolution, and military despotism close the scene."[1] Eight years after these words were written, when the Chartist movement had already grown in strength, these inflated sentiments were actually exhumed and quoted as a wise and accurate prognostication of what was to be expected.[2] The importance of Chartism lies principally in the fact that by that portion of the population of the country which was responsible for its government, every Chartist was regarded as a potential Robespierre. Such was the state of feeling when Stephens was arrested at the end of 1838.

His eloquence had gradually assumed such a dangerous tone that the authorities took alarm. In consequence of a particularly inflammatory speech delivered at Leigh, Lancashire, on November 13, 1838, a warrant was issued for his arrest, which took place on December 27. The speech in question had been delivered in opposition to the new Poor Law, and its offending passages were based on scriptural texts. What frightened the authorities, however, was that in the course of the examination of Stephens at the New Bailey, Manchester,

[1] *Blackwood's Magazine*, February, 1831, p. 185.
[2] Ib., September, 1839, p. 303.

on December 28, a witness named Coward, a constable, declared
that he knew smithies where pikes were actually being made
at the moment, and that the Chartists were preparing for an
armed insurrection.[1] The trial was adjourned, and bail was
granted. Stephens occupied the interval by more declama-
tion. This outbreak of rodomontade was of course taken
seriously, and presently many of those who considered themselves dissatisfied with the existing order of things clutched at
the appellation Chartist, and so brought about demonstrations
entirely contrary to the principles and the spirit of a movement
which had constitutional reforms for its object. We are told
that " it became a practice of some persons calling themselves
Chartists to go in procession to the churches some time before
divine service began, and to take entire possession of the body
of the edifice. The scene was of course anything but decorous.
Some wore their hats—others had pipes in their mouths—but
it was not usually found that their conduct exceeded this
confessedly unbecoming behaviour."[2] For this deplorable
state of things there is no doubt that Stephens, with O'Connor,
was responsible. They had introduced foreign elements into
Chartism, and a very foreign spirit. By doing so, they had
attracted followers whose concerns were distinctly the reverse
of democratic. Although they had widened the audience
willing to listen to Chartist proposals, they had encouraged a
fringe of irresponsible listeners, whose behaviour caused the
intellectual claims of the movement to be swamped in the
outcry at their proceedings. The re-examination of Stephens
began on January 3, 1839, when he was committed to the
Liverpool Assizes, bail being allowed. According to Place,
" The agitation caused by his apprehension was very remarkable. The whole body of Radicals felt it, and in Manchester
and its environs great apprehensions were entertained of riot-
ings and extensive mischief. All the associations called meetings, and a vast number of people came to Manchester ready for
mischief." His examination had disabled Stephens from
attending the National Convention, and a substitute was found

[1] *Annual Register*, 1838, Part II, p. 169.
[2] Ib., 1839, p. 304.

by his constituency. On being released on bail, Stephens once again indulged himself in the full enjoyment of his popularity, preaching political sermons and generally breathing fire and slaughter. Meanwhile his friends had opened a Stephens's Defence Fund, and a sum approaching £2,000 was received in small subscriptions [1] by the time he had to come up for trial. This took place in August and turned out to be a surprising affair. In spite of the fact that the meeting, at which the seditious utterances for which he was being tried had been made, had been decorated by banners inscribed " Ashton demands Universal Suffrage or Universal Vengeance," and a few frankly sanguinolent messages such as " Blood," Stephens made some amazing statements, which may have been partly palinodial, but were to a certain extent undoubtedly suggested by his rhetorical trick of appealing to his audiences by paradoxes in which he appeared to condescend to their views. His biographer, who quotes largely from Stephens's five-hour speech in his own defence, supplies us with this delightful quotation : " I am dragged here . . . as though I were a party to the Convention, and to the disturbances of Birmingham, to the Charter, to annual Parliaments, vote by ballot, universal suffrage, and all the rest of that rigmarole, in which I never had a share. I only came forward to the men of Leigh, and there declared my detestation of the doctrines of Chartism, declared that if Radicals were in power my views were such that my head would be brought first to the block, and my blood would be the first blood that would have to flow for the olden liberties of the country. Gentlemen, this is the individual who is now brought before you as a Chartist. . . ."[2] He was found guilty and sentenced to eighteen months' imprisonment, with sureties for good behaviour for five years after the period of his confinement.

Peter Murray M'Douall was the next to be prosecuted. M'Douall had in 1839 scarcely completed his twenty-fifth year ; he was a surgeon by profession, and an idealist by temperament. He represented Ashton-under-Lyne at the Con-

---

[1] Gamage, *History of the Chartist Movement*, p. 101.
[2] G. J. Holyoake, *Life of J. R. Stephens*, p. 165.

vention. The cause of his arrest was having attended " an
unlawful meeting," held in Hyde, on April 22 ; the case was
held up until August 16, when it was tried in Chester Hill,
the Attorney-General prosecuting. In opening the case, Hill
virtually delivered himself of the popular prejudice against
Chartism. " The object was to overthrow the laws by force,
and to excite the people to a bloody revolution, unless certain
rights which they had demanded were granted by Government."
M'Douall's " object in view was one of great atrocity, it was
one of the worst of objects—that of filling his own pockets at
the expense of the poor."[1] M'Douall seems to have made a
certain sensation as the result of his long speech in his own
defence. After having explained the position taken up by
the Chartists, he alluded to a paper read by him at a meeting
of the British Association on the Factory System. He described
the vile effects of overcrowding factory workers into entirely
inadequate cottages belonging to the factory owners, and
stated the rate of wages paid : a rate he found generally
lay between 2s. 6d. and 5s. per head *per week*. From this
he went on to his own feelings, and to describe the impulse
given to his political views by the sight of the prevailing conditions of the factory system. Finally he brought devastating
criticism to bear upon the evidence brought forward by the
prosecution, but the judge summed up strongly against him,
and the jury returned a verdict of guilty without retiring to
consider. M'Douall was sentenced to a year's imprisonment,
and was bound over to keep the peace for five years.

Early in 1839 Major-General Sir Charles James Napier,
K.C.B., the future conqueror of Scinde, received a summons
from Lord John Russell. He rushed down to London from
the north of England in only twenty-four hours, singing praises
to steam and smoke. On March 30 he saw Lord John, " a
mild person in manner : poor man, he is in an affliction which
makes it hard to judge, but he seems thoughtful and un-
affected."[2] The Home Secretary was in fear and trembling

[1] *Trial of Peter Murray M'Douall.*
[2] *Life of Charles James Napier.* By Lt.-Gen. Sir W. Napier. Vol. II,
p. 5.

of a Chartist insurrection. Napier, being in command of the
northern district, which extended over eleven counties, had
virtually to undertake the responsibility of suppressing Chartism on its native heath. For this purpose he was well suited,
having no fear of either Chartists or of the Government and
a certain amount of sympathy with both. He did not think
the Chartists, for all their pikes and red nightcaps, would be
dangerous, for " they have, seemingly, no organization, no
leaders, and a strong tendency to turn rebellion into money,
for pikes costing a shilling are sold for three and sixpence."[1]
However, on making inquiries in London on the possibilities
of an actual insurrection, he found the Government " strangely
ill-informed." A little later on Napier heard from various
sources that the Chartists were not going to attempt an insurrection, but would rely upon assassination. It is characteristic
of this faithful Tory that he thoroughly sympathized with
this supposed course of action. " What has made Englishmen
turn assassins ? The new poor law. Their resources have
dried up but indirect taxes for the debt, and the poor law
throws them on a phantom, which it calls their resources—
robbery follows, and a robber soon becomes a murderer."[2]
The rumour of forthcoming assassinations spread throughout
the land, and the aged Duke of Portland came tremblingly to
Napier in April to ask if his life was safe. A few days later
Napier heard that in fact eleven men had met and cast lots
for murdering the Duke because of his support for the new
poor law.[3]

During the following May the fear of an insurrection spread.
Napier exercised the utmost caution in avoiding even the
occasions of conflict. There was " a row " at Stone (Staffs)
early in the month, when a body of Chartists attacked a few
yeomen, much to their own discomfiture. England can never
be sufficiently grateful to Napier for having kept his head at
this trying period. In the face of unceasing rumours of

[1] *Life of Charles James Napier.* By Lt.-Gen. Sir W. Napier. Vol. II,
p. 6.
[2] Ib., p. 9.
[3] Ib., p. 10.

immediate outbreaks, each more wildly exaggerated than its predecessor, he went on organizing his soldiers and taking care that they should not be used until it was thoroughly necessary. When he heard that 250,000 armed Chartists were on the verge of revolting in Yorkshire, he did nothing rash. When, a few days later, a million Yorkshire men were, it was alleged, starting on a march on London, Napier planned schemes of outflanking this immense body, should it ever materialize. When the great meeting at Kersall Moor was held on May 25, Napier was present in " coloured clothes,"[1] and found that the opinions expressed by the orators were " orderly, legal . . . pretty much—don't tell this !—very like my own ! " About this time he appears to have proven to an unnamed Chartist leader the utter inadequacy of five brass cannon to which the rebels had pinned their faith, by allowing him to come and inspect the guns at a barrack. He soon found that some of the Chartist leaders were amenable to reason and tactful handling, and the discovery appreciably reduced the risk of bloodshed. Indeed there was nothing so terrible to Napier as the prospect of shedding blood. " Good God, what work ! " he exclaims. " To send grape-shot from four guns into a helpless mass of fellow-citizens ; sweeping the streets with fire and charging with cavalry, destroying poor people whose only crime is that they have been ill-governed and reduced to such straits that they seek redress by arms, ignorant that of all ways that is the most certain to increase the evils they complain of." During the next few months he is continually complaining of the behaviour of the magistrates, who in his opinion were responsible for the Birmingham riots on July 15, and for the generally fevered state of the people. He ridicules the idea that the Sacred Month will actually be carried out. In spite of all the fears expressed by the magistracy, on August 17 Napier is able to report that " all is quiet throughout Lancashire, Yorkshire, Durham, Cheshire, West-

---

[1] *Life of Charles James Napier*. By Lt.-Gen. Sir W. Napier. Vol. II, p. 39. The Chartists claimed that the number present on this occasion was between 300,000 and 500,000. According to Napier, there were only 30,000, many of whom were not Chartists. (Vol. II, p. 43.)

morland, etc. Bolton is the only place where shot has been fired, but only three there, and those from the eagerness of the magistrates." Under his almost inspired guidance, the persons who were demanding blood failed to get it. Napier understood well the connexion between economic distress and rebelliousness, and therefore refused to regard the latter as the symptoms of revolution. It should not be forgotten, however, that Lord John Russell, timid though he may have been, held the same views as Napier on the employment of the armed forces of the crown. " In 1835 Russell agreed with the Irish law officers that soldiers and police should not be used for the collection of tithes except in emergency. He mentioned that in England he warned the Lords-Lieutenant and the Commander-in-Chief not to allow troops to be brought within sight of the people unless actual rioting took place. This was always a valued principle with him, and I have heard him tell how in the Chartist movement of 1848, even at the most threatening moments, he in concert with the Duke of Wellington arranged that the troops should be kept out of sight."[1] This is the testimony of Lord John Russell's son. Lord John Russell's account of his own impressions of the Chartist movement,[2] however, does not convey the conviction of any unusual wisdom on his part. It is indeed open to argument that on Russell's own showing he hardly understood what all the excitement was about, that he gave Napier a free hand to deal with it, and that he did not know how Napier dealt with it.

The Physical Force Chartists relied perhaps overmuch on the counsel of a frequently-mentioned book by a refugee foreign officer, Colonel Francis Maceroni, *Defensive Instruction to the People*.[3] According to the Colonel the armed populace could, under certain circumstances, be more than a match for trained troops, especially in street fighting. At the Convention the possibilities of this form of conflict were enthusiastically dis-

---

[1] *Early Correspondence of Lord John Russell.* Introduction. Vol. I, p. 73. Edited by Rollo Russell.
[2] *Recollections and Suggestions*, 1873, pp. 145–148.
[3] Published 1832, revised and reprinted 1834.

cussed in private by members of the Physical Force party.[1]
Alexander Sommerville, an ex-soldier of Chartist sympathies,
frightened by the militant tone of some of his friends, published
a series of penny pamphlets, *Warnings to the People on Street
Warfare*, in which he argued, with considerable knowledge,
that not the advice of Maceroni, nor the experience of past
revolutions in European cities, nor the utmost possible discipline and organization could enable workmen to resist
trained troops and their artillery. According to the author,
these pamphlets were widely read and did much to neutralize
the prevailing bellicosity of the Physical Force Chartists.[2]

A meeting at Nottingham about April 20, 1839, presented
Oastler with a spear, apparently in the mistaken belief that
it was a weapon. The occasion was marked by an oratorical
outburst of some violence in which the working classes were
advised to arm and to " walk upright." He did not suggest
that the weapons were for use ; first let the working men try
the effect of a petition backed by pikes and then, if the Government remained unexpectedly unafraid or unwilling, then " we
shall fight."[3]

[1] Sommerville's *Conservative Science of Nations*, p. 213.

[2] Alexander Sommerville (1811–1885) was the son of an East Lothian
farm labourer. He enlisted in the Scots Greys in 1832, and was with
his regiment in Birmingham just before the outbreak of the Reform
Riots. The soldiers were ordered to prepare to deal drastically with
the mob, who were contemplating a march on London, and Sommerville
was among those who protested. A few weeks later he was court-
martialled for a petty breach of discipline and flogged. Sommerville
maintained his belief that his previous action had made him *persona
ingrata* to his officers, and succeeded in obtaining an inquiry into the
matter. The consequent notoriety and hero-worship gave him an inflated
idea of his own importance. With the interval of 1835–7, spent on
foreign service, Sommerville henceforth lived in publicity, for publicity,
doing journalistic work in London, Dublin, and in Canada, where he
died. He was an anti-Corn Law Radical by profession, and derided both
the physical force and the " sacred month " proposals. A good ideal
of his writing was signed " One who has whistled at the Plough."
He was subsequently designated by Cobden in a letter to Bright (November 4, 1849) as a most suitable author for a history of Chartism. (Morley, *Life of Cobden*, p. 519, in one-volume edition.)

[3] *The Charter*, May 5, 1839.

While the Convention had been sitting, the more extreme of the Chartists had been making sporadic and ineffective efforts to work up something in the nature of an insurrection. On April 1, Vincent, Carrier and Roberts were to have addressed a meeting in the Market Place, Devizes, but the natives would have none of it—attacked the Chartist procession, and, we are told, only allowed the speakers to leave the town on condition they promised never to return to it. During the same month, an attempt to take arms by force from farmers at Llanidloes, Montgomeryshire, was ascribed to Chartists, but the identity of the men in question was not established, as all concerned succeeded in escaping. Early in May, seven Chartists were arrested in Manchester for drilling, although no weapons were found in their possession. Other arrests were made at Westbury (Wiltshire) and Trowbridge. Vincent was the next prominent Chartist to be arrested. Together with Townsend, a wine merchant, and Dickenson, a pork butcher, he was apprehended for " attending a seditious assemblage at Newport, Mon., which had also been addressed by Frost. The arrest took place on May 8, on the day after the defeat of Melbourne's Government. The whole of England and Wales was in a highly excited state at the time, and numerous arrests were made. Vincent was taken from London to Newport, through Bristol, which seems to have been in a mood reminiscent of the riots of 1832. While the country agitated itself about the " Bedchamber Question " it became necessary to tub-thump with particular force to be heard at all, consequently Chartist propaganda grew in intensity, and arrests were even more numerous. Vincent, we may add, was not tried until August 2, 1839, when he was condemned to twelve months' imprisonment. His case came up in the House of Lords a week later, as a result of which Vincent's imprisonment received the mitigations usually extended to political offenders.[1]

Thirty-two Chartists were tried in Welshpool on July 18 on a charge of unlawful assembly, and beginning to demolish,

---

[1] William Dorling, *Henry Vincent, a Biographical Sketch*, p. 19.

K

pull down, and destroy the dwelling house of David Evans, in Llanidloes, with some other cases of drilling and learning to use arms. The result was as follows :

1 Stabbing with intent to do bodily harm	15 years' transportation.
3 Training and drilling to use arms	7 years' transportation.
1 Seditious words	1 year imprisonment and recognizances for 5 years.
2 Riot and assault	1 year hard labour.
5 Drilling and training . . .	6 months.
17 Riots (including 3 women) .	6 months' hard labour.
8 Riots	3 months' hard labour.
2 Riots	2 months' hard labour.
7 Acquitted or entered into recognizances.	

On May 17, at two o'clock in the morning, two delegates, Brown and Russell,[1] were arrested by the Birmingham police for having " made use of inflammatory language tending to excite her Majesty's liege subjects to a breach of the peace." The occasion of this alleged incendiarism of speech was a meeting at the Bull Ring held as far back as March 21. Both prisoners were brought up before the magistrates the next morning and committed for trial.

Lord John Russell had addressed a circular letter to the magistracy offering arms to any association of the middle classes that might be formed for the purpose of putting down the Chartist meetings.[2] This, coupled with the generally high-handed behaviour of the Birmingham bench, raised the Convention to a pitch of fury which only needed an opportunity to burst out upon its opponents.

After the great series of meetings had been concluded, the Convention reassembled in Birmingham on July 1. O'Connor had started through *The Northern Star* a Defence Fund for arrested Chartists, he now commended it to the goodwill of the delegates. The " missionaries " who had represented the

---

[1] Acquitted August 7.
[2] Lovett, p. 208.

appears that the authorities, thoroughly frightened, attempted to clear the Bull Ring by armed force. Rumours to the effect that armed colliers were coming to the help of the Chartists were met by the importation of dragoons. Dozens of arrests were made. Most of the persons taken up were subsequently discharged or acquitted, but three men (one of whom had a wooden leg) and a boy were tried on the charge of arson and sentenced to death.[1] This was afterwards commuted to transportation on the grounds of possible mistaken identity.[2]

During the Birmingham Riots, Harney, it appears, was " wanted " by the authorities, but could not be found. One man alone, G. J. Holyoake, knew where he lodged, and regarded himself as the keeper of the imitator of Marat.[3] Holyoake and his protégé, it seems, lodged opposite each other in a little street off the Bull Ring,[4] and so actually lived in the centre of the rioting. Harney was, however, arrested at Bedlington at the end of July. Benbow, now a Manchester shoemaker, was sentenced to sixteen months' imprisonment in August on a charge of seditious language.

Collins and Lovett were tried on August 6, before a jury which contained two men who were known to have expressed the wish that " all the Chartists were hanged."[5] The Attorney-General, who prosecuted, was a tactful man and told the jury that that was to be the last case his public duties would ever allow him to take in the county of Warwick, and that he should ever recollect, " with gratitude and with admiration," the firmness and the determination which the juries of Warwickshire had displayed. T. Clutton Salt gave evidence on behalf of Lovett, and said that he had always " exhibited a disgust of all violence, and a desire to produce change only by influencing public opinion. He concluded by stating that the idea of the General Convention originated either with Muntz or Attwood— a sound strategical move, as Muntz had been among those magistrates who committed Lovett and Collins for trial. The

[1] *Northern Star*, August 10, 1839.　　　　　[2] Ib., August 31.
[3] G. J. Holyoake, *Bygones Worth Remembering*, Vol. I, p. 112.
[4] J. MacCabe, *Life and Letters of G. J. Holyoake*, Vol. I, p. 42.
[5] *Trial of W. Lovett*, p. 4.

jury, however, was not to be impressed by such means, and the accused were each sentenced to one year's imprisonment in the County Gaol, Warwick.

Lovett and Collins, once immured, suffered terribly. The local magistracy was determined that such of the many indulgences which were in their power to grant should not be granted. This was in spite of medical testimony and petitions to Parliament from the W.M.A., the people of Birmingham, Francis Place, and Mrs. Lovett. Warburton and Duncombe brought up the matter in Parliament. The Marquis of Normanby (Home Secretary, 1840) also failed to move the magistrates. After six months' petitioning a slight change for the better was effected. Collins and Lovett utilized the permission to use pen and ink by writing a small book entitled *Chartism, or a New Organization of the People.*

O'Brien was arrested in Newcastle-on-Tyne, with several less prominent Chartists, on July 7, 1839, on the usual charge of seditious speaking.[1] The knighthood which was promptly given to John Fife, the Mayor of Newcastle, appears to have been the direct reward of his anti-Chartist activities. The trial did not take place until February 29, 1840, when the only evidence forthcoming against O'Brien was that of a newspaper reporter. All the accused were acquitted on the same day, and the disappointed prosecution forthwith set to work to invent other reasons which should seem good enough to lay a few Chartists by the heels. A few months later O'Brien was tried at Liverpool on a charge of conspiracy and attempted rebellion, and this time was found guilty, and sentenced to eighteen months' imprisonment.[2]

On assembling on July 11, the Convention elected Mrs. Lovett as its secretary, in her husband's place. She does not appear, despite her pronounced willingness, to have ever taken over the secretarial duties. On the 14th of the month, the delegates met once more in Bolt Court to consider the " ulterior measures." Lowery's proposal that the " Sacred Month " or " Month of Rest " should begin some time in August met with general approval, except from a few members who wanted

¹ Gammage, p. 149.   ² Ib., p. 179.

to begin earlier.[1] Subsequent discussions did not reveal the same hearty unanimity. Richardson made the strong point that the industrial classes had had " several sacred months already," and that the manufacturers would now regard it as a godsend if their people went on strike. Other delegates wanted the Sacred Month to begin the very next day. On July 17[2] it was agreed that the Sacred Month should begin on August 12, that " the Convention should call on the trades of the United Kingdom to co-operate with them in carrying out the ulterior measures, and that the Committee on the National Holiday take charge of the business," and that the Convention convert their funds into gold. But even then there was opposition. Frost, a stranger to the Convention since his arrest, wrote from Bristol declaring that the Convention's orders stood at the moment little chance of being obeyed in Wales. O'Connor, as usual abstaining from definitely committing himself, had not attended the Convention during the few days when the general strike was under discussion. On July 22,[3] Bronterre O'Brien made a long speech and moved that in view of the unprepared state of the people, the thinness of the Convention, from desertion as well as from arrests, and the variety of opinions, among the delegates as well as among the general public, the date when the general strike should begin ought to be settled by the people generally, rather than by the Convention. O'Connor virtually supported this, having made the curious discovery that the delegates who had committed the Convention to August 12, a few days earlier, all represented thinly-populated and unorganized constituencies. After several days of a discussion, which at times perilously approximated to a wrangle, the Convention was coaxed into unanimity by the combined efforts of O'Brien and O'Connor, and a committee of seven was appointed, to sit in London, and to carry into effect the decision of the working classes as soon as it could be determined. The seven chosen for this committee were O'Connor, O'Brien, Fletcher, Carpenter, Lowery, Smart and Burns.

[1] *Northern Star*, July 20, 1839.   [2] Ib., July 27, 1839.
[3] Ib., July 27, 1839.

The Northern Star strongly supported O'Connor on this matter, warning its readers, in capital letters, that Any Attempt to Bring about the Sacred Month Before a Universal Arming Shall Have Taken Place will ruin all.[1] O'Connor himself addressed his " dear friends," the " working millions," in its columns, and besought them to do themselves no harm in characteristically hypocritical words. " I never will, with a certainty of my own dinner, recommend a project which may cause millions to starve. No ; I would rather go to battle." The following week, in order to keep up the excitement, the editorial article in *The Northern Star*, with real journalistic *flair*, was made to conclude by warning the House of Commons that " a refusal to grant the people justice will turn their appeal for the Charter into a demand for a REPUBLIC."

While the Council of Seven sat in London, at the Arundel Coffee House,[2] the Convention once more dispersed. The Seven embodied their instructions in a harmless series of resolutions, and finally convened the Convention for August 26.[3] At various places in the north of England, e.g., Dewsbury, Almondbury, and to a slight extent in Manchester, a three days' holiday actually took place. The strikers kept the peace, and everything went off with perfect good-humour and ineffectiveness.

A Scottish Convention sat for three days, August 14–16, in the Universalists' Chapel, Glasgow, to consider ways and means of obtaining universal suffrage. Sixty delegates attended, but business seems to have been confined almost entirely to the reception of reports of progress from those present. O'Connor was present and made a speech on the necessity of co-ordination among the Four Kingdoms.

On August 30 a large Chartist meeting at Newcastle-on-Tyne was broken up by the police with some violence. The next day an affray took place in Stockport, where a quantity of weapons had been seized, said to belong to the Chartists.

[1] August 3, 1839.
[2] Strand, opposite St. Clement Dane's Church. *Northern Star*, August 10, 1839.
[3] *Northern Star*, August 24, 1839.

These retaliated by capturing some arms intended for the use of the military, but these were, after a long fight, recaptured. Again several persons were seriously hurt. Before the end of the year wholesale arrests had taken place at Stockport, Chester, Hulme, Manchester, Bolton, and Nottingham.

Early in the year 1839, a singular correspondence had taken place between Lord John Russell and John Frost. It began by an inquiry on the part of the former whether it was true that Frost, a J.P. of Newport, Monmouthshire, had attended a meeting at Pontypool, at which violent language had been used, and whether he was a member of the Convention. Whereupon Frost replied at great length, but in an altogether dignified manner, to the effect that he had been put upon the magistrates' bench because he was a good citizen, and that in attempting to get the law of the land changed he was acting in a manner perfectly compatible with good citizenship and in which Lord John Russell and the Whigs had themselves acted when necessary. Frost then received what can only be described as a qualified apology, and published it, adding " if Lord John takes my name off, the people will put it on." Another letter followed from Russell's secretary, asking if this addition had been made, as reported. Frost then wrote a spirited letter saying that if he had made any remarks personally objectionable to Lord John Russell he would apologize, but he entirely denied his right to censor his opinions. This closed the matter for the time being.[1] The next thing that happened to ruffle the surface of Frost's constituency was the arrival of two missionaries, delegated by the Convention to work up Monmouthshire and the adjoining counties. These were Burn, a comparatively insignificant man, and Vincent, by this time acknowledged as one of the finest orators of the movement. Before long, in the opinion of Vincent's enemies, he " fully succeeded in establishing his perfect supremacy among the operatives of the coal and iron districts,"[2] especially in the neighbourhood of Newport. So threatening did this " supremacy " appear to the local gentry that they took steps to protect themselves

[1] *Annual Register*, 1839, Part II, pp. 22–26.
[2] *The Rise and Fall of Chartism in Monmouthshire*, p. 16.

in case of any outbreak. An armed association was formed at Christchurch, for the purpose of defending property. Appeals were made to London, and troops were poured into Newport and Monmouth. Thomas Phillips, the Mayor of Newport, having decided to terminate Vincent's career as expeditiously as possible, attended his meetings, collected a mass of evidence showing that a revolt was in contemplation, and laid it before the law officers of the Crown. These decided to prosecute. Vincent was arrested in London, where he had returned, and taken to Monmouth. On May 10, 1839, he was tried, in company with Edwards, a local baker, a pork-butcher, and a tradesman, on a charge of unlawfully meeting in a " malicious, riotous and seditious assembly." They were all promptly found guilty and committed for trial.[1] " The town presented a most excited appearance. Nearly three hundred special constables were sworn in and a large detachment of the 29th Regiment was under arms during the entire day."[2] The reason of this excitement is difficult to credit, but it appears certain that the magistrates believed that the object of Vincent's pilgrimage was the establishment of a " Chartist Kingdom." When, a little later, Frost had made his unlucky attempt at rescue, a contemporary account of it solemnly began by stating : " For a considerable time past, it appears that Vincent, who is now confined in Monmouth gaol for sedition, had pointed out to the ignorant mountaineers of South Wales that there it was that the Kingdom of Chartism should first be erected, and the men of Tredegar, Merthyr, Blackwood, etc., were led to believe in everything which he may have said upon the subject ; the consequence of which was, that ever since his confinement a plan was laid for seizing the whole of South Wales to erect a Chartist Kingdom, and for the liberation of Vincent from prison."[3]

The four prisoners were tried at the Monmouthshire assizes on August 2 ; they were found guilty in spite of a fine defence by Roebuck, and sentenced, Vincent to twelve, Edwards to

[1] Gammage, p. 152.
[2] *The Rise and Fall of Chartism in Monmouthshire*, p. 17.
[3] From *Particulars of the Trial of Mr. John Frost for High Treason.*

nine, and the others each to six months' imprisonment. During
the three months preceding the trial, and during the trial itself,
perfect order is said to have reigned in the neighbourhood.

Towards the end of October the local magistrates began to
have suspicions. The local miners were said to be arming in
secret. An immediate insurrection was expected. Rumours
of disciplined and armed battalions disquieted the minds of
the Monmouthshire gentry. Special constables were once
more sworn in, soldiers were reimported, and all precautions
taken. On the night of November 4 the rebellion took place.
A body of men led by John Frost marched into Newport,
probably from Blackwood or Risca. They were armed in a
miscellaneous manner, with the inevitable pikes (which the
early Radical reformers must have seen in their dreams, so
often did they meditate their employment), and with a large
number of domestic implements, adaptable for offensive purposes—such as billhooks, scythes, saws, hammers, pickaxes,
etc. Phillips, the Mayor, was spending the night at the
Westgate Hotel, which was, of course, defended by soldiers.
Not unnaturally, this hotel was the scene of the first fighting.
The Chartists managed to drive the soldiers into the building
and followed them in, demanding the release of the prisoners.
Shots were fired and several Chartists were killed or wounded
before they were dispersed. Frost was arrested the same
night. The Mayor was wounded by one of the pikesmen and
received a knighthood a few days later. The number of killed
was said to be twenty.[1]

A definite and accurate statement of the total number of
the armed Chartist rioters would be of great interest, were it
obtainable. *The Times* stated the figure at 8,000, *The Morning
Chronicle* at 1,000, another account gives 20,000.[2] It is very
probable that the actual figure is much smaller than any of
these. Fear and darkness cause such statistics to multiply
furiously. The facts are that forty Chartists were taken prisoners, and that a smaller number, say twenty, were killed.
(Only ten bodies were forthcoming when the inquest was held.)

[1] *Annual Register*, 1839, Part II, pp. 222–23.
[2] Gammage, pp. 161–162.

We may assume that others, perhaps fifty, were wounded : some of these would probably be included among those captured. In view of the number of special constables and soldiers in Newport on the fatal night, we have a right to assume that an armed insurgent would stand a very good chance of being captured. The fight at the Westgate Hotel lasted at least twenty minutes, or time enough to allow of the assembly of all the upholders of law and order in the town. We must therefore conclude that the total number has been grossly exaggerated by all concerned, and that 200 would be a generous estimate of the number of rioters. The various accounts of the disorders speak of a body of unarmed Chartists outside the town, waiting on the hills for the news of their comrades' victory ; of an unarmed body of the same which entered Newport when it was too late ; of an armed body which did likewise ; of two bodies, one armed and the other unarmed, which did likewise. When these tales are arranged in an ascending order of magnitude, it seems fairly clear that they owe their origin to a common ancestor, and that this may well have originated by some citizen of Newport losing his way and coming upon a strange man or two in the darkness. For a precisely parallel case, see Falstaff's accounts of his adventure in Shakespeare's *Henry IV*, Part I, Act 2, scene iv.

Of the forty prisoners many were shortly acquitted. Fourteen, including Frost, were indicted for high treason. A special commission of thirteen was appointed to try the case, the Chief Justice being a member of it. The Attorney-General acted for the Crown, Sir Frederick Pollock for the accused, for whose defence large sums of money had been gathered. The trial began on January 1, 1840. Pollock pointed out, in the course of the defence, that the Whigs had, in 1832, done nearly as much, and threatened to do more, than the Chartists in 1839. Both sides seemed to take for granted that the objective of the rioters was the release of Vincent from Monmouth prison. This seems an absurd hypothesis, for Monmouth is at least twenty miles from Newport, and Newport is not on the road from Risca or Blackwood to Monmouth. It is in fact probable that the whole affair was due to the officer in command of the soldiers in the neighbourhood of the Westgate Hotel losing his head at the sight of an apparently armed mob. However, the jury found Frost guilty. Two others, Zephaniah Williams and William Jones, were found guilty shortly afterwards. Five others pleaded guilty on the understanding that their lives would be spared, and as the Attorney-General did not press the prosecution of the remaining prisoners, they were discharged. On January 13, Frost, Williams and Jones were sentenced to death. The five who had pleaded guilty received the same sentence, with an intimation to the effect that they could not expect a commutation to transportation for life.

Sir Frederick Pollock took to town a technical objection on behalf of the convicted prisoners of an irregularity in the proceedings, which, after much argument in the Court of Exchequer, was established as valid. In view of this, the recommendations of the Monmouthshire juries, in all cases, to mercy, the immediately forthcoming marriage (on February 10) of the Queen, the petition of a large number of M.P.'s, another petition to the Queen from twelve Birmingham congregations, and a third petition to Parliament, the sentences were commuted on February 1 to transportation for life. A few days later, he and his fellow-convicts were on their way to Australia.[1]

It is usual to speak of the Newport riot as a Chartist rising, and it is not uncommonly hinted that this was the premature outbreak of a great conspiracy which was intended to put the government of the country into the hands of the Chartists. Whether or not a conspiracy of this character was ever seriously contemplated is matter for argument; the evidence is naturally hearsay. The riot of 1839 is generally attributed to the Chartists, and it is, of course, impossible to deny that they gave it leadership. But it is doubtful whether such a rising could have taken place anywhere but in South Wales.

---

[1] Place tabulates 155 petitions for the reprieve of Frost in Place Collection, set 56, 1840, Vol. II. W. J. Linton, the engraver, in *My Memories*, describes (p. 44) his efforts to get a reprieve. He drafted a petition, and obtained signatures from Birkbeck, Dr. Southwood Smith (the public health reformer), W. J. Fox, Hetherington and Watson. Carlyle, on the other hand, refused to sign.

The conditions under which the South Wales miner lives and works have made his country the seat of unrest ever since mines began to befoul his valleys. Miners all over Great Britain " were in very ill repute for riotous proceedings from 1837–44."[1] Only four years after the Newport rising came the peculiar " Rebecca Riots " in the same area ; ostensibly due to turnpikes, they bore witness to feelings of resentment far deeper than those which the payment of tolls might be expected to generate. There is reason to believe that in this case the riots were controlled by men who actually refused to accept Chartist leadership and help.[2] In our own day the South Wales miners have made similar responses to similar conditions. The strikes of 1893, 1898, 1910 and 1912, the stoppage of work in 1915 in the face of the Munitions Act and the nation at war, and the spread of Syndicalism and Guild Socialism, all come from the same cause. We realize what this cause is when we learn that the indifference on the part of colliery owners and managers, which in the case of the Senghenydd disaster led to the death of 439 men, was punished by fines amounting in all to £24, or 1s. 1¼d. per head.[3] While the miner is allowed to learn in this way that his life is equal in value to the price of a dead rabbit, outbreaks are liable to occur at any moment without the interposition of an agitation for universal suffrage.

Feargus O'Connor's conduct about this time appears in an extremely unfavourable light. While supporting militancy on one hand, he was very anxious to avoid having to abide by its consequences : this desire expressing itself in prevarications of the most unblushing nature. A little later on, when Lovett was in prison, O'Connor, according to Lovett, " had the impudence to boast that he was the man that prevented the Sacred Month from taking place ! although, as described, he was an active party in recommending it. He subsequently on several occasions endeavoured to persuade his dupes that

---

[1] Webb, *History of Trade Unionism*, pp. 149–150.
[2] *Rough Types of English Life*, by J. C. Symons, p. 27.
[3] *Mines and Quarries*, Reports of S. Wales Division, Cd. 8023–IV, pp. 58, 59.

I was the concoctor of this violent measure, although himself and his disciples were the first to talk of arming, of the run upon the bank, and the Attwood project of the Sacred Month. I mention these facts in no way to disclaim the hand I had in it, although I believe that I did an act of folly in being a party to some of its provisions ; but I sacrificed much in that convention for the sake of union, and for the love and hope I had in the cause, and I have still vanity enough to believe that if I had not been imprisoned I could have prevented many of the outbreaks and follies that occurred."[1] To quote Lovett again : " From another communication made to me by J. Collins—who had it from one of the parties—it would seem that in anticipation of this rising in the North a person was delegated from one of the towns to go to Feargus O'Connor, to request that he would lead them on, as he had so often declared he would. Collins's informant was present at this interview, and described to him the following conversation that took place :

DELEGATE. Mr. O'Connor, we are going to have a rising for the Charter, in Yorkshire, and I am sent from —— to ask if you will lead us on, as you have so often said you would when we were prepared.

FEARGUS. Well, when is this rising to take place ?

DELEGATE. Why, we have resolved that it shall begin on Saturday next.

FEARGUS. And are you all well provided with arms, then ?

DELEGATE. Yes, all of us.

FEARGUS. Well, that is all right, my man.

DELEGATE. Now, Mr. O'Connor, shall I tell our lads that you will come and lead them on ?

FEARGUS (indignantly). Why, man ! When did you ever hear of me, or of any one of my family, ever deserting the cause of the people ? Have they not always been found at their post in the hour of danger ?

After which O'Connor blandly assured the unfortunate delegate's fellow-townsmen that he had never promised any-

Life and Struggles of William Lovett, pp. 208, 209.

thing."[1] It is a pleasant story, characteristic even if not true. It is clear that O'Connor was completely acquainted with the preparations for the Newport rising, but he absented himself in Ireland, practically up to the eve of the day fixed.[2] The authorities, however, were thoroughly anxious to have all the Chartist leaders under lock and key, and although O'Connor gave them no chances as a rebel, he allowed himself to be trapped as a writer. Various articles which appeared in *The Northern Star* in July, 1839, were regarded as seditious libels, and after many delays O'Connor was tried, and on May 11, 1840, sentenced to eighteen months' imprisonment.

It may well be asked why the Government, which had so systematically suppressed the Chartist leaders for their alleged seditious utterances, should have thus allowed the press which published and circulated them to continue, or to die from natural causes, unassisted by Whitehall. The answer is simple. It was not on account of strength of faith in the freedom of the press that *The Northern Star* was allowed to live unmolested for nearly fifteen years. This paper had a circulation which in its most " seditious " days sometimes reached the weekly figure of 60,000 ; when it was at this figure it had the largest circulation of any weekly paper, and more than quadrupled the daily sales of *The Times*. On each such issue of *The Northern Star* the Treasury received about £250, exclusive of whatever smaller amounts the advertisement and paper duties might bring in. A clear £250 a week covers a multitude of sedition. On those terms what Government would not be content to close its eyes, the more so when it could point to imprisoned orators and declare that it kept its ears open ?

One after the other the Chartist leaders found themselves in prison. The winter of 1839–40 saw the Home Office prosecutions in full blast, but by the middle of 1840 their work was completed and virtually, without exception, the principal sources of Chartist energy were no longer able to cause the Government any anxiety. About this time the total number

[1] *William Lovett*, pp. 239, 240.
[2] *Northern Star*, May 22, 1842, quoted in D. N. B.

of Chartists thus out of the way was between three and four
hundred.

The outward signs of collapse promptly showed themselves.
A heavy mortality raged among the Chartist periodical publications.   The agitation for the Six Points became inarticulate.
New ideas began to get into the heads of the undisciplined rank
and file of the movement.   In England, in fact, Chartism had
reached its critical stage.   In Scotland, however, the faith
was secure.   Harney, almost the only prominent unincarcerated
Chartist, carried on a propaganda up and down North Britain.
In Glasgow the *Scottish Chartist Circular* was successfully
launched at the time when things in England were at their
blackest ; and in Scotland generally the movement was but
slightly affected.   But in those days of defective communications Scottish influences on Westminster were slight at the
best of times, and Scottish Chartism cannot be credited with
much more than preserving the continuity of the movement
between two phases.   The phase upon which Chartism was
now to enter will be the subject of the following chapter.

L

CHAPTER VI

IDEAS AT A PREMIUM

THE People's Charter had been deliberately drafted for the purpose of supplying a greatest common measure of agreement to the unco-ordinated Radical-Socialist movement. So long as those who had accepted the principles of the Charter were at liberty, their mutual differences were subject to a process of attrition. However wide the gap between the upholders of physical and of moral force, the end in view was always the same. For a period of nearly two years the Chartist agitation succeeded in concentrating the reformers' energies. This period came to an end with the imprisonment of the leaders. Isolated for a time from their colleagues, the principal Chartists' fancies strayed unchecked. A mass of new projects came into existence, many to be promptly forgotten, others to exercise a dominant influence on the future of the movement. Many of the new ideas came, as we shall see not from the imprisoned leaders, but from their rank and file at liberty. For this fact the break in the hectoring dictatorship of O'Connor is largely responsible. The " Lion of Chartism " was apt to snap off the heads of any followers who put any originality into the manner of their following. The " new move " (as it came to be called) which was to exercise the greatest influence on the future of the movement emanated from Lovett and Collins.

While Lovett and Collins were imprisoned in Warwick Gaol they occupied themselves by writing a book. *Chartism: a New Organization of the People*, was the outcome, it would appear, of self-questioning. Lovett must have asked himself :

What course of action can we recommend that will keep our forces together, lead to immediately tangible and beneficial results, and be both legal and likely to remain so, to whatever extremes the weaker brethren take it ? We must promote unity, among ourselves as well as between all classes. We must educate the unconverted. We must strengthen the faith of the converted. The result of these questions was that the greater part of the volume consisted of a Proposed Plan, Rules, and Regulations of an Association, to be entitled, The National Association of the United Kingdom, for Promoting the Political and Social Improvement of the People. The Association was to have several objects, but the third and principal one showed such a deviation from the exclusive demand for the Charter that it may be quoted in full.

To erect Public Halls or Schools for the People throughout the Kingdom, upon the most approved principles, and in such districts as may be necessary. Such halls to be used during the day as Infant, Preparatory, and High Schools, in which the children shall be educated on the most approved plans the association can devise ; embracing physical, mental, moral and political instruction ; and used of an evening for Public Lectures, on physical, moral, and political science ; for Readings, Discussions, Musical Entertainments, Dancing, and such other healthful and rational recreations as may serve to instruct and cheer the industrious classes after their hours of toil, and prevent the formation of vicious and intoxicating habits. Such halls to have two commodious play-grounds, and where practicable, a pleasure-garden, attached to each ; apartments for the teachers, rooms for hot and cold baths, for a small museum, a laboratory and general workshop, where the children may be taught experiments in science, as well as the first principles of the most useful trades.

This statement contains the principle urged by Lovett. Among its other objects, the Association was to establish schools for teachers, schools for orphans, circulating libraries,[1] etc. Elaborate rules were suggested to govern the conduct of the

[1] The Book Box scheme of the Fabian Society might be regarded as Lovett's proposal reduced to practical dimensions.

body, and further were given for the circulating libraries, halls, and schools. The last batch of regulations are of great interest, and show that here, at any rate, Lovett was very considerably ahead of his times. It would have been difficult for one who had often listened to Owen to have refrained from thinking about education. That Lovett's mind had been influenced is shown by his publication in 1838 of an Address to the Working Classes on the subject of National Education, in which the educational ideas of *The Charter* were contained in virtually the same words. That Lovett had at that time already attempted to convince the Working Men's Association of the justness of his views on these matters is shown by the fact that the entire Committee of the W.M.A. put its names to the pamphlet. Corporal punishment was to have no place in the education of the young Chartist. The outline of the teaching of the children in the infant and preparatory schools also contains more than a suggestion of Montessori methods.

The slightly fantastic budget which accompanied this scheme was based on the theory that all the 1,283,000 signatories of the National Petition would be willing to become members of the National Association, and pay a subscription of a shilling per quarter. This would provide an annual income of £256,600, which was estimated to be sufficient to build eight district halls at £3,000 each, and to cover the incidental expenses of propaganda and organization. The advantages which the National Association would have over other political bodies would be, " it would not merely use its energies and resources in meeting and petitioning ; it would not, year after year, be engaged in the useless task of endeavouring to induce corruption to purify itself ; but it would be gradually accumulating means of instruction and amusement, and devising sources of refined enjoyments to which the millions are strangers ; it would be industriously employed in politically, intellectually, and morally training fathers, mothers, and children to know their rights and perform their duties ; and with a people so trained, exclusive power, corruption, and injustice would soon cease to have an existence."[1]

[1] P. 55, *Chartism.*

Lovett, it will be seen, had ceased to believe in the omnipotence of Universal Suffrage. If the condition of the people was to be improved, the people must themselves prepare for the change. The little book concluded with a series of general observations on education, and some specimen " Lesson Cards " to illustrate the teaching of truth, geology, anatomy, rights, and duties. The most interesting anticipation of Dr. Montessori is contained in the suggestion that children should be partly taught, partly teach themselves, to read, with the aid of a case of movable types.[1] The District Halls were planned down to their minutest details and the frontispiece of *Chartism* was a hideously symmetrical design for one of these buildings.

Vincent's new idea, although it was enthusiastically taken up at the time is not in these days associated with Chartism, or, indeed, with working-class politics. He came to the conclusion that Chartists must be teetotallers. While the imprisoned Chartists were treated in most respects with great severity, they were nevertheless allowed ample means of communication with the outside world. Vincent's total abstinence views were therefore not kept hidden until his release ; while he was still in gaol he drafted a teetotal manifesto, and managed to convince a group of his friends of the rightness of his views. On November 27, 1840, this declaration of principle was duly published in the *Dundee Chronicle*, over the names Vincent, Hill, Cleave, Hetherington, and Neesom. The manifesto was afterwards republished as a leaflet, which contained also an article strongly attacking the use of tobacco and snuff as injurious to the cause of Chartism. Hill had already begun to recommend the readers of *The Northern Star* to abstain from drink. According to him, " Teetotalism leads to knowledge—knowledge leads to thinking—thinking leads to discontent of things as they are, and then, as a matter of course, comes Chartism."[2] The same paper records a solemn and

---

[1] Lovett tells us that after he had written this he read, in a life of Pestalozzi, that that educationist had already recommended a somewhat similar contrivance. Lovett's invention was made quite independently, however.   [2] *Northern Star*, September 7, 1840.

largely-attended public discussion, held in Manchester, on temperance and Chartism.[1] The spirit of the proceedings seems wildly removed from what we should imagine to be the reception of an analogous debate in these days. After Vincent's release his time was very largely occupied in oratorical temperance tours, and the administration of the pledge wholesale to Chartist Organization.

Another divagation from undiluted Chartism was known as Bible Chartism. John Collins seems to have been affected by it as well as by the " new move," for he founded a " Chartist Church " in Birmingham after his release, but he was not the only member of this sect. Throughout the south of Scotland, in 1840 and 1841, Chartism adopted a definitely religious basis. This tendency, like the teetotal campaign, was supported by Hill, as a minister. A single issue of *The Northern Star*[2] contains three letters from correspondents, urging the identity of Christianity with Chartism, and also the first of a series of articles on " Scriptural Chartism." One of the just-mentioned correspondents, by the way, signed himself " Christian Socialist " (Was this the first use of the term ?) and demanded, as a part of the Christian-Chartist programme, the restoration of the land to the people.

The new movement spread best in Scotland. Early in 1841 it had extended to such dimensions that it was thought desirable to hold a delegate meeting in Glasgow. *The Northern Star* report of the proceedings[3] gives no clue to the number of either representatives or represented, but says that delegates came " from most of the Chartist Churches in the west of Scotland," and mentions about twenty names. Bronterre O'Brien had already[4] spoken approvingly of this development of Chartism, and said that Chartist Christianity was the same as primitive Christianity. O'Connor, as usual, had views to suit all sides. He declares, " I never knew a grain of good to come out of ' Bible Chartism ' "[5] ; a little later he decides that it is a good thing for Scotland, because Scotland " has no State Church,"

---

[1] *Northern Star*, November 21, 1840.   [2] September 12, 1840.
[3] January 16, 1841.   [4] *Northern Star*, January 2, 1841.
[5] Ib., January 16, 1841.

and " in Scotland preaching unites the, people, and weakens and disunites the enemy."[1] But of English Bible Chartism, O'Connor could not approve. However, as there was very little of it outside Birmingham, his disapproval hardly mattered.

Feargus O'Connor had only been imprisoned in York Castle five days when one Parkin produced an original scheme, which was published in and favourably commented upon by *The Northern Star*.[2] Parkin had drafted a memorial to the President of the United States, asking for his intercession on behalf of the " industrious, and deeply insulted and injured classes of this country," and to help forward the Charter agitation. Nothing *much* seems to have come of this. Almost simultaneously voices in the Chartist ranks were heard to demand " household suffrage and redistribution as a practical compromise."[3] Less than a month afterwards *The Northern Star* published a scheme, drafted by Richardson, for the re-organization of Chartism in Lancashire,[4] to be extended, if possible, throughout the country. Richardson recommended the local branches to federate and work out some benefit scheme, also to register under the Friendly Societies Act.

In the winter of 1840–41 an expected diversion of interests drew a great many Chartists, and especially in the neighbourhood of Newcastle-on-Tyne, away from the movement. David Urquhart, formerly a diplomatic agent in the alternate service of the British and Turkish Government, had returned to this country from the Near East overflowing with hatred of Russia and suspicion of this country's foreign policy. In common with others who in more recent times have attempted to make out a case for the wickedness of secret diplomacy, he illustrated the wickedness by denying the secrecy. Starting with the theory that the Chartist movement was a plot, in the hands of Russian agents, intended to embarrass the British Government, he preached to innumerable Chartist audiences on the depraved aggressiveness of Russia, and finally won over Charles Attwood, Lowery, Cardo, and Warden, who thenceforward concerned themselves with Urquhart's Foreign Affairs Com-

---

[1] *Northern Star*, May 8, 1841.   [2] May 24, 1840.
[3] *Leeds Times*, May 23, 1840.   [4] June 20, 1840.

mittees—curiously close anticipations of the Union of Democratic Control—and had no more to do with Chartism. (See Appendix I.)

Various other Chartists urged new demands about this time, or attempted new experiments. " Newmilns : A Chartist co-operative store has been recently opened in this spirited village, consisting of 248 members."[1] We hear, too, that Scottish Chartists are urging Home Rule for Scotland, perhaps not very vociferously.[2] From other Chartists we hear a demand for woman suffrage. This idea had occupied an inconspicuous position in the background of Chartism since 1838. In and even before that year " Female Political Unions " had come into existence, especially in the neighbourhood of Birmingham, where Attwood's influence prevailed. Sir Edward Bulwer-Lytton in 1838 inquired as to the reason of the exclusion of woman suffrage from the Six Points, and elicited a curious reply from *The Northern Star*. In this the orthodox attitude on the matter of the upholders of universal suffrage was defined ; no serious believer in universal suffrage could refuse the right of spinsters and widows to a vote, but the civil and political rights and interests of a married woman were bound up with those of her husband.[3] The Annual Register for 1839, describing the meeting on Kersall Moor on May 25, says : " The only novelty worth noticing was the presence of several *female* political associations. It was observed by an eyewitness that the appearance of some of the fair sex who figured on this occasion, both as to person and apparel, furnished a stronger argument than any adduced by orators, of the necessity of adopting immediate legislative enactments for improving the condition of the mass of the people." Female Charter Unions sprang up by the dozen after the publication of the Charter, but their members seem to have generally contented themselves with giving moral support to their male relatives and, in some cases, assisting the families and dependents of imprisoned Chartists. Vincent's special popularity among women obtained for

[1] *The Free Press*, October 31, 1840.
[2] *Leeds Times*, November 21, 1840.
[3] *Northern Star*, October 20, 1838.

his Teetotal Chartism crusade a strong feminine support, and led to the formation of many Female Chartist Abstinence Unions, and organizations with similar names. But the air of novelty with which every proposer of woman suffrage explains his or her views shows that the faith was not commonly held. During the period of new ideas, the case for woman suffrage received much attention. It is particularly well stated in a letter signed Laone,[1] which is full of phrases familiar to twentieth-century ears. " Why should not a woman vote ? . . . We are told that *woman's proper sphere* lies in the possession of *indirect influence.*" Laone heartily pounds these ideas (the words are italicized in the original). The letter was followed up by a series of dialogues in favour of Woman Suffrage, by Colonel Perronet Thompson. The only imprisoned Chartist of note from whom barely anything new proceeded was Feargus O'Connor, who condemned all the innovations wholesale. From York Castle he indited a series of weekly letters to *The Northern Star*. To show his irrevocable opposition to all compromise with the middle class, he addressed his letters, not always in exactly the same terms, " To the Fustian Jackets, Blistered Hands, and unshorn chins of England, Scotland, and Wales, and to the Ragged-Backed, Bare-Footed Irish." To these he declaimed in a single commination[2] against " Church Chartism, Teetotal Chartism, Knowledge Chartism, and House-hold Suffrage Chartism." A little later he writes, " Do not think of Reform of the Lords—of sponging the National Debt —of Repealing the Corn Laws—of Free Trade—of the Ballot —of purifying the church—of reducing the army or the navy —of opposing any police bill—of repealing the Poor Law Amend-ment Act—of stopping a war with China, Naples, America, Russia, or the whole world. Never mind what the Queen gives Prince Albert (or rather what you give him), or whether he spends it at Crockford's or other places of debauchery— never mind corporation bills or registration bills, Dissenters' bills or Protestant bills, Canada church reserves or emigration bills ; mind none of them ; for your united force could not

---

[1] *Leeds Times*, March 20, 1841.   [2] April 3, 1841.

affect any of these questions a pin's point, while your interference would weaken your power of laying the axe to the root
of one and all. If every abuse of which you now complain was
abolished to-morrow, your order would not derive a fraction of
benefit from the change."[1] O'Connor's contribution to the
stock of new ideas is briefly told. " My Dear Friends,—I now
proceed to my plan for carrying the Charter. You observe
I do not say for agitating for the Charter, but for carrying the
Charter. Mark its simplicity, and in that you will recognize
its greatest worth. Two short words—DAILY PAPER." So
begins one of his weekly letters " To the Fustian Jackets."[2]
For the most part O'Connor prepared to wallow in self-pity
and self-admiration, irrelevantly enumerating his own good
deeds, and claiming in the most directly possible manner to
be the only honest man in the Chartist movement. " Good
God, how I glory in the rich and consoling reflection ; not one
drop of blood shed through five years and a half of unparalleled
cruelty and persecution upon the one side, and patient suffering upon the other."[3] Or else, "On the eighteenth of November,
1837, I established *The Northern Star*, the first paper ever published in England exclusively for the people ; a paper which
has given a completely new tone to the whole press of the
empire. . . . From September, 1835, to February, 1839, I
led you single-handed and alone . . ."[4]

Lovett and Collins were released on July 25, 1840. A
triumphant series of receptions and dinners had been more
or less arranged for them, but both had suffered severely in
health and needed rest. A week after they had been restored
to freedom, however, the two Chartists managed to attend a
dinner given in their honour in Birmingham. The speakers
on this occasion were Wakley, M.P., Dr. Epps, and Cleave.
Lovett, in making his speech, foreshadowed the course he was
preparing to take by declaring that nothing had rejoiced him
so much when in prison as the news of the erection of some

[1] O'Connor in *The Northern Star*, April 25, 1840.
[2] *Northern Star*, July 18, 1840.
[3] Ib., January 30, 1841.
[4] Ib., January 16, 1841.

Trade Halls by trade unions.[1] The book *Chartism* was placed in the printer's hands, and Lovett went to Cornwall to recuperate.

Chartism promptly made a stir, and went into a second edition in a very short time. It was followed by the launching of the National Association for Promoting the Political and Social Improvement of the People. It goes without saying that Lovett was the moving spirit in this body. The Rules and Regulations published by the National Association are taken wholesale from *Chartism* with scarcely an amendment. Lovett, having drafted the constitution of the National Association, sent it to Place for his opinion ; Place pointed out that the law was against political associations which had " divisions, branches or parts." The N.A. was avowedly political, and it aimed at having branches ; it was therefore illegal. He suggested a large number of modifications, most of which Lovett did not accept. Place pointed out, however, that Government prosecution was most unlikely, and that Lovett might go ahead. Lovett was fully persuaded that his scheme would have immediate success ; Place declared that Lovett " would never be able to establish even one school."[2] Place, in spite of his discouraging opinion, obtained £50 for the Association from J. T. Leader, M.P. Hetherington became the first secretary, followed later by Charles Westerton, " a gentleman who subsequently, as churchwarden at Knightsbridge, rendered great service to the Liberal cause by his opposition to Puseyism."[3] Others who took an active part in starting the Association were Cleave, Vincent, Watson, J. Collins, R. Moore, C. H. Neesom, W. J. Linton, J. Stansfeld, W. Shawn, J. D. Collett, and several middle-class men. The published receipts and expenditure of the year 1842–43 contains the names of subscribers. Dr. Epps, Joseph Hume, M.P., H. Elphinstone, M.P., J. S. Mill, T. S. Duncombe, M.P., H. Warburton, M.P., P. W. Williams, M.P., Lord Brougham, Benjamin Wood, M.P., Sir John Easthope, Lord Radnor, George Grote, R. Wason,

---

[1] *Northern Star*, August 4, 1840.
[2] Place Collection, set 56, 1841, Vol. 3, fo. 220.
[3] Lovett, *Autobiography*, p. 259.

M.P., General Johnson, M.P., W. Collins, M.P., Sir Matthew Wood, M.P., T. Milner Gibson, M.P., R. O. Cave, M.P., The Hon. C. P. Villiers, M.P., Wynn Ellis, M.P., T. Wakley, M.P., and Charles Buller, M.P., virtually all the intellectual liberals, were among those who contributed to start the movement.

The Northern Star began to denounce the National Association even before it was under way.[1] The new move was stigmatized as an endeavour to break up Chartist unity, and to side-track the Charter. " Of course," wrote O'Connor, " the Charter is the object ; indeed nothing else would do to bait the trap."[2] The results of this campaign were soon visible. A great many Chartists had put their names to a manifesto, drafted by Lovett, Collins and Vincent, and circulated among the local organizations. But now, fearing the displeasure of O'Connor, a series of recantations took place. One number of The Northern Star[3] published ten letters from persons withdrawing their signatures. The next week or two the columns of the paper contained innumerable reports of Chartist meetings held all over the country, at which the manifesto was denounced and disclaimed. O'Connor fulminated against the new move regularly once a week, with a mendacity surpassed only by his egotism. He represents Lovett and his followers as traitors, and asks, " Who were the three most physical-force men in the Convention ? Lovett, Collins and Hetherington ? "[4] It is surprising that complete misrepresentations such as this one—and others as bad were invented every week—did not split the ranks of O'Connor's followers. But the fact is that the dictator's reputation had never stood higher than at this moment. During the period of his imprisonment every issue of The Northern Star contained a list, headed More Young Patriots, of the newly-born children of Chartist parents, invariably named after O'Connor. One result of the Chartist movement was that thousands of O'Connors and Fearguses were contained among the Christian names of the English working class of the second half of the nineteenth century. With an

[1] Beginning with the March 27, 1841, issue.
[2] Northern Star, April 17, 1841.
[3] April 24, 1841.
[4] Northern Star, May 8, 1841.

unlimited amount of moral support behind him, O'Connor had no need of mere accuracy. His bluster unfortunately communicated itself to some of his followers with an unpleasant amount of force. John Watkins, for example (the author of *John Frost*, a Chartist Play, in five acts, 1841), preached a sermon on several occasions,[1] demonstrating the entire justice of any assassination of Lovett. Neesom, once a physical-force Chartist, now a member of the National Association, was boycotted by fervent followers of O'Connor until his newsagent's business became completely profitless, and he was brought face to face with starvation.

The subsequent history of the National Association may be shortly told. A year after its foundation it had a library of 800 volumes, a large coffee-room seating 150, and a free Sunday School for children. Men paid a subscription of eightpence a month, women of fourpence. Classes in dancing and phrenology were held, and well attended. In the Hall of the Association, 242A, High Holborn, where these classes, etc., were held, there was room for 2,000. This Hall was triumphantly opened on July 25, 1842, with J. T. Leader, M.P., in the chair. A year later W. J. Fox took the chair at its birthday celebration. Yet in spite of the activity at its centre, the National Association never developed in the way expected by its founder, and Place's pessimistic forecast was completely justified. Lovett says that " efforts were made in some few places to form local bodies, similar to those of the London members, but they did not enroll sufficient numbers to make them effective."[2] The fear that the " new move " would split the Chartist movement was indeed vain. The *Leeds Times*, a neighbour and rival of *The Northern Star*, took up the side of Lovett. It did not attempt to outdo the organ of Feargus O'Connor in scurrility, and, in fact, went no farther than to cast gentle aspersions on the chastity of the editor, the Rev. W. Hill.[3] The editor of the paper at that time was Samuel Smiles, the self-helper. He had a great admiration for Lovett, and once offered him the post of sub-editor. (Lovett, *Autobiography*, p. 245.)

---

[1] Lovett, *Autobiography*, p. 251.
[2] Lovett, *Life and Struggles*, p. 286. [3] *Leeds Times*, May 8, 1841.

On Monday, July 20, 1840, a Convention of twenty-three delegates met at Manchester to consider the reorganization of the Chartist movement, which was rapidly falling into disorder with the imprisonment of the leaders. The delegates were all admirers of O'Connor, and had a physical force bias. The result of their deliberations was the National Charter Association of Great Britain. This was to be a federation of all the local Chartist Societies, which had hitherto remained unco-ordinated on account of the state of the law on illegal associations. The annual subscription was fixed as a minimum of eightpence, payable in quarterly instalments. The delegates paid lip-service to constitutional methods, and decided to adopt a proposal of Bronterre O'Brien and put forward Chartist candidates at the next general election. James Leach and William Tillman were the first president and secretary. Lovett was invited to join, but refused, alleging the illegality of the organization.[1] The real difference between the N.C.A. and Lovett's organization lay in the classes appealed to. Lovett believed that " the principles of Chartism are purely democratical, calculated to benefit all classes, and not the working classes exclusively." He declared that if Sir R. Peel, Lord John Russell and the Duke of Wellington wished to join the Association, he, for his part, would welcome them.[2] Place, as before, was asked for his opinion on the new organization, and gave it, in completely unsympathetic but amply justifiable terms. " The Association is to all intents and purposes an illegal assembly and every member thereof, and every one who aids or abets it, or in any way assists it, or contributes to it by money, or corresponds with it, or any of its branches, or any members thereof as such, incurs the penalty of the Acts of 1798 and 1817, and may be transported for seven years. It does not certainly follow that every one who pleases may, by becoming a member, etc., take the risk—but after what we have seen, he who takes the risk must be more foolhardy than brave. Any one who thus commits himself must be a very silly fellow. . . . If these men should go on, as I suppose they will, and

[1] Lovett, *Autobiography*, p. 252.
[2] Letter from Lovett in the *Perth Chronicle*, May 6, 1841.

in time be prosecuted, what sympathy will they deserve ? What sympathy will they receive ? None. How will they have promoted the good cause ? Not at all. They will have played the game for the only real enemy, the aristocracy, and when they have served their purpose will be treated as the Lower Orders always have been treated by them.

" We shall have the Charter whenever we, the mass of the people, are really fit for it, and not till then, until then we ought not to have it because we should not have kept it. . . . But the Chartists one and all, even the most rational and considerate, have been too sanguine. . . . The annunciation of the Charter has been acted upon by them as if it was something Divine . . ."[1]

The immediate result of the N.C.A. Convention was a manifesto. This reviewed the situation, pronounced against the refusal of the Government to pardon Frost, Jones and Williams, condemned the Poor Law, and referred to " Church-Chartism, Teetotal-Chartism, and Education-Chartism " to recommend those who followed these bypaths to enter the N.C.A., unity of opinion as to the end desired being of greater importance than unity as to the means. The manifesto then embarked upon an excursion in economics. The policy of Free Trade was condemned ; then, curiously enough the total repeal of all duties was demanded, and it was argued that the probable effects of Free Trade upon labour would be deplorable. Then finally a political programme was recommended. " We are natural enemies to Whigism and Toryism, but being unable to destroy both factions, we advise you to destroy the one faction by making a tool of the other. We advise you to upset the ministerial candidates on every occasion." Then . . . " raise a fund by voluntary contributions for election purposes," and appoint committees " in any place where a chartist candidate is likely to be returned or a ministerial hack upset." A special convention in London was also proposed, the members to consist of Chartist candidates. The signatories to this document were —

[1] Place to Collins, February 27, 1841, fo. 259, Vol. I, 1841, set 56, Place Collection.

P. M. M'Douall,	J. G. Barmby,
T. R. Smart,	M. Williams,
John Skevington,	L. Pitkeithly,
W. Martin,	M. Cullen,
T. J. Wall,	Ruy Ridley,
W. Morgan,	John Rose.

The copy of this document in the Place Collection is decorated with a border of acid marginal comments by the man who, quite wrongly, regarded himself as the author of the People's Charter. His note on the last proposal (that recommending the Convention of the People's Deputies) is, " This means, Keep us that we may not be compelled to work." Truly the movement had fallen from grace since it had outgrown the W.M.A. It may be noted that only two (M'Douall and Pitkeithly) of the founders of the N.C.A. had sat in the 1839 Convention. The growth of the N.C.A. during its first year seems to have been regarded as satisfactory by its progenitors. In March, 1841, the Association had less than one hundred branches.[1] Only eighty-three branches took part in the election of the Executive in June, when the largest number of votes cast by a single branch for one candidate was 200 : Merthyr Tydfil cast this number for each of five candidates. The result of this election was as follows : P. M. M'Douall, 3,795 ; J. Leach, 3,664 ; John Campbell (secretary), 2,219 ; Morgan Williams, 2,945 ; George Binns, 1,879 ; R. K. Philp, 1,130.[2] These figures suggest that the total membership of the eighty-three branches in question did not exceed five thousand. The membership increased slowly, but the leaders watched its growth through magnifying glasses. When O'Connor was at last released from York Castle on August 30, *The Northern Star* stated[3] that he was welcomed by " upwards of one hundred and fifty delegates, representing almost the entire labouring population of the United Kingdom. Yet at the beginning of October there were still under two hundred

---

[1] *Executive Journal of the National Charter Association*, October 23, 1841.

[2] *Northern Star*, June 7, 1841.   [3] Ib., September 4, 1841.

branches [1] and only about 16,000 membership cards had been issued. A week later [2] 204 branches are reported. At the beginning of November there were already 263,[3] while at the end of the month the number was 282.[4] The membership, although but a minute fraction of the two million adherents to the Chartist movement constantly claimed by O'Connor, was largely composed of individuals whose subscriptions could not be relied on ; there are such persons at the fringe of every movement, but the Chartist movement certainly had, throughout its existence, an undue proportion of such a fringe. The members of the N.C.A. could not be trusted to support any little side-show got up by the Executive—and it is by these small special appeals that the loyalty of a body of members is best tested. For example ; the Executive of the N.C.A. decided at the end of 1841 to print a little penny weekly sheet called the *Executive Journal of the National Charter Association*, with the object of bringing the members into closer touch with them than was possible in the public columns of *The Northern Star*. Only four numbers of the *Journal* were ever printed. The members refused to respond. Place comments on this that two thousand subscribers would have kept it going.[5]

The membership of the N.C.A. was, in fact, very largely a paper affair. In February, 1842, 40,060 membership cards had been issued, according to an address of the Executive Council.[6] Yet, in spite of the growing numbers, and the most rigid economy,[7] the Secretary found himself unable to pay expenses. In April, 1842, he complains of being £20 in debt.[8] The Branches should pay the Executive a penny per month per member ; this ought to bring in £43 a week, but the sum actually received is much smaller. In July, Campbell publishes

---

[1] *Northern Star*, October 9, 1841.   [2] Ib., October 16, 1841.
[3] Ib., November 13, 1841.   [4] Ib., December 4, 1841.
[5] Place Collection, set 56, 1841, Vol. III, contains a set of the *Executive Journal*, with comments.
[6] *Northern Star*, February 19, 1842.
[7] Lack of means, according to Campbell, was responsible for the failure of the Birmingham Conference in April, 1842.
[8] *Northern Star*, April 9, 1842.

a very pessimistic report.[1] The debt is now £50, and a " black list " is given, showing about 170 branches, all at least three months in arrear. Some are of important places ; Manchester, the very headquarters of the N.C.A., is among the offending branches. The increased membership is illustrated by the number of votes cast at the Executive election of 1842. M'Douall is still at the top of the poll, with 11,221 votes ; Leach follows him with 10,830 ; Campbell gets 9,712 ; M. Williams, 4,410 ; and Bairstow 4,611. Philp receives 2,656, and so loses his seat. Cooper gets only 2,454.[2]

Many of the branches of the N.C.A. were extremely small. A writer in the *Leeds Times*, himself a Chartist, gives an interesting inside account of the movement in 1842.[3] He tells us that " In every hamlet where two or three Chartists can be gathered together an Association has been formed. In most places the Association does not meet above once a quarter, except some business of importance is to be transacted—such as giving countenance to an itinerating missionary, or getting up a petition for a certain purpose." Many of the Chartists are trade unionists, in fact, " the tact which the Chartists have displayed in conducting their affairs was acquired in the same schools in which they learned their political and economical creed—the trades' unions." But " there is a rule in most Chartist Associations that those belonging to them shall join in no agitation but for the Charter." The writer describes the organization of the Chartists in Dundee, where they are comparatively very strong. Here there are 12,350 workmen, members of trade unions ; and 7,000 " odd-fellows," i.e., men working in unorganized trades. Between them they muster 1,050 organized Chartists. There is also a Female Chartist Association, to which the male Chartists ungallantly refuse representation on their local Executive.

The organization, it will be noted, is fragile ; it exists on hope rather than on subscriptions. But the Chartists possessed a virtue which now appears to have been lost by political bodies : in religious circles it is known as faith ; to many of

---

[1] *Northern Star*, July 9, 1842.   [2] *Northern Star*, June 25, 1842.
[3] *Leeds Times*, January 15, 22, and 29, 1842.

us it can only be described negatively, as the absence of cynicism. When O'Connor wrote that " Six months after the Charter is passed every man, woman and child in the country will be well fed, well housed, and well clothed," his followers believed him, although Lovett derided the prophecy.[1] If a thing is said often enough it is believed, and in sticking to the importance of Universal Suffrage, O'Connor, consistent here, if nowhere else, undoubtedly carried his hearers and readers with him. His statements look curious to-day when examined in the cold and critical light of subsequent events. " Let this be borne in mind," he exclaimed, for example, " and never lost sight of, that Universal Suffrage alone will make the thirty-three of each vicious hundred blush and crouch before the remaining sixty-seven "(sic).[2] This tremendous concentration of feeling upon one point, upon which his followers were equally convinced, prevented the most arrant bluster from appearing merely ridiculous. At a time when nearly half of the forty thousand members of the N.C.A.[3] were in arrears with their subscriptions and the stability of the organization was extremely flimsy. O'Connor could grandiloquently declare, " We are 4,000,000, aye, and more. Never lose sight of the fact that we are 4,000,000 and more."[4] Financial difficulties were in the end too much for the N.C.A. Hill got hold of various scandals and printed them in The Northern Star. In one issue he fired a broadside of five charges [5] alleging that the Executive had neglected the duties of their office, that they had violated the organization they were appointed to enforce, that they had done so wilfully, after repeated caution and remonstrance, that they had wilfully appropriated the moneys of the N.C.A. to their own use and benefit, and that they had manifested in their own conduct, and countenanced in that of others, a disregard of Chartist principle. Hill's virulence, here as else-

---

[1] National Association Gazette, April 9, 1842.
[2] Northern Star, January 2, 1841.
[3] The membership was largely duplicate. O'Connor claimed to belong to twenty-eight associations.
[4] Northern Star, May 21, 1842.
[5] Ib., December 12, 1842.

where, probably outran the truth of the matter, but there seems to be distinct grounds for believing that Campbell, in spite of his complaints as to the lowness of the N.C.A.'s finances, helped himself freely to small sums.[1]

It is curious that Cleave should about this time become the treasurer of the City of London Political and Scientific Institute for the Moral and Social Improvement of the Working Classes, which was virtually a branch of the N.C.A.   This body had a hall in the Old Bailey, which it outgrew, and then moved to a larger hall, holding 2,000, at 1, Turnagain Lane, Skinner Street, Snow Hill.   Here as elsewhere Cleave's behaviour suggests that it was inspired by professional motives, rather than by loyalty to Lovett.   Cleave was the London agent for various periodical publications of the N.C.A., such as the short-lived *Executive Journal*, and seems to have dealt in Chartism as a bookseller deals in ideas.   His behaviour is nevertheless peculiar, the more so as his " Lovettite " friends could not have approved of the action of the N.C.A. in wrecking meetings, such as one by the Society for the Propagation of the Gospel in Foreign Parts held in London in October, 1841, or another in January, 1842, when a Leeds meeting of the Society for the Extinction of the Slave Trade was the occasion of a riot.   The General Election of July, 1841, caused an acrimonious discussion on election policy.   O'Brien suggested that Chartists should choose candidates who would address electors, side-by-side with the nominees of the official parties.   They would, however, retire after the show of hands and not proceed to the poll.   O'Connor gave the same advice.[2]   A dispute occurred as to the time to be taken by those Chartists who possessed votes, and as to propaganda generally.   Should the Whigs be supported, or the Tories ?   The Whigs had caused Chartists to be imprisoned, but the Tories were the more strenuous opponents of reform.   Which of the two evils should be chosen ?   O'Connor urged that the Tories be used in order to crush the Whigs.   O'Brien, very forcibly indeed, objected to this course of action.   " There is but one part of the *Star's*

[1] *Northern Star*, January 7, 1843.
[2] Ib., June 26, 1841.

advice I regret to see—one part from which I dissent *in toto*. I mean the editor's recommendation to support Tories against Whigs, in case the Chartists should not be able to return their own candidate. I cannot possibly concur in this advice, nor will any of my friends throughout the country. Our business as Chartists is, I repeat, to disavow both factions alike, even as they have disavowed us, and to make no distinction whatever between them, saving when they choose to make the distinction themselves, by agreeing to coalesce and split their votes with our party. What ! Vote for a Tory merely to keep out a Whig ! Vote for a villain who wants to put down me, and my principles, and my party, by brute force, merely to get rid of another villain who has tried the same game and failed ! No ! d——n me ! if I do. . . . And as to the new *hocus-pocus* policy of promoting Chartism by inundating the next House of Commons with Toryism, I cannot find language capable of expressing my contempt for it. O'Connor is certainly mad, if he imagines it ; for I am certain he could never swallow such a gross lump of Cobbettism in a moment of sober reflection. It is contrary to all his former recorded opinions, and utterly at variance with the policy he so ably and manfully followed up against the *Liberator* and *Champion*. Let the Chartists but once make common cause with the Tories, no matter for what purpose, and that moment they annihilate themselves *morally* as a political party and prepare the way for their physical extinction by the very villains they would league with, covertly supported by the other villains they leagued against."[1] This was the first blast of a controversy which has persisted in the ranks of Labour even to our own day.

O'Connor's first reply[2] to O'Brien was quite courteous, although entirely irrelevant. It was an attempt in eight columns to shuffle the blame for something or other on to that scapegoat of Chartism, Daniel O'Connell. But O'Brien returned to the attack a week later,[3] when Hill tried to keep

---

[1] Letter from O'Brien in *The Northern Star*, June 19, 1841.
[2] *Northern Star*, June 26, 1841.   [3] Ib., July 3, 1841.

the peace by speaking of " the perfect unanimity of purpose " of the controversialists.

It is curious to note that Robert Owen at this stage showed himself to be more wisely political than the Chartists. Holding no illusions as to the value of Universal Suffrage, but keenly alive to the things that mattered most at the time, he published and widely circulated a manifesto begging the electors to demand a graduated property tax, the abolition of all other taxes, free trade, national education for those who desired it, national employment for those who needed it, free speech, a free press, and complete religious toleration. *The Northern Star* printed his address [1] and said nothing.

Various Chartist candidates were duly chosen, of whom only one, not already in Parliamentary circles, went the whole length of a formal rejection by his constituency. This was Vincent, easily the most sanguine of the Chartist candidates. He writes to Place on June 13, after much previous correspondence of a damping description, and asks for money : " If I had but £30, all would be right." Four days later : " My canvass each day has exceeded my most sanguine expectations . . . £10 or £5 would save me."[2] He received 51 votes, against the 154 given to the elected, and 101 to the other candidate. Immediately after the General Election of 1841, the Executive Committee of the N.C.A. published a manifesto [3] claiming that the Chartists had been the principal factor in the defeat of the Whigs. The argument is not quite clear ; the Chartists had found themselves on the horns of a dilemma, from which they made ungraceful efforts to extricate themselves. Thus the manifesto in point contains these somewhat incompatible statements : " Our party was known, but known only to be feared ; hence if the truth must be proclaimed, the terror of Chartism has ended in the triumph of Toryism." But, a little farther on, " Let not the cry of Tory and Chartist coalition be repeated, when the truth is well known that the

[1] July 3, 1841.
[2] These letters, with drafts of Place's replies, are in the Place Collection, set 56, 1841, Vol. II. See also Wallas, *Life of Francis Place*, pp. 379, 380. [3] *Northern Star*, July 24, 1841.

people turned the tide of public opinion against the Whigs, but never in favour of the Tories. What possible interest can the Chartists have in Tory government ? What possible benefit did they even deserve from Whig government ? " There has been the appearance of division in the town of Birmingham, where a collision took place between the local branch of the N.C.A. and the Christian Chartist Church. This is now subsided. " We conceive that the man who is not a member of our Association, and who endeavours to cripple our efforts or weaken our influence, exhibits great malice towards the people, or proves treachery to their cause."

The Executive Council decided on the adoption of a National Petition to the House of Commons. In connexion with the presentation of this, another General Convention was summoned, to be held in London on February 4, 1842. This time the Chartists, in conformity with their own principle of Equal Representation, divided England into constituencies, electing altogether twenty-four members. Scotland and Wales were to return not more than twenty-five others, so that the legal maximum of forty-nine should not be exceeded. Members of the Convention were to be balloted for and paid (except two of the four Yorkshire members). The Convention was not to sit for more than four weeks. The 1842 Petition[1] differs from its predecessor in being a recital of economic as well as of political grievances. The growth of the National Debt in spite of twenty-six years of almost uninterrupted peace, the disparity between the sums paid to the Queen, the Prince Consort, the Archbishop of Canterbury on one hand, and to the working classes on the other, long hours of labour, starvation wages, and the Church Establishment are all complained of, before the Six Points are demanded. Scottish Chartists objected to the introduction of extraneous matter into the Petition,[2] especially the complaints against the English Poor Law, which differed in many important respects from their own, and had nothing to do with the Six Points in any case. By the end of 1841, however, Chartism was astir from causes

[1] First printed in *The Northern Star*, October 16, 1841.
[2] *Northern Star*, November 27, 1841.

more important than the Petition and the forthcoming Convention. Two new men had entered the movement. The first was Thomas Cooper (1805–1892). In spite of a boyhood and youth passed in extreme poverty, Cooper had educated himself with remarkable thoroughness and perseverance, and about 1835 became a journalist in Lincoln. Six years later, after many vicissitudes, he became a newspaper reporter in Leicester. His job led to his frequent attendance at Chartist meetings, and to his conversion—to the Physical Force party. When the election of 1841 came along, Cooper worked at Nottingham for the return of the Tory Walter, the proprietor of the *Times*. Writing his autobiography in 1873, Cooper explains himself : " That old and steady advocates of Freedom should have recommended us to help the Tories sounds very strange to me now. But the poor took up the cry readily. They remarked that the Whigs had banished John Frost and his companions, and had thrown four hundred and thirty Chartists into prison, and therefore the Whigs were their worst enemies. ' We will be revenged upon the Whigs ' became the cry of Chartists."[1] Within a year of his conversion, Cooper had become the leader of a large section of the Leicester Chartists. The remainder, under the guidance of John Markham, disapproved of Cooper's extreme admiration for O'Connor and formed a separate Chartist Association. Cooper's band held its meetings in " Shakesperean Room," at All Saints' Open, and thereafter called itself the Shakesperean Association of Leicester Chartists.[2] Cooper was dubbed the " General " of these Shakespereans, and adopted the term in his signature.[3]

More important, however, was the adhesion of Joseph Sturge (1793–1859), a Quaker. He was born of well-to-do parents and was able to devote himself to philanthropic work from about 1826 onwards—the date when he went on the committee of the Anti-Slavery Society. Sturge was a born reconciler, with an inspiration for making peace. All his life he worked for the maintenance of good relations between man and man.

---

[1] *The Life of Thomas Cooper*, p. 149.   [2] Ib., p. 165.

[3] Appendix (by Cooper) to 1894 edition of Gammage's *History of the Chartist Movement*.

Soon after Lord Brougham had passed the slave-emancipation Act of 1833, Sturge and his friends came to the conclusion that the system of apprenticeship permitted by the Act retained many of the features of undiluted slavery. But Brougham was not to be so easily moved, and demanded definite proofs. Thereupon, it is said, Sturge quietly remarked, " Then I must supply thee with proof," and started at once for the West Indies.[1] He collected much evidence, published some of it in *The West Indies in* 1837, gave evidence before a House of Commons Committee, and a year later the new evil was abolished by Parliament. The United States negro next called for his attention. In 1838 he was as alderman elected to the Birmingham Town Council, newly incorporated under the Municipal Act of 1835. He was therefore one of the City Fathers during the Bull Ring riots, when he frequently appeared as peacemaker and " did much, it is believed, to mitigate the evil he could not wholly prevent. When the crisis was over, his first efforts were directed to save the lives of the unfortunate men who were condemned to die for their share in the riots. By indefatigable exertions, he succeeded in getting their sentence commuted to transportation."[2] He next moved in the Town Council for a committee of inquiry into the disturbances, and was appointed its chairman, and after some time came to the conclusion that the principal cause of the disorder was the misbehaviour of the imported London police.

Sturge's sympathies lay with the working classes during the bad years 1840–42. As a keen democrat, he approved of the Charter, but regretted the anti-middle-class attitude of so many of its followers, partly because this alienated those whose support mattered most, but to a great extent because Sturge was a Christian and believed in peace. A series of articles appeared in 1841 in the newly established *Nonconformist London Weekly Newspaper*. These articles completely expressed Sturge's own views, and were immediately reprinted

[1] *Dictionary of National Biography*. The story is not contained in the official *Memoirs* by Henry Richard.

[2] *Memoirs of Joseph Sturge*, by H. Richard, p. 261.

with a preface by him. Sturge then laboured to convert the Anti-Corn Law League, of which he was a prominent member, to his own views on democracy. Here he found little difficulty. The Free Trade leaders were keenly alive to the importance of the applause they evoked in the provinces becoming audible in the House of Commons. Votes were needed for this. Moreover there were a great many men on the Chartist side with pronounced Free Trade sympathies, who believed that economic legislation did not *ipso facto* proceed from political changes. While Physical Force Chartists were going about breaking up Free Trade meetings, others were thinking and coming over to support Cobden and Bright. " Every day brings us accounts of the union of Chartists with the rest of their fellow-countrymen in a determination to agitate for the repeal of the corn-laws."[1] A good many people seem to have made the discovery in 1841 that a union between Chartists and middle-class Radicals was desirable.[2] The very *Spectator* had an article[3] in which the Six Points were examined one by one, and given general support. This article sagely concluded to the effect that the vote might be extended to " all men, women and children ; and if the prejudices of society did not stand in the way of such an extension, it might be made with perfect safety." Moreover it so happened that the great publicists of the Anti-Corn Law League were good democrats. The influence of Bright, Cobden, and W. J. Fox upon the working classes was not to be nullified because *The Northern Star* called the League the " Plague " and described the break-up of its meetings by Chartists in each case as a " glorious victory."

This tendency towards a union of forces naturally suited Lovett very well. Readers will already have gathered from the list of subscribers to the National Association that its membership was by no means exclusively proletarian. A month or two after the Association had come into existence, Lovett had put forth an Address to the Middle Classes, which

---

[1] *Morning Chronicle*, May 25, 1841.
[2] Wallas, *Life of Francis Place*, p. 389.
[3] *Spectator*, July 17, 1841.

was virtually a disavowal of the Physical Force party.   The
Address began somewhat strikingly, as follows—

" Fellow-countrymen : The political partisans of our respective classes have in too many instances succeeded in awakening our mutual prejudices ; and selfishness and distrust on
the one hand, and violence and folly on the other, have ripened
animosities and fostered the spirit of exclusiveness, to the
dissevering of those links which ought to be united for our
common weal ; while a selfish, corrupt, and oppressive few
have flourished and triumphed by reason of such prejudices
and dissensions.

" Seeing the result of these evils in the social degradation,
the commercial ruin, and political oppression of our country,
we are anxious to see a mantle of oblivion cast over past
differences, and to see the wise and good of all classes resolving
that in future they will labour and reason together to work
out the social and political regeneration of man."[1]

The remainder of this document upheld the principles of
the Charter with dignity.   The one statement to which the
twentieth century political thinker will not readily accede is
made with reference to the evils of the day.   " Satisfied, therefore, that most of these evils can be traced to unjust and selfish
legislation, we have pushed our inquiries still further ; we find
their chief source *in our present exclusive system of representation.*"   It would not be entirely frivolous to comment that
the last statement, if true, knocks the bottom out of the theory
of Lovett's own " Knowledge-Chartism."

About a month later, in January, 1842, Sturge began his
attempt to build the bridge between his own class and Lovett's.
Starting from opposite banks, these two immediately hailed
each other, and entered into co-operation.

Early in February, 1842, the Anti-Corn Law League held
a Conference in London.   Sturge made use of the opportunity
and got up at a day's notice a meeting of the delegates who
entertained " views favourable to ' Complete Suffrage.' "   This
took place on Friday, February 11, at the " Crown and Anchor."
Among those present were Sharman Crawford, M.P., the Rev.

----

[1] *Life and Struggles of William Lovett*, p. 260.

Thomas Spencer,[1] John Bright, Hetherington and Lovett. The object of the gathering was a frank interchange of views ; a series of private conversations presented in the form of public speeches. Sturge took the chair. Two clergymen, Spencer and Young, began the proceedings by emphatically stating a case for extending the suffrage to the working classes. Spencer's argument, nevertheless, must have grated on the ears of a few of those present. " They had laws which meddled with everything, with their money, their religion—(hear, hear, and cheers)—and with their trade ; with everything they could mention. If the working men were admitted to power, he hoped they would guard against meddling with too many things ; the grand thing was to protect person and property, and to leave everything else alone. There were no more important words than ' let alone '—the *laissez-faire* of the French." The speaker then went on to explain why, in his opinion, the working men would leave things alone. Spencer had unwittingly found the frontier line between the different philosophies of the two classes who had met at the " Crown and Anchor " to be reconciled. The Free Traders were conscious and deliberate adherents to the individualist theory of *laissez-faire*. The Chartists, permeated with Socialist ideas, were virtually committed to the opposing theory of State interference. In theory the Six Points could be held by any Whig, Liberal, Radical or Socialist. But in practice the Charter was too closely associated with the demand for factory legislation—to give the crucial instance—to be entirely compatible with the Anti-Corn Law agitation. Lovett, whose speech was the great event of the evening, either did not notice, or affected not to notice, this antinomy. The greater part of his speech was a mere exposition of the Charter. Towards the end he explained the Chartist hostility against the Free Trade movement. " He was an advocate for Free Trade ; and the only reason why he had stood apart from the advocates of the repeal of the Corn Laws, was a conviction that they would never be able to carry it in the House of Commons as at present constituted. (Hear, hear.) It had also been supposed by the working classes that

[1] Father of Herbert Spencer.

the agitation for the repeal of the Corn Laws had been got up as a counter-agitation to the Charter. (No, no.) It was certain that at the time the first meeting was called in London, for the Charter, in Palace Yard, just at that time an article appeared in the *True Sun*, calling on the middle classes to commence the agitation for the repeal of the Corn Laws. The working men had been led to believe that it was meant as a counter movement."

A recent incident, which had caused some hubbub among the Chartists, probably decided Sturge's actions. More than a year before, a large meeting in support of Household Suffrage was held in Leeds,[1] under the auspices of the middle-class Leeds Reform Association. Chartists were present in large numbers ; their intention was to make themselves heard in support of their own case, and to prevent the favourite *bête noire* of Feargus O'Connor, and his former employer, Daniel O'Connell, from getting a hearing. The latter did not turn up, and the Chartists, to their own surprise, found that the speakers almost unanimously confessed a sympathy with the Six Points.

Sturge's efforts to promote the political reconciliation of the middle and working classes crystallized in a Conference held in Birmingham from the 9th to the 13th April, 1842. This took place at the Waterloo Rooms, Waterloo Street. Among those present were Sturge, Rev. Dr. Wade, Rev. T. Spencer, Collins, Vincent, Lovett, Neesom, John Bright, the Rev. H. Solly, and Bronterre O'Brien. Conferences of this nature spend much of their time in the performance of what can only be described as a ritual. There is no need to analyse the entire proceedings.[2] People delivered the usual complimentary speeches, made the customary platitudinous remarks —this time with more than usual sincerity—on the importance of friendly relations between the classes. The Chartists asserted the dogmas of the Six Points, the Free Traders repeated the shibboleths of Free Trade. Lovett moved the essential point to establish " an association, to be called the National Complete

---

[1] The *Leeds Mercury*, January 23, 1841, gives a good account.

[2] An almost verbatim report may be found in Edward Miall's paper, *The Nonconformist*, for April 13 and 20, 1842.

Suffrage Union, for extending an enlightened opinion in favour of the six principles affirmed by the Conference . . ." the Six Points with which we are already so familiar. After much discussion it was decided to avoid direct reference to the Charter. O'Brien supported this decision, wisely refusing to be bound to words. The Conference immediately determined upon a crusade on a national scale, a petition, missionaries, and all the paraphernalia of successful political propaganda.

These preparations for victory deeply annoyed O'Connor, who saw his supremacy in the Chartist movement seriously threatened by this vigorous incursion of intelligent and prominent middle-class men. He had already expressed himself strongly on the subject of the Free Traders, whom, indeed, he had abused week by week for nearly four years. A month before the Birmingham Conference he had taken as his text a resolution passed by the always intransigeant miners of Merthyr. "That every approval towards a union with the Corn Law League must be regarded as a direct step towards a betrayal of the Chartist cause ; and that every public meeting which neglects to affirm the adoption of the People's Charter as the only remedy for the distresses of the people must be considered as compromising the great right of the working class to a share in the making of the laws." O'Connor's comment is summarized in his first words, " This is the true position for the people ; and the only safe one."[1] He decided to break up the Conference if it were possible. With this amiable intention, he summoned an opposition Conference in Birmingham, which met at the same time as the other, and appointed a few " delegates " to the Sturge gathering. These were refused admission. O'Brien managed to attend both meetings, and justified his attitude to the N.C.A. members. Nothing came of O'Connor's intention, except bitterness. Warm hopes of success prevailed as the immediate result of the formation of the N.C.S.U. Vincent wrote, " The Conference has proved the existence of virtue and talent in the persons of men who have hitherto feared or disliked each other ; it has shown that the seeds of democratic principles are sown in the breasts of

[1] *Northern Star*, March 5, 1842.

the Middle Classes." The objectors to the Conference he divides into two classes—" those who live by misrule, and their knavish or blind tools."

The personality of Sturge is reflected in the Rules of the N.C.S.U. Object VIII is " To recommend all classes of Society to refuse to participate in the horrors of war, or to be used for the purposes of cruelty and injustice, and in order that our movement may be peaceably and morally conducted, to recommend sobriety and temperance.

Object XII. To adopt every just, peaceful, legal, and constitutional means for carrying the above resolutions into effect, and only such.

William Morgan was the first Secretary. There was no fixed subscription.

Place, in entire sympathy with the idea of an *entente* between the middle and working classes, on May 20, 1842, formed yet another organization, the Metropolitan Parliamentary Reform Association. P. A. Taylor was Chairman, Dr. J. R. Black, Secretary. The M.P.'s who had already joined so many bodies of the kind, as usual, gave their support. The Committee was a large one, but the work of the Association was virtually left in the hands of a small Business Committee, which included Place (Chairman), Hetherington and Westerton.[1] The annual subscription was fixed at four shillings, payable quarterly if preferred. The objects were the Six Points, but the words Charter and Chartists, by this time so malodorous to the middle classes, were not used in any of the Association's pronouncements. This body was the most abortive of all Place's undertakings. It lived only one year,[2] There is some truth in the comment of a paper, " An extraordinary idea this said Snip must have had of the vigour of himself and his allies." [3] O'Connor's next move was dictated to him by sheer jealousy of the N.C.S.U. He ceased to attack the middle class, and began to canvass them. He drew a distinction between the

[1] Afterwards Secretary of the National Association.

[2] It turns up again a year or two after its demise as the Metropolitan Parliamentary and Franchise Reform Association.

[3] *John Bull*, May 28, 1842.

" middle class " or " shopocracy," and the more numerous
" middling class," the brainworkers, and addressed articles
to the latter showing that, after all, their interests were one
with those of the working classes.   His evolution in this direction was extraordinarily rapid ; it was less a change of opinion
than the manœuvre of a human weathercock.   In April and
May he was cursing Sturge.   In July he was supporting him
at a by-election.

Early in May, 1842, Sturge was asked to contest Nottingham
at a by-election, brought about by the death of Sir G. Larpent.
He accepted, and put forward a Chartist-Quaker-Free Trade
election address, in which he declared, *inter alia*, against capital
punishment, and " not only considered all naval and military
establishments in time of peace as a needless and absurd
expense, but that all war is as inconsistent with true national
safety as it is in direct violation of the spirit and precepts of
the New Testament . . . I am not insensible to the kindness
and favourable opinion of those who are anxious to promote
my election ; but I most strongly deprecate a single word or
expression that can justly excite any angry feeling towards
those who differ from them.   I hope I shall be excused for
giving this caution, because on these occasions the best of men
sometimes forget that charity which in private they usually
exercise towards each other."[1]

The date of the election was deferred for various reasons
until August.   Sturge's opponent was John Walter, then Tory
editor of *The Times*.   On this occasion, however, Sturge's
supporters were of more importance than his opponents.
O'Connor actually came down to support Sturge, for whose
personality he had on recent occasions begun to express a
warm admiration.   His arrival was the occasion of a warm
display of " physical force."   The Tories claimed that O'Connor
was the cause of the mischief.   A poster announced, " An
Irish bully, backed by a band of hired ruffians, strangers to
your town and neighbourhood, has insulted, outraged, and
severely maltreated a number of your fellow-townsmen. . . .
Be not deceived.   Sturge the pacific and O'Connor ' the

[1] *Nottingham Review*, May 20, 1842.

brave' have one common object in view—the subjugation
of your town by brute force to the intolerable tyranny of
strangers."[1] It need hardly be said that this declaration could
be paralleled by others emanating from O'Connor's side.
Cooper, Vincent and M'Douall also turned up to support Sturge
—Cooper having supported Walter at the General Election of
the previous year. The Rev. J. R. Stephens, since his release
from his eighteen months' imprisonment, had been strangely
silent. Now the silence was broken in a sufficiently noisy
manner, for Stephens, remembering his erstwhile Toryism,
came down to support Walter. Hence the free fight to which
allusion has already been made, resulting in the arrest of O'Connor and several others. Evidence is cheap and plentiful at
election times, and no convictions were made. The Sturge
party worked fiercely, but the Tories prevailed. Walter received 1885 votes, Sturge 84 less.[2]

The result of the election mattered little. From the point
of view of every side of the Universal Suffrage movement its
importance lay in the achievement of unity. To outward
appearance the Nottingham by-election was the occasion of
the consolidation of the liberal forces of the country, and to
the strengthening of Chartism. Unfortunately this was not
to be the case. While most people regarded the election campaign of the Chartists as a matter of unity, O'Connor was
regarding the whole affair as a matter of leadership.

[1] *Northern Star*, August 6, 1842.
[2] A few months later Walter was unseated on a charge of corruption.
Sturge was offered the seat but refused to accept it, as he had not been
elected by a majority.

APPENDIX TO CHAPTER VI

The 1842 Convention duly met at Dr. Johnson's Tavern, on April 12, and talked for nearly three weeks. The absence of Lovett's and Attwood's followers might have been expected to have produced unanimity, but this was not the case. Even a convention of twenty-five may contain dissidents. O'Brien and Philp were there and fought with O'Connor over the relations of the N.C.A. with the middle class. O'Brien, O'Connor, M'Douall, Pitkeithley, Lowery, Duncan and Moir were the only delegates present who had attended the first Convention. The other eighteen were mediocrities, and the whole assembly had neither the personalities nor the hopes of its predecessor. The Petition was said, when completed, to have 3,317,752 signatures. On May 2 it was taken in procession to the House of Commons and handed over to Duncombe. According to Place only 3,000 marched in this procession, one-third of whom were not male adults.

On May 3, 1842, Duncombe moved that " the petitioners, whose petition I presented yesterday, be heard by themselves or their counsel at the Bar of the House."[1] He sketched the history of the movement for franchise reform, since the beginning of Major Cartwright's propaganda, and then went on to describe the state of the country in 1842, quoting from letters he had received from all parts. After a long account of the terrible sufferings then being experienced by the poor, Duncombe soberly ended by assuring the House that they would not have to listen to more than six Chartists or to spend more than two days in doing so.

The motion was seconded by Leader, who protested the sincerity underlying Chartism, and declared that the dissection or dismissal of the Petition would in no wise stop the movement, which was based on real economic grievances. Bowring followed him, supporting the Petition on Benthamite principles. Dr. Fielden also spoke in favour, basing his argument, as usual

---

[1] Hansard, Vol. 63, cols. 13-91.

with him, on factory conditions. Sir John Easthope added his voice to the same effect. Then the opponents began. Sir James Graham (Home Secretary) vaguely intimated that " the subversion of all our great institutions must inevitably result from the granting of the prayer of the petition," and criticized Easthope's apparent fickleness, as that gentleman had previously voted against the Six Points. Then Easthope had to explain that he was really opposed to the Charter, but did not think that the Chartists should be denied a hearing at the Bar of the House.

Perhaps the most interesting speech of the day was that of Macaulay, who followed. He declared himself to be in favour of parts of the Charter, and to entertain " extreme and unmitigated hostility," to one point only—to Universal Suffrage. " I believe that Universal Suffrage would be fatal to all purposes for which government exists, and for which aristocracies and all other things exist, and that it is utterly incompatible with the very existence of civilization. I conceive that civilization rests on the security of property, but I think that it is not necessary for me, in a dis-cussion of this kind, to go through the arguments, and through the vast experience which necessarily leads to this result ; but I will assert, that while property is insecure, it is not in the power of the finest soil, or of the moral or intellectual constitution of any country, to prevent the country sinking into barbarism, while, on the other hand, while property is secure, it is not possible to prevent a country from advancing in prosperity." Macaulay then attacked the least defensible clauses of the Petition, and concluded by urging the necessity of resisting " spoiliation."

Roebuck replied to Macaulay, and urged that 3,500,000 people had a right to be listened to, more so when their cause was just, and their sufferings were great. " Yes, it was from these sufferings that he judged of his fellow-countrymen, and not from the trashy doctrine contained in the Petition, which would be of itself ridiculous but for the grandeur of the multitude of names appended to it." Matters were serious, and if 3,500,000 people rose up against the Government, it would " not have physical force adequate to put them down."

The next speaker was Lord Francis Egerton who was gently sarcastic at the expense of Roebuck.

Hawes (Lambeth) also opposed. He was " a warm advocate for the progressive improvement of the people," but he disapproved of the " language made use of at certain public meetings which had been held of late throughout the country."

Hume supported the motion, pointing out that the utterance of subversive and revolutionary sentiments was not a Chartist monopoly, that the working classes were " taxed infinitely more in proportion to their means than the possessors of extensive property. . . . He was prepared to place confidence in the working classes, as they had always acted as honestly, or perhaps more so, than the richer classes."

Wakley, also speaking in support, tried to get the discussion back to the point. Was the existing constituency the best that could be devised ? He could not support annual parliaments, but the question before the House was, were the representatives of the petitioners to be allowed to state their own case ?

Lord John Russell followed. He declared his sympathy with " the sufferings and privations of the working classes," and argued that venerable institutions ought to be preserved. He denied that anybody had any " right " to a vote. " For my own part, I think it is very likely that at many elections, even if universal suffrage were in operation, you would find that respect for property, respect for old habits, and general regard for the constitution of the country, would produce results not very different from those which are produced when property is one of the qualifications required for the franchise." The matter was virtually reduced to, Is it expedient ? In the present uneducated condition of the working classes it undoubtedly was not. Russell ended up by saying that it would take more than a few working men to convert him to a faith in the Six Points, and that he would therefore vote against the motion.

He was followed by Peel. The Prime Minister sheltered himself behind the clauses of the Petition which seemed to him to speak of the Monarch and the Established Church with insufficient respect. " I say the Petition is altogether an impeachment of the Constitution of this country, and of the whole frame of Society." Peel expressed his fear of the power of demagogues should universal suffrage come to be established, and claimed that the existing state of things " has secured for us during 150 years more of practical happiness and of true liberty than has been enjoyed in any country excepting the United States of America, not excepting any other country whatever."

Macaulay briefly corrected a misapprehension.

G. F. Muntz supported in a few words, and J. Oswald as shortly opposed the motion.

The Hon. Charles Villiers, in supporting, said that the rejection of the Charter would make the working classes mistrust the House.

Lord Clements opposed ; as an Irishman, he wished to protest as emphatically as possible against the reference in favour of repeal contained in the Petition.

O'Connell supported. He claimed to be " a decided advocate of universal suffrage," and declared that nobody had yet explained where and why the line between voters and the voteless should be drawn.

Duncombe replied to the discussion. He dissented from many parts of the Petition, but said that confiscation was not in the minds of those who asked for universal suffrage. " Three millions of men are entitled to a hearing, and so far from the communication of political rights to the working classes endangering your constitution, it would, in my opinion, strengthen its stability."

The House divided—Ayes, 49 ; Noes, 287 ; Majority, 236.

Cobden was among the Ayes, Palmerston and Gladstone among the Noes. Disraeli was absent.

CHAPTER VII

THE DICTATORSHIP OF FEARGUS O'CONNOR

IN a brief account of Chartist organization, contained in the last chapter, it was stated that Chartists did not, as a rule, belong to organizations other than their own. The Chartist leaders, in fact, discouraged the participation of their followers in trade unionism, just as they objected to any demand not covered by the Six Points. The Executive of the N.C.A. published an address[1] very soon after the formation of that body, criticizing the principles of trade unionism on the grounds that without political power the members of a trade union were helpless. Chartism, however, cannot be considered apart from economic conditions. This was quite realized by the leaders. We have Stephens' well-known dictum, " Universal suffrage is a . . . knife-and-fork question, a bread-and-cheese question."[2] O'Connor talks of[3] " A means of insuring a fair day's wages for a fair day's work, which, after all, is the aim and end of the People's Charter." The opponents of Chartism realized this too. When Gladstone retired from the Presidency of the Board of Trade in 1845, he had a farewell audience with Queen Victoria. The Queen spoke " of the reduced condition of Chartism, of which I said the chief feeder was want of employment."[4]

The avidity with which the population of Lancashire flung

---

[1] English Chartist Circular, No. 46.

[2] *Northern Star*, September 29, 1838.

[3] From the Introduction to *The Trial of Feargus O'Connor and Fifty-eight others at Lancaster*, 1843.

[4] Morley, *Gladstone*, Vol. I, p. 204, Popular Edition.

itself at the anything but succulent Six Points was due to no philosophical creed. It was caused by hunger and fear. Let us very briefly review the economic facts which determined this ready acceptance of the Charter as a panacea.

The gradual replacement of hand labour by machinery had made the condition of the remaining hand-loom weavers critical in 1840. The general acceptance of the power-loom had originated in the cotton branch of the textile trades. Here the immediate distress was less than in the branches where, as yet, the hand-loom persisted. The displaced hand-loom cotton weavers simply drifted into linen- and silk-weaving and overcrowded these industries. To add to the distress caused by this invasion, Irish immigrants, displaced in their own country, came and sought employment in England. The introduction of the machine-loom into linen-weaving completed the sorrows of the original employees. Wages fell. The hand-loom weavers were not, on the whole, town labourers. The machine-loom weavers, on the other hand, could obviously not work in cottages and farms. A rapid transfer of population therefore was taking place. Uncontrolled as regards their buildings or their sanitation, the new towns were slums from the first. Engels, in his *Condition of the English Working Class in* 1844, describes a new Manchester that is virtually a sink of all the foulness known to civilization. The case of Lancashire and cotton is typical of what was happening over all the industrial districts of the Four Kingdoms. In Yorkshire the woollen trade was passing through a similar set of conditions.

Low wages and insanitary and insufficient houses were not the only evils rampant in 1842, the year with which the progress of this narrative leads us to be specially concerned. In that year only, the Coal Mines Act was passed, prohibiting the underground employment of women and of children under ten. The Commission whose Report led to the passing of this Act had a ghastly tale to tell of the vicious conditions under which women and children earned their insufficient wages. Long hours of labour (the maximum for children was reduced to *twelve* only in 1846) ; falling wages (in the cotton trade wages fell consistently for some thirty years after 1810) ; a high rate of infantile mortality and the prevalence of epidemics were among the accessories of the new capitalism.

These facts make the state of mind of the Chartists comprehensible. The Chartist saw himself hemmed in on all sides. The philosophy of the time was against him. If he wondered why wages could not be raised, he came up against the Iron Law of Wages, the Wage Fund Fallacy. Malthus was against him : " The principal causes of the increase of pauperism . . . are, first, the general increase of the manufacturing system, and the unavoidable variations of manufacturing labour ; and, secondly, and more particularly, the practice . . . of paying a considerable portion of what ought to be the wages of labour out of the parish rates."[1] If he asked why his hours of labour could not be shortened, he was told that shorter hours would be worth lower wages, and would cause higher prices. The Free Trade movement, founded by the manufacturers whom he regarded as his enemies, naturally failed to attract him. He felt that only by some drastic and revolutionary measure could his situation be improved. That is why Physical Force Chartism got its attractiveness.

In August, 1842, the strain became excessive. A great series of strikes or " turn-outs " seems to have started on the 4th of the month, when over 20,000 Stalybridge weavers marched on Manchester in consequence of an attempt to reduce their wages. Immediately the whole district around Manchester was on fire. In Ashton-under-Lyne, Stalybridge, Dukinfield, and Hyde a general strike appears to have taken place. Oldham followed. At the same time the miners on the Tyne and in the Glasgow district also went on strike. They had good reasons for doing so. Their wages were low, and subject to deductions, on account of the iniquitous truck system. John M'Lay, the Glasgow secretary of a miners' union wrote this statement of the case.[2] " The average wages of the miners of coal and iron vary from 1s. 7½d. to 2s. 5½d. for putting out one-third of more labour than they did, one year ago,

---

[1] Malthus, *An Essay on Population*, Seventh Edition, Book III, chapter vii.
[2] *Northern Star*, August 13, 1842.

receive 4s. per day for ; and at same time could, in many instances, get their money when earned, while now we go to our masters' store and take our labour in goods ; or if the employer has not a store, he, according to his laws, makes us pay one penny for each shilling lifted before pay day."

The Northern Star soon had reasons to rejoice. " We are glad the miners, like other trades, have hoisted the banner of the Charter. In the principles of that invaluable document must centre all their hopes. . . . Trade Unions in times past were deemed the only panacea for the complicated evils endured by the operative classes—the specific was tried but its virtues were undiscovered or practically unknown."

O'Connor's first endeavour after the outbreak was to turn it to his own strategic advantage by declaring that the Anti-Corn-Law League was responsible for the disorder and should be made to pay the bill. " Every succeeding day furnishes additional proof of the villainy inherent in the despicable middle classes ; of their hostility to the interests of the masses ; of their hatred of justice, and, consequently, of the absurdity of the doctrines propounded by the defunct ' New Movers,' and the expiring League, who profess to desire an amalgamation of the middle and working classes."[1] It was surely inconsistent to allege that an " expiring " body could work such evil. But O'Connor was not to be turned from his purpose. The League might be a dead donkey, but it had to be flogged. The next week *The Northern Star* returns to the charge : " They have gotten the people out. How will they get them in again ? How will they compensate for the loss of life and the personal injuries—the shootings, and cuttings, and slashings ; the imprisonments, and the transportings that are to follow ; how will they compensate for these things which they, and *they alone*, have caused ? "[2] On Tuesday, August 16, a mob entered Cleckheaton and attempted to make the employees at the various mills stop work. They met with brickbats, but gained a partial success. The strikers are thus described by the historian of Spen Valley. " Many of the men had coarse

[1] *Northern Star*, August 13, 1842.
[2] Ib., August 20, 1842.

grey blankets strapped to their backs, and were armed with formidable bludgeons, flails, pitchforks, and pikes. Their appearance as they came pouring down the road in thousands, was one which it would be impossible to forget—a gaunt, famished-looking, desperate multitude, many without coats and hats, hundreds like scarecrows with their clothes in rags and tatters, and amongst them were many women. Some of the older men looked footsore and weary, but the great bulk were in the prime of life, full of wild excitement."[1] On their second appearance the strikers were able to stop work at several factories by drawing the boiler-plugs, before the soldiers arrived and put an end to the proceedings by sabring part of the crowd and arresting those of its members who did not act on this hint and disperse. The same writer tells us elsewhere that the Spen Valley was the centre of an insurrection which would not have broken out had it not been for O'Connor's shiftiness.[2] The movement swiftly spread through the North. In Halifax, Skipton, Keighley, the Potteries, Chorley, Bingley, Stafford, Preston, Heywood, Rochdale, Bacup, Ashton-under-Lyne, Sheffield, Wigan, Blackburn, and innumerable other towns, men went out on strike. In some places—e.g., Rochdale —no breach of the peace appears to have taken place. In others—e.g., Preston—the military were called out and were ordered to fire on the crowd. Even lethargic London was affected. A meeting was held on Stepney Green, and the police, frightened thereat, made many arrests, although the intentions of the speakers seem to have been peaceable. Thomas Cooper went on a crusade in the Midlands and preached the Charter to the colliers of Wednesbury, Wolverhamton and Stafford. He was arrested at Burslem, but released almost at once. These risings made an impression difficult to account for at this time of day. An old Chartist, describing his recollections of the movement,[3] tells us that he was in Bourne (Lincolnshire) in August when news was received of the riots in the North. "In the course of the day a rumour spread

---

[1] *Spen Valley, Past and Present*, p. 326.
[2] Ib., p. 314.
[3] Sketchley, *To-day*, July, 1884.

through the town that a Chartist army of several thousands was collecting at Nottingham, intending to march through Lincolnshire on its way for Dover. The greatest alarm prevailed." ‚It appears on the evidence of the same writer that the shopkeepers and farmers belonging to the villages in the neighbourhood of Bourne were so terror-stricken that they invariably attended to casual callers with a loaded gun in their hands, fearing that he might be a precursor of the direst.

On August 16, 1842, Cooper, M'Douall, Leach, Bairstow, O'Connor, and other Chartists, some sixty in all, had assembled in Manchester. Cooper, who throughout his tour in Staffordshire had been preaching " Peace, Law, and Order," now told this conference that he wanted a universal strike, " because it meant fighting." O'Connor protested against this ; they had met, he said, to try to turn the strike to the advantage of the Charter, and not to talk about fighting.[1] Hill supported O'Connor, and so, curiously enough, did Harney. M'Douall, on the other hand, was out for trouble. He drew up a fiercely worded address to the strikers " appealing to the God of Battles for the issue, and urging a universal strike."[2] This was printed the same day, and circulated on the responsibility of the executive of the N.C.A.—of which, of course, O'Connor was not a member.

The police promptly got on to the tracks of the signatories. Bairstow was arrested at once ; the others managed to escape, either for the time being, or altogether. M'Douall got away to America. Bussey, a truculent member of the 1839 Convention, a Bradford grocer and beershop keeper by trade, also fled to America about this time. Cooper was arrested and tried at Newcastle-under-Lyne on a charge of aiding in a riot at Hanley, but was acquitted. Later on Cooper was found guilty on a charge of conspiracy, and eventually sentenced to two years' imprisonment in Stafford Gaol.

By the second week of August the deliberate attempts made by the followers of O'Connor to turn the strikes for higher wages into strikes for the Charter already showed signs of

[1] *Life of Thomas Cooper*, p. 209.
[2] Ib., p. 211.

success. Trade unionist after trade unionist was excavated from a previous nonentity by *The Northern Star* reporters and made to give testimony to the intentions of a union, of a trade, or of a town, to strike for nothing but the Charter, to declare that he would not strike for wages, as these were sufficient, but for the Charter that alone could keep them from falling. A meeting of 200 delegates from Lancashire and Yorkshire was held in Manchester on August 12, and passed two resolutions. " We "—the delegates—" do most emphatically declare that it is our most solemn and conscientious conviction that all the evils which affect society, and which have prostrated the interests and energies of the great body of the producing classes arise solely from class legislation ; and that the only remedy for the present alarming distress and widespread destitution is the immediate and unmutilated adoption, and carrying into law, the document known as the People's Charter." The second resolution was, " That this meeting recommend the people of all trades and callings to forthwith cease work, until the above document becomes the law of the land."[1]

All this time the Chartist interventionists never ceased to assert that they were wholly opposed to the use of physical force. In Manchester a number of them enrolled as special constables the better to be able to keep the peace. Lovett published a characteristic address, on behalf of the National Association. " To the Working Classes of England, Scotland, and Wales, now on Strike for additional wages." The writer's insistence, even at this critical hour, on the necessity of employing only moral force, illustrates the finest trait in his character. " To you who have declared for the Charter we would say, *avoid violence*. The enemies of liberty have their emissaries among you ; do not allow them to betray you into wrong, do not furnish a pretext for their letting loose their hired bravoes to cut you to pieces. The loss of life has already tainted our glorious cause ; we pray you use your efforts to restrain outrage, and by your wise and peaceful conduct win all good men to your cause." The end of this outbreak of strikes was followed by a large number of arrests, on charges of sedition.

[1] *Northern Star*, August 20, 1842.

Feargus O'Connor and John Campbell were arrested in Manchester on September 30, 1842.[1] Harney, with ten Manchester Chartists, were next apprehended. Within a week or two, the Rev. W. Hill, Thomas Cooper, and several other prominent Chartists of the Midlands and the North, had followed them. A Special Commission sat at Stafford to try 180 alleged incendiaries, during the first week of October, 1842. The total number of prisoners for trial was 274. Of these no fewer than fifty-four were sentenced to transportation, eleven for life, thirteen for twenty-one years, and the remainder for shorter periods. A hundred and forty-six were sentenced to imprisonment and hard labour for periods varying from two years to ten days. Eight were sentenced to various terms of imprisonment without hard labour, and fifty-five were acquitted, two discharged on entering into recognizances, six discharged by proclamation, and finally, three, among them Cooper, traversed till the next assizes.[2]

The attempt of the N.C.A. to dominate this industrial unrest had come to an unsuccessful end. A few leaders had been imprisoned, a few others had fled, and the People's Charter seemed as unattainable as ever. After the collapse of the August " Turn-out" only one thing kept the Chartist movement from drifting into complete apathy. This was the hope that, after all, something might come of the proposed " union " with middle-class reformers. O'Connor's invective on this account is relatively subdued after August.

On April 21, 1842, Sharman Crawford had moved in the House for a Committee to consider the demands contained in the second National Petition. On that occasion, in spite of Sir J. Graham's declaration on the part of the Government, that the Charter, if conceded, would endanger the monarchy, the reformers, if they did not have things their own way, at least put up a better case than they had ever done before, or were to do again in the course of the Chartist movement. Sir Charles Napier supported the motion. So too did Cobden, who tried to show that the support for the Six Points did not

---

[1] *Northern Star*, October 1, 1842.
[2] *Annual Register*, 1842, Pt. 2, p. 163.

come from one class alone, and concluded his speech by glowingly eulogizing Joseph Sturge. On the division, 67 members followed Crawford into the Aye Lobby, against 226 Noes, among whom were both Gladstone and Disraeli.[1] Sixty-seven supporters were not to be despised. If the House could be made to feel that Sharman Crawford was the mouthpiece of but a small minority of reformers, who knows how many M.P.'s might be coerced into supporting the Charter ? This, roughly speaking, was the moral drawn by the Chartists from the debate and the division.

The practical union of the forces of the Chartists and of the N.C.S.U. had been left to a Conference, which was to meet in Birmingham on December 27. The members of this were to decide on a common plan of action, to take the form of " deciding on an Act of Parliament for securing the just representation of the whole people ; and for determining on such peaceful, legal, and constitutional means as may cause it to become the law of these realms." Lovett and the Council of the N.C.S.U. had then to face the practical difficulty of providing for the fair representation of all parties at this Conference. A scheme of Lovett's was adopted which fixed the number of delegates each town was to send, and contained this proviso, " That one-half of the representatives shall be appointed by the electors, and half by the non-electors."

O'Connor's chief anxiety at this time was the representation of his followers. If these could but form a majority of the Conference, all would be well. He therefore went about denouncing the plan of representation as undemocratic, and stirring up his followers to elect delegates. The result was that by way of a prelude to their future unity, " a fierce battle was now fought between the Complete Suffragists and the Chartists in the election of delegates. The Chartists were anxious to get their men elected if possible at the Complete Suffrage meetings, in order to avoid the expense falling on themselves alone, and in many cases they succeeded in so doing. At Leicester the electors held a separate meeting, but the redoubtable Cooper and his ' Shakesperians ' were at

[1] Hansard, 1842, Vol. 62, 907–984.

tion in favour of the suffrage, and for seeking to secure the legal enactment of which vast numbers have suffered imprisonment, transportation and death, has, in the opinion of the meeting, a prior claim over all other documents professing to embrace the principles of just representation. It is, therefore, resolved that we proceed to discuss the different sections of the people's charter, in order to ascertain whether any improvement can be made in it, and what these improvements shall be, it being necessary to make that document as clear and perfect as possible." O'Connor seconded in an able speech. He said that the Charter had the moral support of three and a half million persons, who were not in way committed to the Bill. After which he denied most emphatically that he had ever advocated or recommended a recourse to physical force. Then the N.C.S.U. began, and the squabble lasted the whole day. The division was taken; 193 supported Lovett, 94 supported the Bill. Sturge thereupon announced that " After the most minute consideration he felt that he would now best promote the cause they had in view by no longer occupying the chair. At the same time he earnestly hoped that although they could not work together in exactly the same steps they would not consider each other enemies, but as men all working heartily and anxiously in the same road." Answering a question put by O'Connor, Sturge said that they would best promote the cause of the people by discussing the bill in another room. Lovett said that he blamed himself for having led people to believe that the Complete Suffrage movement was in any way connected with the Anti-Corn Law League, and regretted the course that had been adopted by Sturge and his followers, whom he believed to be actuated by the best motives. He moved the cordial thanks of the conference to Sturge for taking the chair. He was seconded by O'Connor, who once more became fulsome in praise of the Quaker. Vincent walked out with Sturge. The next day the minority met at the Temperance Hotel, Moore Street, and there went ahead with the Bill, which Sharman Crawford was to present to Parliament. The majority Conference discussed a plan of Cooper's as to the reorganization of the N.C.A. Lovett withdrew. The remaining members indulged in acrimony, and their numbers rapidly fell to thirty-seven on the fourth and last day.

The Conference has an intensely pathetic side. It represented the downfall of the hopes of so many decent men that we cannot laugh at its futility. " The whole affair has proved so abortive," wrote a local paper, " that, had it depended on us alone, we should have preferred to bury it at once in the oblivion to which in a few weeks it will be certainly, and with universal consent, consigned."[1] *The Northern Star* leading article of the issue following the Conference begins : " We presume that by this time at all events the mind of the people will be pretty well settled upon the fact that our worst suspicions of the Sturge men have been more than realized."[2] In a similar feeling of peace and goodwill, Francis Place spent Sunday, New Year's Day, 1843, in the composition of an extremely acid but far-sighted Memorandum on the Conference.[3]

The fate of the N.C.S.U. Bill may be briefly described here. It was introduced by the indefatigable Sharman Crawford on May 18, 1843, before a small and bored House. The usual speakers spoke. Ross, M.P. for Belfast, surprised those present by asserting that he " was in the manufacturing districts in the north of England [near Rochdale, it was subsequently explained] for some time last year, and there he heard doctrines propounded which appeared to him so monstrous, and, he was sorry to say, so widely spread, that if this Bill became law the country would have such a deluge of these doctrines as would carry all before it." The Bill was lost by 101 to 32.[4]

On January 31, 1844, the Complete Suffrage Union held its first important public meeting in London after the failure of Sharman Crawford's Bill. The Crown and Anchor Tavern was, as usual, the scene. Crawford himself took the chair ; Sturge, Spencer, and in fact all the prominent members of the N.C.S.U. were present. Lovett and Vincent were also there ; the presence of the former is significant. The meeting had been called to give moral support to a proposal for moving

[1] *Birmingham Journal*, December 31, 1842.
[2] *Northern Star*, January 7, 1843.   [3] See Appendix II.
[4] Hansard, 1843, Vol. 69, 500–530.

amendments on motions of supply until the grievances alleged by the N.C.S.U. members of Parliament had been heard and redressed. O'Connor and Duncombe were however present, with a large number of disciples, and the meeting was compelled to listen to O'Connor and much uproar.[1] The N.C.S.U. is little heard of after this. If it, working in the name of democracy, was opposed by O'Connor, also in the name of democracy, obviously there was little to be done.

The movement over which O'Connor had established his predominance had sadly degenerated from its original enthusiasm and vigour. The years 1843-45 are marked by apathy, declining numbers, and the absence of a definite programme. The N.C.S.U. men, in their withdrawal, took the agitation for the Six Points with them. This was soon recognized by Lovett who once more begins to appear on Complete Suffrage platforms. For a while O'Connor was in the position of a hermit-crab which has come into possession of an empty shell of uncomfortable largeness. His denunciations are chastened ; he is less keen to detect and to denounce heresy ; in his speeches and writings the quality of flamboyant egotism is softened down. Even the optimism evoked for the purpose of arousing enthusiasm for another year's campaigning is qualified by regrets and the admission of past futility. " 1843 was the year of slumber : 1844 the year of waking and thought."[2] Six months later O'Connor significantly heads an article " The Revival of Chartism."[3]

What were the Chartists doing in these dead years ? So far as the followers of O'Connor are concerned, the answer is : Extremely little. The pages of *The Northern Star* are opened to the discussion of innumerable matters outside the four corners of the People's Charter. The arrest of Daniel O'Connell, his trial, conviction, and subsequent acquittal, as well as the whole new Repeal agitation, are the subjects of innumerable articles. The Maynooth grant, the Young England party, the failure of the potato crop, and the Young Ireland party,

---

[1] *Times*, February 1, 1844, and *Northern Star*, February 3, give accounts. [2] *Northern Star*, December 28, 1844.
[3] *Northern Star*, June 7, 1845.

are all studied. O'Connor made an attempt to promote an interest in Chartism among trade unionists. *The Northern Star*, indeed, becomes very largely an organ of the working-men's societies. O'Connor's sympathies are extended towards the National Association of United Trades for the Protection of Labour, of which body Duncombe became President. This had an ambitious programme, but its active life was only three years,[1] and is mainly of interest on account of the experiments with which it was associated.

Experiments, indeed, alone redeem this period from complete uselessness. There are three classes of these : (1) the experiments in co-operative production encouraged by the National Association of United Trades ; (2) the great experiment in co-operative distribution ; (3) the experiments in the co-operative ownership of land, with which O'Connor is specially concerned. The first group were all failures ; their history is difficult to chronicle, as records of the death and dissolution of such undertakings are not kept. An interesting example of the type is supplied by *The Northern Star* of June 14, 1845. Four days before the date of issue, a little ceremony had taken place in a field three miles from Oldham. In consequence of reductions of wages and general ill-treatment, a body of miners on strike, members of a Miners' Protective Association, had borrowed £1,250, and bought the right to mine for coal under 18 acres. W. P. Roberts, a solicitor, raised the first clod of the shaft. The attempt to run a self-governing mine, like the Christian Socialist attempts, a few years later, to found self-governing workshops, appears, from the absence of subsequent news, to have unostentatiously failed.

We now come to the humble birth of the most prodigious child of the Chartist movement. A small group of working men in Rochdale had got into the habit of meeting in a room in Mill Street. Here many opinions were discussed, and many schemes nurtured with a fierceness stimulated by the poverty prevailing in the town. A strike of flannel weavers in 1843 had been a failure ; some other line of advance was eagerly sought for. Chartists, Socialists, and Free Traders met to

---

[1] Webb, *History of Trade Unionism*, pp. 168–177.

argue, and at last decided on something positive. They saved hard for a year, and collected £28 capital. With this, twenty-eight Rochdale working-men opened a shop in Toad Lane, the Rochdale Equitable Pioneers' Society, and spent their capital on a stock of flour, salt and bacon, bought at wholesale prices. Here they made their purchases, sharing part of the profit, using the remainder to extend the business. The majority of the twenty-eight were Chartists; the remainder were mostly Socialists, although a few had no definite political colour.[1] This shop, at first opened only on two week-nights, derided by the passers-by and the local children, was the herald of the co-operative movement as we know it to-day. From the Toad Lane experiment the great Wholesale Societies gradually developed. In 1914 the English Co-operative Wholesale Society alone had a capital of £6,196,150, a reserve fund of £1,883,921, and sold goods to the value of £34,910,813. In the same year the 1,390 retail distributive societies had a total membership of 3,054,297, a capital of £46,317,939, reserve and insurance funds of £2,912,853; did a trade of £87,964,229 and employed 103,074 persons.[2]

The growing distress had directed the attention of the Chartists' leaders to possible remedies. The land naturally suggested itself. In November, 1841, Bronterre O'Brien recommended small holdings, in a speech in London, as a partial solution of the prevailing difficulties.[3] *The Northern Star* took up the subject and discussed the relation between unemployment and agriculture without suggesting anything definite. John West, of Halifax, produced a scheme for buying up waste land and planting Chartists on it; this was condemned by Col. T. Perronet Thompson.[4] O'Connor then took up the subject and declared that Great Britain was capable of supporting her own population, if only her lands were properly cultivated,[5] and published a variant of West's scheme,

[1] G. J. Holyoake, *History of the Rochdale Pioneers*, pp. 79–87.
[2] Figures taken from the *Labour Year Book*, 1916.
[3] *Northern Star*, November 27, 1841.
[4] Ib., December 25, 1842.
[5] Ib., January 1, 1842.

in a pamphlet *The Land*. This appears to be now lost, but Col. Thompson's Letters [1] quote the most important passages. In the United Kingdom there were fifteen millions of acres of waste land capable of reclamation. The expenditure of £100 on a million small farms of 15 acres each would make these waste lands productive. The sale value of this territory would be about £120,000,000. The Government would buy the lands and allot them to tenants, who would pay a rent of £5 for eleven years. After that they would pay £10 yearly. Twenty-one years after the scheme had been started the original £120,000,000 would have been paid off, with interest at 4 per cent. After that the tenant need only pay the original chief-rent, a mere trifle estimated at one shilling and fourpence an acre, unless Government decreed otherwise.

During 1842 O'Connor's interests were absorbed in the growth and development of the N.C.A., and the struggle with the Complete Suffragists, and the land schemes had little attention paid them. In 1843, the Sturgists had been disposed of, interest in the Anti-Corn-Law League was thin, and another bone of contention was required to enable O'Connor to prove once again that his were the strongest jaws. Again, therefore, did he direct his followers' attention to land, and to the marvellous things that might be expected of it, if only they were to have the use of it. *The Northern Star*, towards the middle of the year, fairly overflowed with estimates of what could be done with a four-acre holding. As was only to be expected, a certain amount of expert ridicule was at once forthcoming. The *Leeds Mercury* was especially caustic in its criticisms. However, luck enabled O'Connor to turn the tables, in a dialectical sense, upon this particular opponent. In 1819, a number of Leeds gentlemen had been appointed a committee by the Overseers of the Poor of the town for the purpose of inquiring into the causes of poverty and into the best means of providing some productive work for the unemployed. The secretary of this committee was one Baines, of the *Leeds Mercury*. Baines produced a Report, which O'Connor now exhumed. This interesting document declared that machinery

[1] *Exercises*, Vol. 6, p. 410.

was the principal cause of unemployment, and that " as to manufacturers—we cannot get a glimpse of hope respecting them." The Report asserted that " The Soil—the Earth, is our last, our only resource," and recommended the cultivation of wastes, quoting Arthur Young and Robert Owen as authorities for suggesting this remedy.[1] O'Connor probably did not realize that the progress of enclosures and the intensified difference between those who worked on the land and those who did not, had invalidated this remedy, if indeed, it ever had been a remedy. However, here, in the kernel was a promising scheme and O'Connor set to work to get it put into operation.

A Conference convened by the N.C.A. was held in Birmingham from September 5–8, when this body converted itself into the National Charter Association, established for the mutual benefit of its members. This had two objects : to better " the condition of man " by peaceful and legal means only, and " to provide for the unemployed, and means of support for those who are desirous to locate upon the land." The principles of the new N.C.A. were those of the Charter. The subscription was to be a penny a week. The organization was complicated, branches were grouped into districts, and the highest authority lay in an annual convention, which was to elect the Executive Committee. A special Land Fund was to be started : members were to subscribe 1d. a week upwards for £1 shares. This was to be applied to the purchase of land, stock, and the erection of dwellings. The land bought by means of the fund was to be divided into four-acre farms, to be distributed among the applicants by lot.[2] The first Executive of the new N.C.A. contained among its twenty-eight members, O'Connor, Harney, Joshua Hobson (the publisher of *The Northern Star*), a handful of the old N.C.A. members, Bairstow, Marsden, etc. The rest were nonentities : Morrison, Clark, M'Grath, Doyle and Wheeler were supposed to be in O'Connor's pocket. To enable O'Connor to get absolute control over the agitation, now converted, so far as he

[1] *Northern Star*, September 9, 1843.
[2] Ib., September 16, 1843.

was concerned, for ever into a movement into settling people upon the land, only one thing was necessary. If only Lovett could be won over, all the Chartists would be with him—or under his thumb. All the working-class leaders of Chartism would be united into one body, with O'Connor in undisputed and indisputable command.

Since the Birmingham Conference of December, 1842, had found him on the same side as O'Connor, Lovett had been waiting for an opportunity of publicly dissociating himself from the Dictator. The Birmingham Convention gave him his chance. A. H. Donaldson and J. Mason, two of the principal delegates, wrote to Lovett on behalf of the N.C.A., asking him to become its General Secretary. Their letter was all that such a letter should be. It tactfully hinted at the loss entailed upon the " furtherance of the principle of Democracy " by Lovett's virtual withdrawal, and urged the importance of the " union of all the ablest spirits of the age." It assured him that his election would be unanimous, and implored (its own word) an immediate answer. Lovett politely acknowledged the complimentary tone of the invitation, and went on to talk about his *bête noire*. " Whatever may be the merits of the Plan you are met to discuss, I cannot overlook O'Connor's connexion with it, which enables me at once to form my opinion as to any good likely to be effected by it, and which at once determines my course of action. You may, or may not, be aware that I regard Feargus O'Connor as the chief marplot in our movement in favour of the Charter ; a man who, by his personal conduct, joined to his malignant influence in *The Northern Star*, has been the blight of Democracy from the first moment he opened his lips as its *professed* advocate. Previous to his notorious career there was something pure and intellectual in our agitation. There was a reciprocity of generous sentiment, a tolerant spirit of investigation, an ardent aspiration for all that can improve and dignify humanity ; which awaked the hopes of all good men, and which even our enemies respected. He came among us to blight those feelings, to wither those hopes." The rest of the letter is in a less lofty strain ; but it reads throughout as the work of a passionately honest and indignant man, to whom the Cause was an ideal so high that it claimed the utmost of truth and energy in its service. With this letter Lovett renounced his hold upon the Chartist movement. Truth and honesty were not, as it seemed to him, likely to have an influence ; he would withdraw and let O'Connor do as he would. Perhaps the future would offer him another opportunity of leading the movement back to its original decency.

On November 23, 1844, O'Connor announced the removal of *The Northern Star* from Leeds to London. The paper had been running at a loss since March, 1840, O'Connor paying up the deficit. It had been started before the establishment of the penny post, and it had consequently been at first a mere local paper. Seven years later the introduction of railways had changed that. " From London," said O'Connor, " I shall be able to give a portion of my readers two days' later news than they have hitherto had, and some, four days' news. In London *The Star* will be the means of rallying the proper machinery for conducting the Registration Movement—the Land Movement—the National Trades' Movement—the Labour Movement—and the Charter Movement." The title was to be changed to *The Northern Star and National Trades Journal.* Hobson and Harney were to continue in charge. The price was raised from fourpence halfpenny to fivepence. The editorial office was to be 340, Strand ; the printing was to be done at 17, Great Windmill Street. But for some time O'Connor could not make up his mind definitely to start a land movement. He looks longingly at the trade unions, with the eye of a would-be leader : " I invite you to keep your eye steadily fixed upon the great Trades' Movement now manifesting itself throughout the country, and I would implore you to act by all other trades as you have acted by the Colliers. Attend their meetings, swell their numbers, and give them your sympathy ; but upon no account interpose the Charter as an obstacle to their proceedings. All labour and labourers must unite ; and they will speedily discover that the Charter is the only standard under which they can successfully rally : but don't interpose it to the interruption of their proceedings. . . . I assert, without fear of contradiction, that a combination of the Trades of England under his (Roberts') management and direction, would be the greatest move ever witnessed within the last century. It would be practical Chartism ; and therefore it is our duty to aid and assist it, and not to mar it by imprudent interference."[1] However, at last he made up his mind to take the plunge. " I have been much thwarted and harassed on this subject. When the Birmingham Conference unanimously, and wisely, adopted the Land plan in 1843, the acrimony of the knavish for a season triumphed over the judgment of the prudent ; and I, among others, was compelled to ' bide my time ' till common sense had resumed its place."[2] The National Charter Association held its Annual Convention at the Parthenium, St. Martin's Lane, on April 21, 1845. It was attended by only fourteen delegates, of whom six represented London districts. On the second day a long Report on the Land was read. This document had been drafted by O'Connor and was enthusiastically received. It was rich in suggestions, but, as usual, committed its author to nothing definite. The Convention, again in accordance with the ritual practice of Chartist conferences, gave birth to The Chartist Land Co-operative Society. This was to consist of shareholders, number not limited, holding shares of £2 10s. each, which were to be paid in weekly settlements of 3d., 6d., 1s. and upwards. The " Means " is interesting. " Good arable land may be rented in some of the most fertile parts of the country at the rate of 15s. per acre, and might be bought at twenty-five years' purchase—that is, at £18 15s. per acre ; and supposing £5,000 raised in shares of £2 10s. each, this sum would purchase 120 acres, and locate 60 persons with 2 acres each, besides having a balance of £2,750, which would give to each of the occupants £45 16s. 8d., £30 of which would be sufficient to build a commodious and comfortable cottage on each allotment ; one-half of the remaining £15 16s. 8d. would be sufficient to purchase implements, stock, etc., leaving the residue as a means of subsistence for the occupant until his allotment produced the necessaries of life. These allotments, with dwellings,

[1] *Northern Star*, November 16, 1844. [2] Ib., July 26, 1845.

might be leased for ever to the members of the society at an annual rental of £5 each, which would be below their real value. The gross annual rental would thus amount to £300. This property, if sold at 20 years' purchase (which would be far below the market value), would yield to the funds of the society £6,000, which sum, if expended in a similar manner to the first, would locate other 72 persons on 2 acres of land, provided with homes. These 72 allotments, sold at the rate of the first, would bring £7,200 ; and this sum, laid out in the purchase of other land, buildings, etc., at the original rate, would locate 86⅖ persons. These 86⅖ allotments, if sold, would realize £8,634, 8s. ; and with this amount of capital the society could locate other 103⅙ persons. These 103⅙ allotments would produce £10,317 3s. 4d. ; and the last-named sum expended as before would locate 123⅓ persons. Thus the original capital of £5,000 would more than double itself at the fourth sale ; and so on in the same rates. The benefits arising from the expenditure of the funds in the manner stated may be seen at a glance in the following summary :

	£	s.	d.	Purchase acres	Local persons
Original Capital	5,000	0	0	120	60
First sale produce	6,000	0	0	144	72
Second Do.	7,200	0	0	172	86
Third Do.	8,634	8	0	206	103
Fourth Do.	10,317	3	4	246	123

Continuing to increase in the same proportion until the tenth sale, which would realize £37,324, and locate 372½ persons. Thus the total number which could be located in ten sales— which, if the project be taken up with spirit, might easily be effected in four years—would be 1,923 persons ; in addition to having in possession of the society an estate worth, at least, in the wholesale market, £37,324, which estate could be resold, increasing at each sale in value and capability of sustaining the members, until, in the space of a few years, a vast number of the ' surplus labour population ' could be placed in happiness and prosperity upon the soil of their native land, and thus become valuable consumers as well as producers of wealth."

The Executive of the N.C.A. appointed five of their number as a Board of Directors. These were O'Connor, T. M. Wheeler (Secretary), P. M'Grath, T. Clark and Christopher Doyle.

Money began to come in almost immediately ; of criticism, plentiful outside the N.C.A., scarcely a breath was heard within. The Coventry N.C.A. hazarded the suggestion that the proceeds of the tenth sale, £37,324, might be used to buy up some of the smaller estates previously sold, and so keep them in the hands of the N.C.A. Wheeler replied [1] that the rent which the N.C.A. would be receiving after the tenth sale, amounting to about £2,000 yearly, could be used, if thought fit, towards the repurchase of the first estates. O'Connor was no doubt influenced in his advocacy of the Land Scheme by the success which the Owenite communities were then appearing to enjoy. In 1837 Owen had formed the National Community Friendly Society. In 1841 this body had started the Queenwood Hall colony at Tytherly, and made a very good show there until 1845, by which time even Owen had come to the conclusion that the Millennium, whenever it chose to make a start, would not make it at the Queenwood settlement.[2] Three months after the formation of the Chartist Land Co-operative Society, O'Connor came out with another version of his Scheme. This time he asked for £5,000 in shares of £2 10s. as before, but estimated its expenditure differently. Fifty persons were to be located, each on two acres, bought on the same terms.

	£	s.	d.
Two acres of land @ 15s. an acre at 25 years' purchase	37	10	0
Cost of cottage	30	0	0
Capital advanced	15	0	0
	£82	10	0

The cost of fifty holdings would therefore be £4,125, leaving £875 capital in hand. The tenants would each pay £5 rent ;

[1] *Northern Star*, June 7, 1845.
[2] G. J. Holyoake, *History of Co-operation*, Vol. I, p. 305.

total, £250. The estate would not be sold, but mortgaged for £4,000. With this sum, plus £125 taken out of the £875 in hand, fifty more tenants would be located. The mortgaging process would then be repeated until seven payments of £125 had exhausted the £875. Then the society would own eight estates, seven of which would have been mortgaged for £28,000 secured upon rents totalling £2,000 per year. This would seem to be pretty good going for an undertaking with a capital of only £5,000, but the ingenious brain of O'Connor saw even wider possibilities. " And now, what I do assert is this, and I will abide by the decision of any twelve men of common sense. I do assert, that whereas the first allotment, if sold at once, would be dear at twenty years' purchase, or £5,000, though it would fetch it, that at the end of the first two years it would fetch thirty years' purchase, or £7,500," so that at the end of four years upon that amount of purchase alone the society would be able to sell its estates for £60,000. Having paid off the mortgages and the £5,000 original capital, it would then be left with £27,000 clear profit in hand. A small Land Conference of the National Chartist Co-operative Association was held at the Carpenters' Hall, Manchester, in the week beginning December 8, 1845. Most of the talking was done by O'Connor, who flung masses of figures and estimates at the heads of the delegates and succeeded in getting the discussion, acrimonious at times as it was, confined strictly to details. W. P. Roberts had resigned the post of treasurer, and O'Connor refused to accept it for himself, " though the office had been offered to him, not all the land that could be purchased by the society would induce him to accept it."[1] He would, however, consent to act as " sub-treasurer." Wheeler presented a financial report showing total receipts of £3,266, and an expenditure of £184. Seven trustees were elected : Duncombe, Titus Brooke (of Dewsbury), James Leach (of Manchester), W. Sewell, Duncan Skerrington (of Scotland), William Dixon (of Manchester), and J. G. Dron. Hardly anything had previously been heard in the movement of five of these men. Roberts was subsequently re-elected treasurer. In his *Practi-*

---

[1] *Northern Star*, December 20, 1845.

cal Work on the Management of Small Farms, O'Connor's optimistic ingenuity is so fertile in schemes as to be beyond summarizing. He bristles with suggestions and throws upon every other page a mass of recommendations guaranteed to enable the Chartists to settle on the land to their eternal profit. O'Connor does not definitely bind himself anywhere to any estimates of profits or expenditure, he merely outlines general principles, and illustrates them. Certain things are always postulated, the chief one is that a hand-loom weaver with a family can make a profit from a small holding, if he gives his whole time to it. It is always assumed that the value of the holding will grow from year to year, so that after one year's working a mortgage can be raised upon a farm very nearly, if not quite, equal in value to the original capital outlay. The tenant is required in all the schemes to pay a yearly rent equivalent to 4 per cent. upon the capital outlay, the expenditure of the income from this source is, however, the subject of several suggestions. The tenants are, in all the schemes put forward, to be selected by lot from the subscribers to the fund which is to pay for the land. O'Connor produced a delightfully optimistic statement as to what could be done with these acres. Somebody wrote to him saying that all that was required to convince him and many of his class of the practicability of the Land Scheme was some definite light on the ability of the occupants of even a four-acre holding to live and pay rent. O'Connor replied : " I will take three acres for consideration, that being the mean ; and what I state three acres will do, two will do, as I am going to place it before you in the roughest aspect of husbandry, stating the lowest price for produce to be sold, and the most extravagant for outgoings." He recommended that the three acres should be disposed of as follows : 1 acre of potatoes, 1 acre of wheat, 3½ roods cropped with cabbages, mangel-wurzel, turnips, tares, clover, and flax, and the remainder kitchen-garden. The produce was estimated as follows :

> Produce of acre of potatoes, 15 tons.
> Produce of acre of wheat, 200 stone.
> For growing stuff for cows, 2½ roods.

For flax, 1 rood.

For kitchen garden, ½ rood.

This absurdly exaggerated crop was to be disposed of as follows :

For cows—from November to March, two tons of potatoes, or nearly one and a half stone each per day.

For family—one and a half tons of potatoes, or about nine pounds per day.

For six fatting pigs—from November to March, eight tons of potatoes, or nearly two stone each per day.

For sale—3½ tons of potatoes.

   ,,   milk of two cows.

   ,,   100 stone of wheat.

   ,,   produce of quarter of acre of flax, pounded, scutched, heckled, and spun by the family, during the winter.

   ,,   4 bacon pigs in March.

The prices to be paid on this basis for the produce to be sold were to bring in a tidy little sum.

	£	s.	d.
Milk of two cows, at 8 quarts a day each : 16 quarts at 1½d. per quart	36	10	0
Four bacon pigs in March	20	0	0
100 stone of wheat, at 1s. 6d. per stone	7	10	0
3½ tons of potatoes, at 6d. per stone.	14	0	0
¼ of an acre of flax, spun	12	10	0
Fruit and vegetables	5	0	0
	£95	10	0

This would leave over various items of produce for the consumption of the family.

2 bacon pigs, 3 cwt. each, or nearly 14 lb. of bacon per week.

1½ tons of potatoes, or 4½ stone of potatoes per week.

100 stone of flour, or 1½ stone of flour per week.

Six ducks, or 20 eggs a week.

Fruit and vegetables.

2 hives of honey, or 2 lb. per week.

The annual expenditure would be :

	£	s.	d.
Rent, rates, and taxes	13	10	0
Two tons of best hay for cows, December to March . .	8	0	0
Clothing of family	15	0	0
Fuel, soap, candles	8	0	0
Repairs	1	0	0
Six pigs in May	6	0	0
	£51	10	0

This amount, deducted from the selling-price of the produce, left £44 per annum, " after consumption, and the best of good living."

The value of the produce consumed by the family itself was estimated at 17s. a week, so that living would be at the total rate of about £1 17s. a week.

Finally, O'Connor estimated the employment of time of the family at only 157 days in the year.

John Revans, secretary to the Poor Law Commission of 1832–34, who was examined as an expert witness by the Select Committee of 1848, declared that the estimate was utterly absurd, the more so when considered in reference to the exhausting nature of the cropping proposed. He also pointed out various details which the lay eye is liable to overlook. The fact a cow is generally dry for about three months before calving would either reduce the total output of milk by one-quarter, or else force the unhappy creature to supply at least ten quarts daily during the available period. Moreover, O'Connor was ignorant of the fact that a cow fed as he proposed his tenants' cows to be fed, would produce milk of an extremely unpalatable flavour, that is, so long as it did not die of diarrhœa. Finlaison, an actuary, examined by the Select Committee on the National Land Company, also pointed out various flaws in the scheme. If it took two years to buy, settle and mortgage any estate to its full value, with the original capital of £273,000, a hundred and fifty years would be required to " locate " the 75,000 shareholders. The scheme was therefore " utterly impracticable in point of time."[1] O'Connor had probably confused Irish with English acres ; the former being three-fifths as large again as the latter.

[1] Fifth Report, p. 27.

In any case he had allowed for an impossibly high degree of productivity.[1]

However, mad as the scheme was, money began to come in. That it should have done so is to be explained by two reasons. The first is O'Connor's extraordinary domination over the movement. The second is the fact that among the factory workers who followed O'Connor the agricultural tradition was not yet dead. The vast majority of the Lancashire cotton operatives, for example, had agricultural fathers or grandfathers. " Back to the land " did not sound in their ears as an invitation to take up the simple life, but to return from their own hated surroundings to the work which a long line of forefathers had carried on before their descendants were gripped by the lengthening tentacles of the towns, and dragged away from their original employment. By the end of March, 1846, over £7,000 was in hand ; money was coming in quickly and a new account was started for a second experiment. On April 10, in Manchester, O'Connor conducted the ceremony of selecting by ballot the winning allottees. Thirteen persons became the " landlords " of 4-acre holdings, five of 3 acres each, and seventeen of 2 acres. An estate of 130 acres was immediately bought at Herringsgate, near Rickmansworth. For some weeks *The Northern Star* re-echoes the praises of those who visited the place. O'Connor constituted himself the " bailiff," and went down to put things straight, sharing a cottage with a " Chartist cow " named Rebecca. A few weeks later,[2] O'Connor bought, for £3,900, a second estate, " Carpenter's Farm," also of 130 acres, near Pinner, and promptly sold it again for £5,250, giving the profit to the Chartist Co-operative Land Society. The Herringsgate estate was renamed O'Connorville and exhibited on August 17, 1846. According to the *Daily News*,[3] not less than 12,000 persons attended the demonstration ; according to O'Connor, over 20,000. The wildest enthusiasm seems to have been felt by all save Rebecca, the Chartist cow, which had been decorated for the occasion, and was annoyed. Besides the abundancy of speeches and

[1] Fourth Report, pp. 24–36. [2] *Northern Star*, June 20, 1846.
[3] Ib., August 18, 1846.

P

refreshments, there were present a number of minstrels to cheer the hearts of the demonstrators. Songs were sung such as :

> Those beautiful villas, how stately they stand,
> A national honour to this our land,
> Triumph of labour itself to employ,
> And industry's fruits fully to enjoy ;
> Let fame on thy founders her laurel bestow,
> And history's page their true value show ;
> We have seen many schemes, none can rival thee,
> Thou beautiful villas, the pride of the free.

O'Connorville was duly opened on May 1, 1847. O'Connor made a marvellous speech which began : " And must I not have a cold and flinty heart if I could survey the scene before me without emotion ? Who can look upon those mothers, accustomed to be dragged by the waking light of morn from those little babes now nestling on their breasts——(Here the speaker was so overcome that he was obliged to sit down, his face covered with large tears, and we never beheld such a scene in our life ; not an eye in the building that did not weep.)" The greatest enthusiasm was aroused by O'Connor's promise that " I am not afraid to tell you, that no man who is industrious, sober, honest, and affectionate, shall ever leave the castle in which I have placed him, so long as I have a coat to sell, or a second shirt to pawn." All this time the scheme had no legal basis. The Chartist Co-operative Land Company was provisionally registered on October 24, 1846. On December 17 its name was changed to the National Co-operative Land Company. On March 25 it changed again to the National Land Company. Complete registration was refused by Tidd Pratt, Registrar of Friendly Societies, as he contended that the Land Company was not a Friendly Society, and was an undertaking of a form not sanctioned by law.

The Chartist Land Company held another small Conference in Birmingham in the week beginning December 7, when O'Connor was able to report that total receipts amounted to £22,799. The chief decision at which the delegates arrived was that the Company's lands should not be sold, nor mortgaged to outsiders, but that a bank of deposit should be established.

It was also resolved that the maximum-sized cottage should not contain more than four rooms, of twelve feet square each. The directors were empowered to build school-houses and to appoint teachers, dismissable by a vote of two-thirds of the occupants of the estate on which they were to teach. The location of the Herringsgate allottees was deferred to May 1, 1847. This resolution implied that things would take a longer time to adjust themselves than originally planned, hence O'Connor came in for a little adverse criticism. He, however, pinned the responsibility for the future upon the bank, and claimed that with its assistance, 20,000 Chartists would be settled upon the land within five years.

In conformity with the resolution of the Conference, the National Land and Labour Bank was founded. It was to consist of three departments : a deposit, a redemption, and a sinking fund department.

The deposit department was to be open to all " who wish to vest their monies upon the security of the landed property of the National Co-operative Land Company." $3\frac{1}{2}$ per cent. interest was to be paid.

The redemption department was to be open to the members of the Land Company, who were to get 4 per cent. The funds collected by this department were to be used for purchasing land, or, in the case of occupants' deposits, to " fining down their rent-charge," until, presumably, he could have his allotment, if he wished, free of rent.

The sinking fund department was to be credited with a capital equivalent to five-sevenths of the deposits received by the first department. The theory was that the bank could afford to pay 6 per cent. on the security of the land, but only paid $3\frac{1}{2}$ per cent. The balance of $2\frac{1}{2}$ per cent. was to go to the sinking fund department, to be used for the same purposes as the funds of the redemption department.

The first effect of these three departments was expected to amount to this : they would borrow money from the public at $3\frac{1}{2}$ per cent., and make it earn 5 per cent. by investment in the Land Scheme. How firmly O'Connor believed in the possibility of perpetual motion in the economic sphere ! The plan of the bank had to be explained over and over again.

The prospectus of the Bank made things no clearer. " The National Land Company has been called into existence to pioneer the way in the glorious war of social emancipation. . . . The company aims at the realization of its purpose by the location of its members upon the land, and by aiding them with funds for the cultivation of their farms." The manner in which this was to be achieved is thus explained : " Suppose the company make a purchase of 300 acres of land at £40 per acre (£12,000), and built 100 cottages at £100 each (£10,000), besides advancing aid money to 100 allottees at £22 10s. each (£2,250), the aggregate cost of location, including land, building and aid money, would amount to £24,250. In order to locate a second hundred of its members, the company purpose to reproduce the sum of £24,250 by making the land, buildings, etc., liable to the National Land and Labour Bank, for deposits to that amount ; the depositors in the bank having a legal claim upon the property of the company for the amounts advanced by them."[1] The National Land and Labour Bank was the private property of O'Connor, and was housed under the same roof as the National Land Company. It did all the business of the Land Company, and, in addition, received a considerable amount of deposits at 4 per cent., from sources unconnected with the Land Scheme. The Company, in fact, was to mortgage its estates with the Bank, and buy another estate with the money.

Such comments as have been made on O'Connor in the course of this work have been invariably adverse. A succession of such criticisms may not be unjust in themselves, but nevertheless convey, in sum, a false impression. It is desirable in the interests of justice to make an attempt to present O'Connor to ourselves in the light in which his followers saw him. In the years 1846 and 1847 he was at the summit of his leadership, and his intellectual force was at its strongest. We shall not attempt to look for the early traces of the insanity which subsequently overcame him. It is clear that there were periods

---

[1] *First Report from the Select Committee on the National Land Company,* p. 51.

when O'Connor's reasoning faculties were not in working order. One instance of this is supplied by the wretched fiasco of his debate with Cobden in Northampton on August 5, 1844. Accounts of what actually took place differ considerably.[1] We only know that O'Connor's argument broke down, that he wandered away from the point, and that the majority of the meeting voted in favour of Free Trade. The wildest rumours grew up around O'Connor's maunderings on this occasion ; principally to the effect that he had been bought over by the Anti-Corn Law League. O'Brien declared[2] that O'Connor had danced to the tune of two thousand golden sovereigns. This explanation seems most unlikely. Cobden, who presumably must have known of this, was not the man to bribe O'Connor, or anybody else. Nor was O'Connor the man to accept a bribe ; he would have been far more likely to publish an attempt to buy him and so discredit his adversaries and bask in the warm glow of the righteous indignation of the Chartist movement. In point of fact O'Connor was quite extraordinarily and inexplicably disinterested in the pursuit of his chimeras. He demanded limelight, but scorned lucre. He was undoubtedly careless, and in consequence provoked the wrath of Joshua Hobson and many another, but his carelessness always left himself and not the movement out of pocket. No charge of actual dishonesty was ever proved against him. The Land Scheme had its critics, and the charge of dishonesty was made by them, but demonstration never accompanied it. Many were these critics even in the early stages of the Scheme and its heyday. O'Brien disapproved on economic grounds, preferring his own plan of land nationalization, which, according to O'Connor, would make the people the serfs of the Government.[3] John Watkins objected on the strongly individualist grounds that the owners of the soil have prescriptive rights, and that dispossession was immoral—an argument which would seem to apply to land nationalization rather than to the scheme. Carpenter also assailed it. The *Man-*

---

[1] *Northern Star*, August 5, 1844.

[2] *National Reformer*, April 17, 1847.

[3] *Northern Star*, July 19, 1845.

chester Examiner appointed Alexander Somerville as its special commissioner, and he, signing himself as usual, One Who Has Whistled At The Plough, first picked holes in the economic, then in the agricultural side of the business. Finally he went down to Herringsgate, had a talk with some people in a public-house, and returned to Manchester with the feeling that he had devastated the Scheme. He was wrong : it was Somerville who was devastated, for O'Connor produced newspaper evidence[1] showing that he had in 1841 committed quite a respectable number of little forgeries before severing his connexion with the army, and was, in fact, not as virtuous as he might have been. His criticisms thereupon followed his character overboard. Later on, however, the Land Scheme became a staple topic of the newspapers. The *Daily News* headed a chorus of protest.[2] The *Globe, Chronicle,* and *Dispatch* followed it : the provincial, as usual, taking up the note.

Yet O'Connor had never in his life worked so hard and so sincerely as in connexion with the Land Scheme. He had given it birth, and the ever-changing forms and names he gave it indicate his fears that it might never arrive at maturity. He spared himself no effort to make it a success, describing himself on one occasion as the " Land Company's Bailiff, Contractor, Architect, Engineer, Surveyor, Farmer, Dung-maker, Cow and Pig Jobber, Milkman, Horse Jobber, etc."[3] His writings and speeches during this period are seldom efforts to raise a horse-laugh at somebody's expense ; they show considerable restraint and closeness of reasoning. He no longer generalizes wildly in order to drive home each point, however minute, by sweepingly stating a probably irrelevant and frequently inaccurate proposition. Typical of this habit is his dictum that Locke was the most profound politician that ever lived,[4] which may be easily paralleled.

Under the energetic guidance of the revived O'Connor, the response to the Land Scheme grew in a most extraordinary

[1] *Northern Star*, October 23, 1847.
[2] Ib., September 11, 1847.
[3] Ib., October 23, 1847.
[4] Ib., April 25, 1840.

manner. O'Connor was fully alive to the strategical importance of the Land Scheme. " The great advantage of the Land movement is this—that it supplies food for sensible agitation in good times and in bad times. Good times have always been destructive of Chartism, but now assist it, because it is then that the working classes have the best opportunity of subscribing to the Land plan ; while bad times compel them to think about the land as the only means of escape."[1] Was this merely cynicism ? We think not ; a cynical O'Connor could not have been so energetic.

Money flowed in. On October 31, 1846, O'Connor announced his purchase of a second estate : Lowbands, in Worcestershire, nine miles from Gloucester and the same distance from Tewkesbury. Lowbands, costing £8,100 for its 160 acres, is " one of the most heavenly spots in creation." In February, 1847, he buys for £10,878, 297 acres at Minster Lovel, ten miles from Lowbands, and eight from Worcester, " in the loveliest valley in the world," in June another 270 acres are bought at Snig's End, 2½ miles from Lowbands, and 6½ from Gloucester.[2]

During 1846 subscriptions came in in small but increasing amounts. In 1847 there was a leap upwards. Between December 7, 1846, and August 14, 1847, no less than £49,520 was received by the National Land Company and by the Land Bank.[3] In November there were 42,000 shareholders, who had paid £80,000.[4]

But we are anticipating. In July 1847 the attention of England was distracted by a General Election. Lord John Russell had become Prime Minister in succession to Peel. Fielden had at last got his Ten Hours' Bill through the Commons, while Lord Ashley guided it through the Lords. Peel had embraced Free Trade. O'Connell had just died, leaving this life at the moment when Ireland was in the throes of the Potato Famine. The Repeal agitation had surged up to such an extent that the frightened Government had asked for repressive powers, and being refused them, had resigned.

---

[1] *Northern Star*, December 19, 1846.
[2] Ib., June 12, 1847.
[3] Ib., September 4, 1847. [4] Ib., November 13, 1847.

Maynooth still echoed in parliamentary ears. A great trade boom was hastening, unsuspected, to its collapse. Parliament was dissolved.

The Chartists resolved once more to contest a few seats at the hustings, but not to proceed to the poll. With the admirable intention of making themselves as conspicuous and objectionable as possible to the members of the Government, O'Connor fought Sir John Cam Hobhouse (President of the Board of Control) at Nottingham ; Harney went down to Tiverton, to oppose and to be taken very seriously by Lord Palmerston ; Ernest Jones opposed Sir Charles Wood, the Chancellor of the Exchequer, at Halifax, and so on. W. P. Roberts at Blackburn, Sturge at Leeds, Vincent at Ipswich, and M'Grath at Derby, stood against smaller fry. O'Connor went to the poll. Nottingham was a two-member constituency, and was being wooed by John Walter, the son of Sturge's erstwhile opponent, and Gisborne, in addition to the two others. The day before the poll, the elder Walter died. Nottingham expressed itself by giving the son 1,830 votes, and O'Connor 1,340. Hobhouse, at the bottom of the poll, received only 974. Truly the *Times* was justified in observing on the next day : " The result of the Nottingham election is about as surprising an occurrence as could possibly arise from the mere movements of human opinion and feeling."[1]

So now O'Connor was an M.P. The country had chosen him, had given its endorsement to his claim for leadership. Is it to be wondered at that during election week the receipts of the Land Company reached the record figure of £5,099 ?[2]

We now see O'Connor at the height of his power, and inclined to magnanimity. Immediately after his election, he published an address to the " Old Guards of Chartism," exulting in his victory, which he magnified into the victory of his cause. " These are events which call for a reunion of all the dissevered elements of Chartism. The O'Briens, Lovetts, Vincents, Coopers, and all. Now is the time, if their honest fears have been dissipated, to return to the popular embrace and join in a national jubilee. A good general takes care that

---

[1] *Times*, July 31, 1847.   [2] *Northern Star*, August 7, 1847.

execution shall follow upon the heels of design ; and now is
the time to sign your petition sheets, to prepare for the election
of your delegates who shall meet the new parliament as a
national Convention of Chartism. . . . Will you, then, Old
Guards, join with me, in spite of derision, in winning our old
friends back to our cause ? . . . Without the slightest
recollection of the past I will cheerfully shake hands with
every man who has honestly differed from me, and I will
zealously struggle with him, a good soldier in the good fight."[1]

The end of the Land Scheme may be told here, as after 1847
it ceases to be an integral part of the Chartist movement. As
a result of the newspaper campaign, a Select Committee of
the House of Commons was appointed early in 1848 to consider
the Land Company. Financial irregularities had been alleged,
and things were going none too well at Lowbands, while the
Snig's End allottees never paid a pennyworth of rent for at
least three years. O'Connor published an attempt at excul-
pation, describing in detail how he had spent £90,837 of the
Land Company's money, in the course of which expenditure
he had paid large sums out of his own pocket, and charged
nothing for his own time and labour. The Select Committee
on the National Land Company reported in August, 1848.
They found that the Company was not consistent with the
general principles upon which Friendly Societies are founded,
and therefore was strictly speaking illegal, and should not
have the protection of the Friendly Societies' Acts extended
to it. " The Committee was of opinion that the Company's
minutes and accounts had been most imperfectly kept . . .
but Mr. Feargus O'Connor having expressed an opinion that
an impression had gone abroad that the monies subscribed
by the National Land Company had been applied to his own
benefit, this Committee are clearly of opinion, that although
the accounts have not been kept with strict regularity, yet that
irregularity has been against Mr. Feargus O'Connor's interest,
instead of in his favour ; and that it appears by Mr. Grey's
account there is due to Mr. Feargus O'Connor the sum of

[1] *Northern Star*, August 7, 1847.
[2] Ib., June 24, 1848.

£3,298 5s. 3½d., and by Mr. Finlaison's account the sum of £3,400."

The Committee went farther than merely to exonerate O'Connor from the charges of malversation. The Report went on to state that in view of the large number of persons interested in the scheme, and the *bona fides* with which it appeared to have been carried on, the parties concerned ought to be granted powers to wind up the undertaking, and relieved " from the penalties to which they may incautiously have subjected themselves." The Committee merely put this out as a suggestion, leaving the future of the Scheme an open question, and pronouncing, after discussion, no verdict as to its practicability.

The Land Company did not collapse as rapidly as might have been anticipated after the publication of the Report of the Select Committee. Feargus O'Connor, in Hilary term, 1849, made an application to the Court of Queen's Bench for a mandamus to the Registrar of Joint Stock Companies. This writ was duly granted, and the Registrar, Tidd Pratt, was thereby ordered to register the National Land Company. He refused to do so, and the matter came up for argument a year later, when the Court of Queen's Bench finally decided that the Company was not entitled to registration, and gave judgment for the defendant. On July 9, 1850, Sharman Crawford, M.P., presented a petition to the House of Commons asking for leave to present a petition for a Bill to dissolve the Land Company.[1] This roundabout method was due to the expiration of the time within which, according to the rules of the House, petitions for leave to present Bills could be deposited. This petition was signed by O'Connor, Doyle, Clark, Dixon, and M'Grath. Things had been going badly at Minster Lovel, and no rent was being paid. O'Connor, raging against the " located ruffians," had them ejected by process at the Oxford Assizes, " and now the estate will be sold, and thank God for it."[2] Still he did not lose his hope of making an ultimate success of the idea. " I will carry out the Land Scheme, until I see it become the national system whereby your order

[1] *Northern Star*, July 13, 1850.   [2] Ib., July 20, 1850.

will cease to be slaves," he declares in August.[1] The situation at O'Connorville, as a matter of fact, was such as to promise eventual success to the most optimistic of leaders. In August the allottees at this estate sent him a letter expressing their sympathy with him, and their indignation with Minster Lovel. The O'Connorville settlers, indeed, somehow or other managed to keep going, in spite of defections—perhaps because of them. In May, 1851, O'Connor and T. M. Wheeler started the National Loan Society, which had a short and unprofitable existence,[2] and was wound up in 1852. This body was to fulfil the orthodox functions of a building society, and to buy up the Land Company's estates. It only illustrated O'Connor's tenacious hold upon his idea, and his complete inability to recognize its superabundantly demonstrated weaknesses. In August, 1851, the Royal Assent was at last given to the Bill which had followed the petition, which had succeeded the one mentioned above.[3] *Bona fide* purchasers of land through the Land Company were to remain in possession ; the portions of the estates not bought by allottees were to be sold, and the scheme liquidated. But many years were to elapse before the last was heard of the scheme. Throughout the 'fifties and early 'sixties newspaper references are to be met with. It would appear that the winding-up involved heavy costs, which fell upon the estates, and that the tenants had to be dealt with individually : after the first year's working of the scheme, many of the allottees had complicated matters by subletting or selling their land. In 1875 the *Newcastle Daily Chronicle* sent a special commissioner to O'Connorville.

It should be remembered that the land scheme was one of many experiments in the same direction. Building Societies, as we know them to-day, are a result of this experimentation. A more modest attempt in the same direction as the land scheme was initiated by one James Hill, who founded the National Land and Building Association. The members of this were to take up twenty-pound shares, payable in small

[1] *Northern Star*, August 31, 1850.
[2] Stevens, *Life of Wheeler*, p. 60.
[3] *Northern Star*, September 6, 1851.

instalments. The Association was to build with the capital, and convey one room per share, in perpetuity, to each investor. On payment of smaller amounts, proportionate to the expectation of life of the investor, he could buy the use of a room, rent free, for the rest of his life. A man of sixty, to give an example, would pay £9 5s. 9d. for his room, or £18 11s. 6d. if he desired two rooms. The plan was based on the assumption that the cost of erecting a house would average £20 per room. T. Wakley, M.P., was enthusiastic over the plan, and Richard Moore also gave it his support at a meeting held at Lovett's hall, on March 25, 1846.[1] The Association bought its first estate of 100 acres in July, 1846.[2] There were many other such attempts made about this time, the most productive of ideas and the least studied in the history of the English working classes.

This chapter should not conclude without some reference to O'Brien's activity in the formation and dissemination of ideas. In 1846–47 he edited, from Douglas, Isle of Man, *The National Reformer and Manx Weekly Observer*. The reason of its habitation was the freedom of the Isle of Man from the operation of the Newspaper Tax. Here he spent much energy attacking O'Connor and his ideas, and drawing up a Chartist-Socialist programme. " The National Charter Association is no National Charter Association. It is neither National nor Chartist. It does not include one in a thousand of the Chartists who signed the National Petition, nor ever will, and its object is not the Charter, but the bolstering up of that demagogue and the hunting down of every man of worth and spirit who will not submit to his dictation . . ."[3] Like so many predecessors, he expects great things of paper money, or " symbolical currency." " Paper money, like machinery, and science, and religion, etc., has hitherto worked only for the rich. It has never been made to work for the poor. In no country have the working classes been allowed any of the advantages of paper money. In no country has there been allowed a sym-

---

[1] *Morning Advertiser*, March 26, 1846.
[2] *The Commonweal*, July 11, 1846.
[3] *National Reformer*, October 17, 1846.

bolic currency to represent the products of their labour, and to enable them to interchange, at sight, with one another their respective productions, on the equitable principle of equal labour for equal labour.   Till this is done the inestimable value of symbolic money, as an instrument of exchange, must remain unknown.   The paper money which excited the suspicions and hatred of Paine and Cobbett was, generally speaking, the paper money of schemers and usurers, often that of needy adventurers and desperate blacklegs.   It did not represent actual wealth.   It did not represent houses, railways, merchandise, or any other valuable production of skill and labour. It represented only the credit of certain great names. . . . This is not the sort of paper money we counted for, though even that might be better than no paper money at all.   What we contend for is, equitable Labour Exchanges, between man and man, through the medium of a paper currency that shall represent the exact value of the goods deposited, measured or estimated by the labour expended in producing them."[1]   He attacks private ownership of land, and, as a corollary, the Land Scheme.   " Instead of forming a National Organization to improve the hellish principles of Landlordism and Usury from the soil, they are actually incorporating themselves into Societies, under Government licence, to extend those principles downwards to the working classes, by erecting petty fractions of working men into petty landlords and usurers, to prey upon the rest. . . .   Every man who joins in these Land Societies is practically enlisting himself on the side of the Government against his own order.   He is trying to get interest for his pence and shillings at the expense of those who can save nothing ; and he is trying, by becoming a part owner of the soil, to make that his private property which ought to be no man's private property, but ought to be public property, as much for the use of him who can save nothing as for him who can."[2]   Instead, he advocates nationalization.   " On the subject of land you cannot have honest laws—i.e., laws founded upon first principles—without making the land public property ;

---

[1] *Northern Star*, October 24, 1846.
[2] *National Reformer*, January 9, 1847.

the only rational way of doing which is to make the State sole landlords, the rents applicable to public uses, and the right of occupying the soil (as tenant-farmers under the State) the same, or equal, for every citizen or subject, without that you inevitably have monopoly, injustice, and eventually despotism."[1]   And to conclude this series of quotations, O'Brien draws the distinction between his own Socialism—which the twentieth-century Socialists have adopted—and the Socialism of Owen and the Communists, of whom William Morris was perhaps the best exponent, outside the ranks of the philosophic anarchists. " Mr. King, like a great many others, appears to lose sight of this great essential difference between all such systems as that of Owen, and Mr. O'Brien's, namely that Mr. O'Brien contends only for what are strictly the rights of the people, and what any people may establish practically by law ; whereas the systems of Owen, Fourier, St. Simon, etc., transcend the capabilities of all human legislature, and may, for all we know to the contrary, be incompatible with the essential character of man, and therefore impossible of realization on a universal scale."[2]   But events, as usual, came in and upset every calculation.   Once again Chartism was to change its form, but not as foreseen by O'Connor or O'Brien.

[1] *National Reformer*, February, 20, 1847.
[2] Ib., January 30, 1847.

CHAPTER VIII

1848

THE last important manifestation of Chartism drew its inspiration from abroad. A number of circumstances had tended to draw the attention of Chartists towards foreign revolutionary movements. The Polish rising of 1830–31 had scattered refugees all over Europe. To England Poles came in small numbers ; France held greater attractions for them. Their greatest poet, Adam Mickiewicz, had in 1840 received the professorship of Slavonic literature in the College de France, which became a political centre forthwith. Several years, therefore, had to elapse before London contained many Polish revolutionists with sufficient knowledge of the English language to have any practical influence. But by 1844 this was beginning to show quite distinctly. One Pole, Major Beniowski, went so far as to incur the suspicion of being a police agent, but lived this down. Among the Poles there exists to this day a tradition of participation in Chartism and a memory of past sympathy received from English Radicals.[1] Poles not domiciled in England acted as connecting links in all the European revolutions of 1848. " The exiles of Poland, being scattered far and wide over the Continent, formed a cosmopolitan network of conspiracy, and were the means of bringing into a loose communion the disaffected portions of the European proletariat."[2]

In 1844, Nicholas I of Russia paid a visit to England. The National Association held a meeting of condemnation directly

---

[1] *La Revue de Pologne* 1915, Nos. 5, 6, pp. 196–199.
[2] H. A. L. Fisher, *The Republican Tradition in Europe*, p. 213.

the project was mooted. The sympathies of Lovett had never been confined to the sufferers of his own country. He, with Moore and several others, addressed a packed and enthusiastic meeting, which listened with horrified astonishment to the long list of detailed charges laid against the Emperor.[1] Several Poles, we are told, were present at the meeting. *Punch*, of all papers, came whole-heartedly to the side of the revolutionists, publishing, in addition to the inevitable cartoon depicting Nicholas as a bear, a list of toasts, suggested as appropriate to the occasion.[2] " To the immortal memory of Nero," is a fair specimen of these. The toasts were reprinted, with admiring comments, by *The Northern Star*. Such was one of the lines along which the Chartists were led to take an interest in the revolutionary movements of Europe.

Lovett had for many years been contributing to the same object, and had taken a strong interest in nationalist movements. As far back as 1839, the Working Men's Association sent an address to " The People of Canada," drafted by the indefatigable Lovett on the occasion of the risings of the two previous years. This was warmly acknowledged by the Permanent and Central Committee of the County of Montreal, in another address. A point of interest, which appears to have escaped the notice of Canadian historians, lies in the signatures to this reply. They include L. J. Papineau, Andre Ouimet, and G. E. Cartier, the latter as a joint-secretary. The future Premier of the Dominion on this occasion put his name to a declaration which was extremely near to being a declaration of independence.[3]

By the middle of the 'forties Frederick Engels had settled in England, and was hard at work formulating the theories he was to teach his friend, master, and pupil, Karl Marx. The German struck up a friendship with the editor of *The Northern Star*, and proceeded to educate him in international politics, and the crimes of living rulers. In 1844 the paper begins to show signs of this instruction. Articles appear on such subjects

---

[1] *Weekly Dispatch*, June 9, 1844. [2] *Punch*, June 8, 1844.
[3] An Address to the People of Canada, with their Reply to the Working Men's Association, *u.d.*

as Chartism in Sweden,[1] and on the internal affairs of Spain and Switzerland, in which no previous interest had been shown.

In the same year Duncombe, still the parliamentary agent of O'Connor, exposed the Mazzini letters scandal. The Government, in particular Sir James Graham, had ordered the private correspondence of Mazzini to be opened and read, in the interests of the Papal States. The indignation aroused by this exposure was altogether to the taste of the Chartists, for Graham, as Home Secretary, had come in for all the unpopularity which democratic movements seem inevitably to bestow upon the holder of his post. Chartists were perforce made to take an interest in Mazzini, and his ideals.[2]

And so we find that foreign revolutions and revolutionists gradually become the centres of new groups. Chartists are, as it were, reshuffled and mixed with men belonging to other groups. We have an illustration of the process at work in the accounts of two suppers held in 1845. In the August of that year, a supper was held to celebrate the anniversary of the formation of the Democratic Association of 1838–39. Harney took the chair, and was supported by Rider (a member of the Convention of 1839) and Cooper, who had but recently been set free from Stafford Gaol. Beniowski was also a guest. Harney talked extreme republicanism, and Cooper moved the toast of Joseph Mazzini in an oration which suggested that his excellent and copious sentiments had been stimulated by the refreshment he had taken.[3] The conjunction of speakers is curious in the light of their past history ; the sentiments are also curious. This festivity was so successful that those present unanimously then and there resolved to have another such supper on November 6, the birthday of Henry Hunt. On this second occasion, O'Connor took the chair. Among the speakers were Michelot and Berrier Fontaine ; and two Germans, Schapper and Weitling. Harney spoke on the sorrows of Poland.[4] The first three of these foreigners were to attain

[1] *Northern Star*, September 14, 1844.
[2] Lovett and Hetherington were largely responsible for the facts upon which the exposure was based. Lovett, *Life and Struggle*, pp. 297, 298. [3] *Northern Star*, August 11, 1845.
[4] *Northern Star*, November 15, 1843.

a minor celebrity in 1848, when Michelot fell at the barricades during the June counter-revolution. Weitling (1808–1871) was an extraordinary tailor who spent the first forty years of his life in wandering over Western Europe preaching and organizing the incipient revolutionary Socialism which came to a head in 1848. The Chartist leaders, in fact, were on the way to regarding themselves as participants in a movement which, if not world-wide, was at least European.

Then there were the Fraternal Democrats. This was a small body, but it greatly influenced the Chartist movement in its next phase. It may be described in the words of Thomas Frost, whose brief description commands more confidence than do many of his other accounts, even when they relate to matters nearer than these to the time of writing. " I was at this time a member of the Association of Fraternal Democrats, meeting monthly at a dingy public-house in Drury Lane, called the White Hart. It was composed of democratic refugees from most parts of Europe, but chiefly of Frenchmen, Germans, and Poles, with a sprinkling of such advanced reformers of this country as, like Julian Harney and Ernest Jones, were ' Chartists and something more.' "[1] Oborski was a prominent member of the Fraternal Democrats, and appears to have enjoyed the confidence and friendship of the leading Chartists. He was a Polish refugee, who had been a colonel in the days before 1831. In the year of revolutions he served under Mieroslawski in Baden, where it is presumed that he fell, as this is the last we hear of him.

References have already been made to Ernest Jones, who was to be one of the main supports of Chartism in and after 1848. He was born in Germany, in 1819, and was the son of Major Jones, equerry to Ernest, Duke of Cumberland (afterwards King of Hanover), who stood godfather to young Ernest. The boy was educated in Germany and soon showed himself to be extraordinarily prococious. At the age of eleven he had published a book of poems, and had made a fruitless endeavour to run away from home and walk across Europe " to help the Poles." In 1838 father and son took up their

---

[1] Frost, *Forty Years' Recollections*, p. 125.

abode in England.   Ernest read law, wrote romance, and lived the life of the fashionable youth of the time.   By the middle of the 'forties he had however developed an unmistakable Radicalism, and in 1846 attached himself to O'Connor, throwing up the prospects of a brilliant if conventional future for the advocacy of what he considered right.   His knowledge of foreign languages and continental affairs naturally brought him into touch with the radically-minded refugees in London.

Another influence tending in the same direction is that of Mazzini, who had in 1847 been living in England for ten years, had mastered the language and was well known to all the liberal intellectuals of the time.   It was he who held all the wires of the People's International League, which was started at a public meeting held on April 28, 1847, at the Crown and Anchor Tavern in the Strand ; Dr. Bowring, M.P., in the chair. This organization was founded at Mazzini's direct instigation and had the following objects :

1. To enlighten the British public as to the political condition and relations of foreign countries.

2. To embody and to manifest an efficient public opinion in favour of the right of every people to self-government and the maintenance of their own nationality.

3. To promote a good understanding between the peoples of all countries.

The Council appointed at the above meeting for the first year is as follows :

W. Bridges Adams,	Dr. Bowring, M.P.
W. H. Ashurst,	William Carpenter,
Goodwin Barmby,	Thomas Cooper,
William Cumming,	J. Humphreys Parry,
T. S. Duncombe, M.P.	William Shaen,
Dr. Epps,	James Stansfeld,
W. J. Fox,	P. A. Taylor,
S. M. Hawkes,	P. A. Taylor, Junr.,
Thornton Hunt,	Richard Taylor,
Douglas Jerrold,	Joseph Toynbee,
W. J. Linton,	Henry Vincent,
Richard Moore,	James Watson.

The personnel of this Council shows with unmistakable clearness the changed direction of thought of the ablest founders and friends of the Chartist movement. In the first place we find three of the six working men of the W. M. A. Charter Committee—the exceptions are Lovett and Hetherington, who were both fully in sympathy and acquainted with Mazzini, and Cleave, who apparently died about this time. Linton, too, we have met : he had been in the Chartist movement from the start, although he rose to prominence only after 1848. With Cooper we are also acquainted, and we have nodded at Carpenter (1797–1874), who had made his reputation, well before the days of the Charter, by the publication of unstamped periodicals, which were held to be newspapers within the meaning of the Act. Ashurst, Hawkes, Parry, Shaen, and Stansfeld were all able young lawyers in sympathy with Chartism and frequent speakers at Chartist meetings.[1] Parry (1816–1880) had edited the *National Association Gazette* with Lovett, and became Serjeant-at-law. Stansfeld (1820–1898) was the Liberal M.P. for Halifax from 1859 to 1895, held several posts between 1863 and 1874, and was the first President of the Local Government Board (1871–4) : he was knighted in 1895. He is now perhaps best remembered on account of his fine support of Josephine Butler's crusade. Thornton Hunt was the son of Leigh Hunt ; Dr. Epps was a friend of Lovett and, it may be remembered, was one of the speakers at the dinner held to welcome Lovett and Collins on their release from prison in 1841. Joseph Toynbee was another doctor, and the father of Arnold Toynbee. The P. A. Taylors, father and son, were well-known as anti-Corn Law leaders. Richard Taylor was one of the founders of University College, London. Barmby (1820–1881), like Fox and the younger P. A. Taylor, was a Unitarian, who spent his intellectual life in gradually working his way from undiluted Owenism to the politics of the Liberal party.

These biographical data, relating mainly to a body of men who are outside the necessary narrative of events, may seem

---

[1] W. J. Linton, *Memories*, pp. 99, 100.

superfluous. All these people, however, should be taken as random specimens of the new blood which was suddenly being infused into the Chartist movement. Although Mazzini had founded the People's International League, he had taken care to have a purely British Committee, and he himself, although he drafted the first manifesto, was ostensibly unconnected with the management of the League. The Council, in fact, was a foreigner's effort to mingle the most vigorous and progressive Englishmen with one another. The mingling of such Englishmen with similarly-minded foreigners, as we have seen, had been proceeding for some time.

As far back as February, 1840, a group of German working men had formed a little Communist Society, holding its meetings at the Red Lion, in Great Windmill Street. This club had an anniversary dinner in commemoration of its sixth birthday, at which Harney again held forth. So, too, did Michelot, Colonel Oborski, Schapper, Heinrich Bauer, and some others. A few days later the insurrection of the Polish Republic of Cracow against Austria, in February, 1846, aided the process. The N.C.A. convened a meeting at the " Crown and Anchor," where O'Connor, Harney, W. J. Linton and lesser lights held forth. Mazzini was expected to attend, but sent a letter of apology. For months *The Northern Star* gave up a large proportion of its columns to such accounts of the progress of the struggle as could be obtained. On May 20 a meeting was held at the National Hall, among the speakers on this occasion being Hetherington, T. M. Wheeler, Ernest Jones, Harney and G. J. Holyoake.

It will be seen that O'Connor's participation in this new internationalism was scanty, and almost unwilling. To Engels and Marx, this appears to have been a cause of regret. Foreseeing the events of 1848, they regarded the Chartist movement as an organization of the proletariat, numerically unsurpassed in any country, which only needed a dose of republicanism to make it take its place possibly at the head of the coming European revolution. O'Connor, more than any other man, could satisfy their wishes and effect the conversion of the British working man from a domestic to an international political faith.   And since O'Connor would not come to Engels and Marx, Engels and Marx came to O'Connor.

In July, 1846, a by-election took place at Nottingham on the appointment of Sir John Cam Hobhouse to a Cabinet post. O'Connor turned up and was nominated as the Chartist candidate, made a great speech attacking the Whigs, and defeated the newly-fledged minister on the show of hands.   He did not go to the poll, and Hobhouse was therefore duly elected.   But O'Connor's interference, even though for all practical purposes it amounted only to one speech, supplied an opportunity to his wooers.   He promptly received an Address from the German Democratic Communists of Brussels.[1]   This congratulated him on a number of things.   " The ground is now cleared by the retreat of the landed aristocracy from the contest ; middle class and working class are the only classes betwixt whom there can be a possible struggle."   The Address further congratulated O'Connor on his victory over the calumnies of Thomas Cooper, on the noble and enlightened manner in which *The Northern Star* is conducted, etc.   The signatories are three : Engels, Ph. Gigot, and Marx.

A year later the attack, still unsuccessful, was renewed. On November 27, 1847, the Fraternal Democrats, in conjunction with the Democratic Committee for Poland's Regeneration, held a meeting to celebrate the anniversary of the Polish Insurrection of 1830.   J. Arnott was in the chair. Stallwood moved a resolution of sympathy with Poland, which was seconded by Ernest Jones, supported by Michelot, and carried unanimously.   Then Schapper moved the second resolution, and explained that it was to be seconded by " Dr. Charles Marx," vice-president of the Brussels Committee of the Democratic Society, who had been delegated by it to the Fraternal Delegates " for the purpose of establishing relations of correspondence and sympathy between the two societies."   The delegate from Brussels, in fact, had a much more serious task on hand than the mere moving of an academic resolution, identical in spirit with the first.   Marx came forward and was tumultuously acclaimed.   Speaking in German, he told the

[1] Printed in full in *The Northern Star*, July 25, 1846.

meeting that the Democrats of Brussels had delegated him to speak in their name to the Democrats of London, and through them to the Democrats of Britain, to call on them to cause to be held a congress of nations—a congress of working men, to establish liberty all over the world. (Loud cheers.) The Democrats of Belgium felt that the Chartists of England were the real Democrats, and that the moment they carried the Six Points of the Charter the road to liberty would be opened to the whole world. " Effect this grand object, you working men of England, and you will be hailed as the saviours of the whole human race." Marx sat down to tremendous cheering, having said of Poland not a word.

Harney next moved the meeting's approval of the plan of a congress of the nations, and was seconded by Stallwood.

Charles Keen then moved a resolution to the effect that, given the Charter, the Democracy of England would be able to help Poland, otherwise it would not. He was seconded by " Citizen Engels (from Paris)," who " had resided for some time in England, and was proud to boast himself a Chartist, name and all. . . . (Rapturous applause.)" Citizen Tedesco (from Brussels), and Oborski followed ; after which Engels, Harney, and Schapper spoke for the second time, the *Times* was hooted, the Marseillaise sung, and the proceedings closed. As the immediate result of this meeting arrangements were made " to render effective the union of the two associations," i.e., the Fraternal Democrats and the Brussels Democrats.[1] The nature of these is undisclosed. The Fraternal Democrats, who had been hitherto rather an unorganized body, now adopted a constitution, and set to work to induce the Chartists to send delegates to the first congress of the nations, which had been fixed for September 25, 1848, in Brussels (the anniversary of the Belgian Revolution). The second congress, in 1849, was to be held in London.[2]

With enormous energy Harney, Keen, and the other Englishmen set to work to create the desired response from the Chartists. Events abroad were beginning to take definite shape.

[1] *Northern Star*, December 11, 1847.
[2] Ib., December 18, 1847.

Crowns were becoming suddenly evasive and slippery things. The prophecies of Mazzini and Marx were to be fulfilled. Yet still the leader of the Chartist movement would not define his attitude. Perhaps Engels had overrated his importance : he had certainly over-estimated his intelligence. In a letter to Marx, written apparently in November, 1847, he says : " Just read the article by O'Connor in the last *Star* against the six Radical newspapers. It is a masterpiece of inspired abuse, in places better than Cobbett, and approaching Shakespeare."[1] Yet this alleged approximation did not enable O'Connor to understand foreign politics. The gradual absorption of the other Chartist leaders in internationalism left him uninfluenced. Near the end of 1845 he had spent two months travelling in Belgium, France, Italy, Germany, and Austria, ostensibly in order to study the land systems of those countries. He had seen the preparations made by the Austrians in Milan to quell any possible rising ; he had visited the capitals where the storms of 1848 were already gathering, and at the end of the journey he had reported that in the countries he had seen " people possessed less liberties, but were more contented and happier, because each possessed more or less of the land."[2] He had, it is true, made advances to the Irish. But the leaders of the Repeal movement rejected them. The *Nation*[3] wrote : " We desire no fraternization between the Irish people and the Chartists—not on account of the bugbear of ' physical force,' but simply because some of their five points [*sic*] are to us an abomination, and the whole spirit and tone of their proceedings, though well enough for England, are so essentially English that their adoption in Ireland would be neither probable nor at all desirable. Between us and them there is a great gulf fixed ; we desire not to bridge it over, but to make it wider and deeper." Thus repulsed, O'Connor spent much labour in trying to win over the Irish by iterated explanations of the Six Points in *The Northern Star*, which probably had no Irish circulation to speak of.

[1] Engels-Marx, *Briefwechsel*, Vol. I, p. 79.
[2] *Northern Star*, November 15, 1845.
[3] The *Nation*, August 15, 1846.

So it came to pass that the Cracow insurrection left O'Connor unmoved, and unconcerned because Switzerland had got over the Sonderbund trouble. The first days of the Year of Revolutions find him planning a scheme to raise £5,000 to erect a Chartist Hall in London, M'Grath acting on this occasion as principal understudy. Yet the attention of the public was being directed abroad by a variety of circumstances. The *Times* was confidently predicting a more or less immediate invasion on the part of France, having been led to this con- clusion by the Duke of Wellington, who in his dotage had suddenly decided that England was defenceless and undefen- sible. Everybody clamoured for a larger army, when a dead duke would have met the case equally well. The agitation lasted exactly two months. Then Lord John Russell proposed to raise the income-tax by fivepence in the pound in order to cover the cost of increased armaments. Brought face to face with the stern realities of war the panic-mongers suddenly, and quite literally, held their peace. A month later, on February 24, the situation was farcically ended by the abdica- tion of Louis Philippe, who came to England, not as an in- vincible invader, but as a very tame refugee.

During January, 1848, crowded meetings were addressed in many parts of England by Samuel Kydd, John West, and W. P. Roberts. The directors of the National Land Company and various others, especially Dixon, Ernest Jones, Harney, Clark, Skelton, Fussell, and Keen, spoke in London. O'Connor addressed meetings in Birmingham and London, but talked no internationalism. By February the course of events in France had become obvious to all except O'Connor. On the 12th he made another great speech, but still had nothing to say on foreign events, although by this time Palermo had given Sicily the lead and the Neapolitan garrison had been expelled from the island, and revolutionists in France, Prussia, Bavaria, Austria, Hungary, Italy, Denmark, and Holland were giving the finishing touches to their plans.

At last the current overcame O'Connor, who had to change his course accordingly. The leading article of *The Northern Star* of February 26, 1848, is headed " The Tossin," and ends up

with a P.S. : " Amiens is in full revolt ; insurrection, began on
the 22nd, is spreading." O'Connor addresses an article " To the
Old Guards." He believes a revolution is to swamp the
governments of Europe, but " I tell you as long as I live the
Charter and the Land shall never be lost sight of, nor placed
in abeyance by any foreign excitement or movement, however
we may use events for the furtherance of those great objects.
Old Guards, the mind of England is now astir, and though
mine is absorbed in the consideration of those means by which
I can insure happy homes, and protection for all—the release
of women from slave labour, and the release of little children
from the abodes of pestilence, disease, immorality, and death—
yet if a greater sphere of action should open upon us, I pledge
myself that I shall not be found backward in moulding passing
events to future advantage." February ended, but still
O'Connor was unruffled. On the other hand the members of
the Government were beginning to show signs of a nervous
disposition. Revolution in France and talk of war were not
the only uncomfortable features of the time. 1847 had been
a bad year. The price of wheat had risen from 50s. 10d. per
quarter in 1845 to 69s. 9d. in 1847. A period of over-invest-
ment in railways had ended in a financial crisis. The Bank
Act had been suspended. Unemployed workmen began to
accumulate in the towns. The Government could not make
up its mind whether the rumblings of discontent might not
end in revolution.

On March 6 the Government showed its hand. One Charles
Cochrane had organized a meeting protesting against the
proposal to raise the income-tax, to take place in Trafalgar
Square on this day at 1.30 p.m. The Home Office informed
him of the rule that meetings were prohibited within one
mile of the Houses of Parliament during their sittings. On the
morning of March 6, therefore, Cochrane published his intention of not holding the meeting. A crowd nevertheless turned
up ; G. W. M. Reynolds[1] leaped on to the plinth and made

---

[1] G. W. M. Reynolds (1844–1879) was at the time of his sudden incursion into the Chartist movement an industrious manufacturer of sensa-

himself chairman, and all went well for the time, although the police were present in large numbers. At 3 p.m. the crowd began to disperse, when an altercation took place : somebody had called somebody else a lazy fellow, and the person addressed had resented it with some emphasis. This developed into a stand-up fight which lasted until midnight. The battle proliferated itself along every street within a mile of the Square, and skirmishing continued for three days. Innumerable arrests were made. During the same week commotions in Glasgow were caused by the local unemployed, five of whom were killed by the soldiers called out to calm things down. In Manchester a riot took place outside a workhouse. In various parts of Ireland sundry rowdinesses occurred. A few days later[1] disturbances were expected in Liverpool, but nothing serious happened.

And the Chartists ? Ernest Jones, P. M'Grath and Julian Harney were sent to Paris to convey congratulations to the new Government. In great haste a National Convention was convened for April 3 and the following days, to arrange for the presentation of a monster Petition to the House of Commons. The Petition was also hurried up.[2] Forty-nine delegates were to meet. Mazzini and Linton also went over to Paris, where they met Lamennais. Linton, like Ernest Jones and the others, returned bubbling over with republicanism.

A revolution was now seriously regarded as imminent. Owen published a set of " Practical measures required to prevent greater political changes in Great Britain and Ireland." These were as follows :

1. Full liberty of thought, speech, writing, and publication on all civil and religious subjects.

2. Representation co-extensive with taxation ; the voters to be protected by the ballot, and the representatives to be paid for their services.

3. No connexion between the State and any one creed, but

tional novels. He was a strong republican and a democrat, but before March 6 had never declared his sympathies with Chartism.

[1] *Times*, March 18, 1848.   [2] *Northern Star*, March 11, 1848.

equal protection to all ; and admissibility of men of all creeds to offices of trust and influence.

4. National education, unexclusive and practical ; and profitable employment to all who require them.

5. Graduated property-tax, to the exclusion of all other imports ; customs and excise to be gradually abolished.

6. National Bank with branches wherever required ; and national currency in notes secured upon the whole property of the British Empire.

7. No other bank or currency to be legal, but reasonable compensation to the " Bank of England " and all other banks, unless employed by the national bank.

8. National notes, in convenient amounts, to be issued in payment of the " national debt," and to the extent required for the currency, or circulation of the Empire

9. Free trade in all things, with all the world.

10. Organizing and training of the people, in local districts, as being the most effectual and the cheapest national defence.

These preliminary changes by the British Government the state of public opinion in Great Britain and Ireland and over Europe renders immediately necessary to prevent greater changes being forced upon the Government from without.

ROBERT OWEN.[1]

LONDON, *March* 15, 1848.

After the middle of March it became difficult to keep count of the revolutionary movement in Europe. Charles Greville writes in his diary on March 25 : "Nothing is more extraordinary than to look back at my last date and see what has happened in the course of *five days*. . . . Within these last four or five days there has been a desperate battle in the streets of Berlin between the soldiers and the mob ; the flight of the Prince of Prussia ; the King's convocation of his States ; concessions to and reconciliation with his people ; and his invitation to all Germany to form a Federal State ; and his notification of what is tantamount to removing the Imperial Crown from the head of the wretched *crétin* at Vienna, and placing it on his

[1] *Northern Star*, March 25, 1848.

own. Next, a revolution in Austria ; an *émeute* at Vienna ;
downfall and flight of Metternich, and announcement of a
constitutional *régime* ; *émeutes* at Milan ; expulsion of Austrians
and Milanese independence ; Hungary up and doing, and the
whole empire in a state of dissolution.   Throughout Germany
all the people stirring ; all the sovereigns yielding to the
popular demands ; the King of Hanover submitting to the
terms demanded of him ; the King of Bavaria abdicating ;
many minor occurrences, any one of which in ordinary times
would have been full of interest and importance, passing almost
unheeded."[1]

Wilhelm, Prince of Prussia, grandfather of Wilhelm II, was
over here as a refugee, having been hastily sent abroad by his
more popular father. At a meeting on Kennington Common
on March 13, fourteen or fifteen thousand men (according to
the conservative estimate of the *Times—The Northern Star*
put the number at over 20,000) had listened to revolutionary
though not inflammatory harangues by Reynolds, Jones and
others, at the expense of Louis Philippe and Guizot. *The
Northern Star* had adopted the meaningless but terrifying
slogan, " France has a Republic : England must have the
Charter." Fear had made it impossible to ignore the Chartists,
and ignorance multiplied their numbers, exaggerated their
power, and overlooked their objects. At the beginning of
April O'Connor's dominance began to waver. Rumours
reached him of his own expected defection. He learned that
many of his followers feared that on April 10 he would not
be present. He protests against this [2] : " I would rather be
taken a corpse from amid that procession than dishonour
myself, disgrace my country, and desert you, by remaining
away." In point of fact he had outrun himself. He had,
unwittingly perhaps, reduced demagogy to a science. He
had discovered that the quickest and surest way to the leadership and applause of numbers was high-flown blather and
magniloquent promises. The fulfilment of the promises would
have redeemed the oratorical excuses, but it never came. He

[1] *Greville Memoirs*, Vol. 6, pp. 158, 159.
[2] *Northern Star*, April 1, 1848.

had spoken of fleshing swords to the hilt in order to obtain leadership, and now he was counselling peace and, very nearly, goodwill. It is curious to read in *The Northern Star*[1] letters from O'Connor and Duncombe urging the utmost propriety for April 10, side by side with a flamboyant manifesto signed by the three faithful ones, Clark, M'Grath, and Doyle. It is pretty certain that the influence of such men as Mazzini and Engels on the periphery of the movement had a great effect upon O'Connor's position. A movement demands intellectual leadership as well as figureheads ; O'Connor provided Chartism with the former alone. As a consequence of the revolutionary movement in Europe, the rank and file of the Chartists had become suddenly infected with republicanism. O'Connor's response to this new idea was so slight that it is in a sense true to say that he was rapidly placed outside the pale. Ernest Jones and G. W. M. Reynolds, moreover, were middle-class men of good education, and not easily to be detached from his side. Besides, he had rid himself of so many capable supporters, turning them into opponents, that further detachment may well have seemed undesirable. Five years later Jones gave evidence to the effect that it was about the beginning of 1848 that his leader's mind began to show signs of shakiness.[2] An insignificant incident about the same time had helped to draw together the Chartists who had not attached themselves to O'Connor. On March 17 the *Times* published an attack on the Socialism of Robert Owen, who forthwith summoned a meeting at the John Street Institute to explain his principles, to denounce the *Times*, and to congratulate France. The meeting was addressed by Owen (for over an hour), by Lloyd Jones, Hetherington, Watson, and Bronterre O'Brien.

On Tuesday, April 4, the Convention met at the John Street Institute. M'Grath was elected chairman and Doyle secretary. The first incident related to the election of G. W. M. Reynolds, who admitted he " had only become a Chartist within the last few days." Then a slightly stormy discussion ensued on the position of the Executive. O'Connor, foreseeing

---

[1] *Northern Star*, April 8, 1848.
[2] *The People's Paper*, April 16, 1853.

trouble, did not wish to be entitled to vote ; by waiving his right to vote he would bear no share in the responsibility for any illegality proceeding from the Convention. He was, however, overruled, and it was resolved that the Executive should be entitled to speak and to vote, and to sit *ex officio* as members of the Convention. The afternoon of the first and the morning of second day were taken up with the verbal reports of the delegates on the political and social state of their constituencies. The Lancashire delegates unanimously testified to the terrible industrial conditions prevailing in their county. The Scottish delegates gave, comparatively speaking, more cheerful accounts. As might be expected, the representatives of the most distressed areas uttered the most revolutionary sentiments. O'Connor made his first important speech in an endeavour to suppress the incipient intransigence of these speakers. He began, as usual, by self-glorification on an autobiographical basis. Thence he passed on to declare that " he was now becoming a quasi-minister, and doubtless would be asked what they intended to do on Monday. On the faith of that Convention, he should reply that not one pane of glass nor one pennyworth of property would be injured. That peace and good order would prevail while their grievances were under discussion." Having thus committed himself to good behaviour, he concluded by blusteringly promising to be in the front row of the first rank ; and now they might shoot away. Then he left the Convention, announcing that he must go to the House.

On Thursday the Convention discussed a programme, wasting many hours by inconsecutive argument and bad chariman-ship. At last an amended programme was drafted and unanimously accepted amid immense cheering. This was as follows :

1. That in the event of the National Petition being rejected by the House of Commons, this Convention prepare a National Memorial to the Queen to dissolve the present Parliament, and call to her council such ministers only as will make the People's Charter a cabinet measure.

2. That this Convention agree to the convocation of a

National Assembly, to consist of delegates appointed at public meetings, to present the National Memorial to the Queen ; and to continue permanently sitting until the Charter is the law of the land.

3. That this Convention call upon the country to hold simultaneous meetings on Good Friday, April 21, for the purpose of adopting the National Memorial, and electing delegates to the National Assembly.

4. That the National Assembly meet in London on Monday, April 24.

5. That the present Convention shall continue its sittings until the meeting of the National Assembly. On the Friday the Convention was brought up against a proclamation published by the Commissioner of Police declaring the procession proposed for April 10 to be illegal. The previous day O'Connor had argued the matter in the House against the Attorney-General and Sir G. Grey. He had pointed out that on several occasions within the last ten years processions had marched down to the House of Commons and there presented their petitions, and had gone on to assure the House that the Chartists had no intention of overawing it, and to plead the generally pacific nature of his intentions. The Convention, faced with the proclamation, met it with another one to the effect that it was based on a " statute passed in the arbitrary reign of King Charles II," that it was " an infringement on the right of petition and public meeting," and declaring a " firm determination to hold such meeting and procession," promising that the whole affair would be " an unarmed moral demonstration," and calling on the inhabitants of London to come to the support of the Chartists. On Saturday O'Connor solemnly harangued the Convention and warned them that there must be no display of force. After a discussion on what was to be done in the event of the wholesale arrest of the delegates, the Convention adjourned until 8 a.m. on Monday morning. Innumerable circumstances had been contributing to the excitement of the public. Events in Ireland seemed to be getting uncontrollable. At a crowded Chartist meeting in Liverpool a Matthew Somers had declared that there were

organizations in Liverpool, Manchester, and " at the foot of the Throne itself," which, in the event of " an attempted massacre of my countrymen," would cause the skies to be " reddened with the blaze of the Babylons of England."[1] The *Times* was declaring that " the Chartists, in fact, are but tools in the hands of a gang of desperadoes. The true character of the present movement is a ramification of the Irish conspiracy. The Repealers wish to make as great a hell of this island as they have made of their own." The Queen left London for the safety of the Isle of Wight on Saturday. Innumerable meetings had been held in London throughout the week. The members of the Inns of Court and the clerks in Government departments were swearing themselves in wholesale as special constables. O'Brien left the Convention, refusing to be associated with illegal proceedings, and by so doing he gave the remaining delegates a definitely illegal stamp to the eyes of the non-Chartist world. The theatres announced that they would be closed on the night of the 10th.

Lord Campbell, Chancellor of the Duchy, writing to his brother on Sunday night, said : " This may be the last time I write to you before the Republic is established ! I have no serious fears of revolution, but there may be bloodshed. . . ." The day before the Cabinet had requested Wellington to attend, and " we had then a regular Council of War, as upon the eve of a great battle. We examined maps and returns and information of the movements of the enemy. . . .[2] It was not I alone who was struck with the consultation yesterday. Macaulay said to me that he considered it the most interesting spectacle he had ever witnessed, and that he should remember it to his dying day." Fortunately the Duke had the sense to order the forces under his command to remain in ambush, in fact, safely out of the way.

Harriet Martineau in her *Autobiography* gives us another glimpse of the panic-stricken state of political circles. The wife of a Cabinet minister wrote to her, " under her husband's

[1] *Times*, April 10, 1848.
[2] G. Lathom Browne, *Wellington*, Vol. II, p. 297.

sanction," to enlist her help in bringing the working classes to reason [!], fearing that the Chartists were about to " hold the metropolis." Lord Malmesbury, in his *Memoirs of an Ex-Minister*, supplies more evidence of the state of feeling in London. On April 5 he writes in his diary : " The alarm about the Chartists increases. Everybody expects that the attack will be serious." On April 9 : " The alarm of to-day is very general all over the town. . . . The Duke of Wellington is to command the troops, and the orders he has given are that the police are to go first to disperse the meeting ; if resistance is offered and they are likely to be beaten, then the troops are instantly to appear, and the cannon to open with shell and grenades, infantry and cavalry are to charge—in short, they are to be made an example of." On the morning of The Day : " My five keepers have arrived at my house this morning, armed with double-barrelled guns, and determined to use them if necessary."[1]

At last the 10th dawned upon the waiting world. Prodigious preparations had been made by the authorities. Four thousand policemen guarded the bridges, Palace Yard, and Trafalgar Square ; 1,500 Chelsea pensioners had been fetched out from their retirement and entrusted with the defence of Battersea and Vauxhall. Eight thousand soldiers were distributed over various strategic points along the Embankment between the Tower and Millbank. Twelve guns were in readiness at the Royal Mews. Three steamboats had been procured in order to move soldiers about from point to point should occasion arise for their services. The clerks at the General Post Office had been equipped with rifles. And, finally, over one hundred and fifty thousand special constables had been sworn in to protect property behind the firing line.[2] Among these was Louis Napoleon, who paced a beat in the West End in the company of the cook of the Athenæum Club, meditating the while, one likes to imagine, on the theory and practice of *coups d'état*. It is certainly one of the minor humours of history that while the last King of the French was painfully adapting

---

[1] Lord Malmesbury's *Memoirs of an Ex-Minister*, Vol. I, pp. 223 *et seq.*   [2] *Times*, April 11, 1848.

himself to life in a London suburb, the future (and also the last) Emperor of the French, with a white band on his arm and a stave in his pocket, was acting as an amateur London police-man.   At four o'clock in the morning the special constables were at their posts.   The late Sir Spencer Ponsonby-Fane,[1] then a junior clerk in the Foreign Office, has described the inter-nal defences of his Department on the great day.   " The ground-floor windows of the office were all blocked up with the huge bound volumes of the *Times* newspaper, which it was supposed would resist bullets."   The clerks were armed with new service muskets and ball cartridges.   We gather from the *Greville Memoirs* that similar precautions had been taken in the other Government offices, where the joyous clerks were improvised into ready-made garrisons, provisioned to stand a short siege. Special trains brought up Chartists, wishing to march in pro-cession, from all parts of England.   The papers published bulletins from hour to hour, by staffs of correspondents dis-tributed all over London.   At eight o'clock the Convention met, principally in order to hear O'Connor deny that he had ever intended not to be present, and to read aloud anonymous messages he had received from friends, to the effect that his life would be certainly ended by a bullet, should he insist on marching.   At ten o'clock a car drawn by six horses arrived, decorated with flags and mottoes, and the delegates mounted and were driven to Kennington Common, *via* Holborn, where the Petition was fetched out of the offices of the N.C.A. and loaded into another car, and Blackfriars Bridge.   At eleven o'clock they arrived, almost at the same time as a small pro-cession of trade unionists.   Within the next hour a number of other processions from various parts of London had congregated. What was the total number of Chartists present ?   According to the *Evening Sun*,[2] " at least 150,000 " ;   according to the next day's *Times*, about 20,000, only about half of whom were Chartists.   According to *The Northern Star*, 250,000.   There is no reason to doubt the correctness of the official estimate of " 15,000 to 20,000."   Before the speeches began a police

---

[1] Died 1915 ; the facts are from a letter published in the *Times* of April 14, 1914.   [2] April 10, 1848.

officer approached the car and said that Mr. Richard Mayne, one of the Commissioners of Police, wished to speak to O'Connor. The latter immediately left the car and spoke to Mayne. The crowd showed a hostile attitude towards the messenger, who was saved by O'Connor's declaration that Mayne was his "best friend." Then the Duke's strategy was revealed. O'Connor was told that the meeting could be held, but that the bridges were closed by the police, and no procession would be allowed to cross. O'Connor at once promised to abandon the procession. He returned to the Common from the Horns Assembly Rooms, where the interview with Mayne had taken place, and the speech-making began. Doyle was put in the chair, and started proceedings. Then O'Connor broke the news. In accordance with his usual tactics he first allowed his prestige full play, adding to it for the occasion. Posing as a revolutionary of the deepest dye, he told the astonished crowd that his father had been tried five or six times for high treason, and was in prison for seven years of his life, that his uncle "is now in the fifteenth year of his banishment, and is about to be made the first President of the Republic in France. My brother is Prime Minister and Commander-in-Chief of a Republic in South America." Having by these means sufficiently impressed his listeners with the sense that he, O'Connor, was a man whose advice was well worth taking, he explained the situation as regards the police, and urged those present to pin their faith to the moral force of the six million signatures to the Petition, and to do nothing rash. Ernest Jones followed, echoing his leader's exhortations. O'Connor left the Common on the conclusion of Jones' speech, and the last speakers, Clark and Reynolds, were not very well listened to. About 2 p.m. the meeting dispersed. The Petition was packed into three cabs and, accompanied by Doyle, Clark, and M'Grath, was driven off to the House of Commons. They were refused a safe-conduct across Westminster Bridge, and had ignominiously to reach Westminster through back streets and over Blackfriars Bridge. A few Chartists stayed behind to listen to an Irish meeting in a corner of the Common, which Harney, West and Reynolds were invited to address. The remaining Char-

tists slowly dispersed, wondering greatly. The demonstration
was at an end.   At 2 p.m. Lord John Russell wrote out a report,
and sent it to the Queen.   " Lord John Russell presents his
humble duty to your Majesty, and has the honour to state that
the Kennington Common meeting has proved a complete
failure."[1]

Yet the demonstration of April 10, 1848, has grown into a
curious legend, easily explicable by anybody with the slightest
acquaintance of crowd-psychology.   Thus in the preface to
Kingsley's *Alton Locke* it is stated that " on the 10th April the
Government had to fill London with troops, and put the Duke
of Wellington in command, who barricaded the bridges and
Downing Street, and other public buildings."   Dean Stubbs
in his book on Kingsley is under the same hallucination.
" On the 10th of April, 1848, a revolution was threatened in
England.   One hundred thousand armed men were to meet on
Kennington Common and thence to march to Westminster,
and there to compel, by physical force, if necessary, the
acceptance of the People's Charter by the Houses of Parliament."[2]   The preposterously extensive arrangements made
by the Duke to keep the peace vanish into insignificance beside
the exaggerated memories which the demonstration left behind
it.

The Duke of Wellington, speaking in the House of Lords on
April 10, said that the effect of the meeting on Kennington
Common was " to place all the inhabitants of the metropolis
under alarm, paralysing all trade and business of every description, and driving individuals to seek for safety by arming
themselves for the protection of the lives of themselves and
of their neighbours, and for the security of their property."
The recent revolutions supply the explanation of this timorous-
ness.   It is apparently an instinct of the crowd to hope for the
worst, and this instinct is communicable to individuals.

The fate of the Petition was even more ignominious than
that of the projected procession.   Even before its presentation

[1] *Letters of Queen Victoria*, Vol. II, p. 168.
[2] Quoted in Holyoake's *Bygones worth Remembering*, chap. vii.

voices had been heard to suggest that the alleged total number of signatures—5,706,000, according to O'Connor's most frequent estimate—was largely inflated. Some ingenious but anonymous person wrote to the *Times* to point out that the total number of adult males in Great Britain was just 300,000 less than the number of signatures. The Government worked on the line suggested by these doubters. The Petition was immediately on its arrival handed over to a staff of clerks, who counted up the signatures and found that there were no more than 1,975,496. On April 13 the Committee on Public Petitions presented its report. It stated that large numbers of signatures on consecutive sheets were in the same handwriting ; and that a large number of distinguished individuals whose allegiance to Chartism had been completely unsuspected had put their names to the Petition. Among these, the Committee grieved to find Victoria Rex [*sic*], April 1, the Duke of Wellington, Sir Robert Peel, and Colonel Sibthorp. Another class of signatures was represented by a few specimens, such as No Cheese, Pugnose, Flatnose, Punch. And " there are other words and phrases which, though written in the form of signatures, and included in the number reported, your Committee will not hazard offending the House and the dignity and decency of their own proceedings by reporting, though it may be added that they are obviously signatures belonging to no human being." The Committee did not even give O'Connor's estimate of the weight of the Petition the benefit of the doubt. He had declared that it weighed five tons ; the Committee, after trial, reduced the estimate to five hundredweight and three-quarters.

O'Connor was in the House when these devastating facts were published. He immediately rose and challenged them, suggesting that the bogus signatures had been inserted by spies for the purpose of discrediting the remainder, and that the thirteen clerks employed by the Committee on Petitions could not possibly have counted nearly two million signatures in the time. He was, however, entirely unsupported by any sympathizers. One member after another rose to denounce the Petition and the petitioners. Cripps, a member of the Com-

mittee on Petitions, declared that he could never believe O'Connor again, whereupon the latter protested against being held
personally responsible for the affair and left the House. A
wrangle then took place on the subject of the dignity of the
House, which was terminated by the arrest of O'Connor by
the Serjeant-at-Arms, and apologies to the House from him
and from Cripps.[1] On Tuesday, April 11, the Convention
reassembled, and confessed itself neatly trapped on the
previous day, by the valve-like action of the bridges. O'Connor was away, ill, after the strenuous days he had passed in
and out of the House. The Convention decided that the
National Assembly should consist of 100 members, seventy-
eight of whom would be delegates chosen in the same manner
as the members of the Convention, and the other twenty-two
of whom would be elected by the trade unions. There was
some talk of joining forces with an Irish National Assembly
of 300 members which was being mooted, but nothing was
decided. On Wednesday the Convention received the offer
by letter of a large bribe from O'Connor, who offered to give
up the profits of *The Northern Star* for the support of the
Convention. Acceptance of this would, of course, have placed
the Convention in O'Connor's pocket, but the delegates knew
better and unanimously declined the offer. O'Connor put in
a brief appearance in the afternoon and declared that " between
400,000 and 500,000 people " had been present on Kennington
Common. He referred to the Crown and Government Security
Bill, denouncing it vigorously. If it was passed, he promised
to become a republican, although he had always previously
contended for a constitutional monarchy. Once more he
spoke of the benefits which the Charter would bring, in terms
remarkably similar to those in which Shakespeare makes Jack
Cade address his followers. On Thursday, the Convention

---

[1] Hansard, Vol. 98, 284–301. O'Connor, in the course of his speech,
is reported, e.g., in *The Northern Star* of April 15, 1848, to have said
" he did not believe he would have any difficulty in obtaining a petition
upon the same subject by 10,000,000, or double or treble that number."
It should be pointed out that Hansard reports no such statement,
which presumably emanated from a hostile source.

decided to send Leach, Kydd and M'Grath over to Ireland as
missionaries, to invite the middle classes and the Irish to be
represented in the National Assembly, and to ask the trade
unions to support the Charter. On Friday, the 14th, O'Connor again appeared and attempted to explain away the fiasco
of the Petition, which had been exposed in the Commons the
day before. He repeated the argument that 1,900,000 signatures could not have been counted by thirteen clerks in the
time stated, and attempted to make out that the report of the
Committee was deliberately fraudulent. The Government
was verging on a financial crisis, therefore his advice to the
Chartists was to go on petitioning, as the Cabinet would have
to make concessions to the people to avoid coming down with
a crash. His statement appears to have met with a slightly
critical reception ; several delegates did not like either the
suggestion of more petitioning, or that of memorializing the
Queen. A discussion ensued as to the actual number of signatures, and it appeared that many thousands had not been presented, having been delayed. On Saturday, April 15, a memorial
to the Queen was adopted ; it was to be laid before the country
at the simultaneous meetings. This document briefly recited
the grievances of the working classes of Great Britain and
Ireland, and declared that the Government was attempting
to take away the liberties of the subject, " arraying class against
class," and bringing forward " the Gagging Bill, falsely deno-
minated a Bill for the better security of your Majesty's Crown
and Government . . . conceived in the spirit of that tyrannical
dynasty, whose expulsion led to the introduction of your
Majesty's family to the British throne." The memorial therefore prayed for the dissolution of the present Parliament, and
for the appointment of a Cabinet in sympathy with the Charter.[1]
During its third week the proceedings of the Convention de-
scended to complete triviality. The National Assembly was
postponed until May 1. On April 22 the Crown and Government Security Bill, having passed through all its stages, was
made law. O'Connor addressed meetings in Manchester and
Nottingham. The Convention adjourned on April 25, the

[1] *Northern Star*, April 15, 1848.

majority of the delegates having already left London in order
to address the simultaneous meetings.

On Monday, May 1, the National Assembly met at the John
Street Institute. Dixon was put into the chair, and Shirren
was made secretary. The delegates at first numbered twenty-
nine, and had virtually all been members of the late Convention,
the exceptions were quite unimportant. The members of the
Assembly met as the chosen of public meetings, and were
therefore entirely unrepresentative. The first two days were
mostly occupied with the reports of the delegates as to the
conditions of their constituencies, as observed in the course
of their lecturing tours. On its third day the Assembly considered the necessity of a programme. M'Douall moved that
the Assembly should receive a programme stating the Chartist
policy in relation to social and political grievances, industrial
and commercial questions, education, the Church, the criminal
code, and the freedom of the press, in addition, of course, to
the business for which the Assembly had been brought into
life. Led by Ernest Jones, however, the majority refused to
touch anything not immediately connected with the enactment
of the Charter, and adopted a programme drafted accordingly.
During its second week the Assembly reorganized the N.C.A.
and elected a provisional new Executive, consisting of M'Crae,
Jones, Kydd, Leach, and M'Douall. The prevailing atmosphere
was distinctly unfriendly to O'Connor, who stayed away,
addressing meetings in his defence in the provinces, and attemp-
ing to organize a fund to run a daily paper, to be called the
Democrat. On Saturday, May 13, the Assembly dissolved itself.
The memorial to the Queen was presented through the post,
as the authorities, in accordance with the " established practice," would not allow it to be handed over by the delegates
in person. Resolutions, more or less academic, were adopted,
and an address to the people was unanimously passed for
publication. The one achievement of the Assembly was the
reconstitution of the N.C.A., in the circumstances an altogether unconstitutional action, as the authority of the body
was not derived from the N.C.A., and the delegates were not
necessarily members of it. This move, however, had much to

recommend it. The new N.C.A. was to consist of groups of ten : each group to select a leader, who with nine other leaders, formed an upper circle, which was again under a tenth of its members and so on. This scheme had the advantage of keeping the members in touch with the central organization. *The Northern Star* began to devote itself to the affairs of Ireland and of Europe, and Chartism sank rapidly into a lethargic condition.

It was awakened suddenly at the beginning of June by reports of the arrests of several of its leaders for violence of language regarded as equivalent to sedition. Ernest Jones was one of the first, and with him Fussell and three others. A number of arrests were made in various parts of Yorkshire. Towards the end of May the Government once more began to fear a Chartist outbreak. Inflammatory meetings on Clerkenwell Green were coming to be of nightly occurrence, and were as often as not accompanied by minatory processions into the City and towards Westminster. The result of these prosecutions was to drive the insurrectionary section of the movement underground. North of England Chartists met in cellars and came out of them armed with pikes. Several arrests were made in Manchester, Liverpool, Birmingham, and Bradford ; in each case the police seized a quantity of these picturesque but harmless weapons. In September a Committee of fourteen Chartists was arrested in the Angel Tavern in Webber Street, Blackfriars, on the information of certain police spies. A small quantity of arms and ammunition was found on this occasion. Other arrests and seizures were made in Great Ormond Street, Holborn, and York Street, Westminster. Powell, the informer responsible for these arrests, was an obvious and blatant perjurer, and came out very badly in cross-examination. He had acted as *agent provocateur*, and had himself made and given away bullets and powder to the Chartists against whom he afterwards informed. However, four prisoners were sentenced to transportation for life, and fifteen, Ernest Jones among them, were sentenced to two years' imprisonment. A larger number received lighter sentences, or were merely bound over. In Manchester, about the same time, P. M. M'Douall was sentenced to two years' imprisonment. Towards the end of the year almost wholesale arrests took place in the North, the attempted rising of Smith O'Brien in Ireland having by this time reduced the Government to a condition bordering on hysteria. In Liverpool John West was sentenced to one year's imprisonment, and James Leach to nine months. There were in all sixty-five Chartists tried here at a single special assizes in December, on charges gently graduated from conspiracy downwards. In Edinburgh and Glasgow the same thing happened. The greater number of these trials depended on the evidence of police spies and *agents provocateurs*. By the end of the year these had exhausted their information, and the prosecutions ceased. It is possible that these arrests were the result of the Government's fear of something more dangerous than a demonstration. Both Thomas Cooper[1] and Thomas Frost[2] have fearsome tales to tell of individuals who, assisted by police spies, attempted to work up violent outbreaks. Certainly some new motive had been brought into action. As in 1839 wholesale arrests were made, and in that year the judges and magistrates who tried the prisoners were unanimously severe in inflicting sentences.

It is not necessary to record at length the different stages of shattered helplessness into which the Chartist movement degenerated with the arrest of its leaders. Hume attempted to bring the Government to accept a compromise—the " Little Charter," or household suffrage. On Tuesday, May 23, 1848, he brought forward a motion in the House of Commons with reference to the extension of the franchise to householders. The moment was not propitious. The day's proceedings had begun with a motion by Lord George Bentinck for the adjournment of the House from its rising until the following Thursday, on the ground that Wednesday was to be Derby Day. There had been a little opposition, from Hume, Bright, and Fox Maule, on the ground that the House had its time very fully occupied. This plea, however, was regarded as frivolous by Lord John Russell, who could not understand how anybody

---

[1] *Life of Thomas Cooper*, chap. xxvii.
[2] *Forty Years' Recollections*, pp. 143–165.

could possibly wish to discuss such things as the Law of Entail in Scotland on a " national *fête*," and the House agreed with him, 103 voting for adjournment and 90 against. With the prospect of a holiday before them, members were not, by the time Hume's motion was brought on after 11 p.m., in a mood to discuss household enfranchisement with any enthusiasm, and the mover had to content himself with a promise to try again on June 20. O'Connor followed, and attacked Hume for this postponement. Cobden rose to Hume's defence and told the House that O'Connor " has done more to retard the political progress of the working classes of England than any other public man that ever lived in this country." Lord John Russell then stepped in, and the subject dropped.[1]

For the rest, Ernest Jones was grossly ill-treated in prison. O'Connor, after the exposure of his ill-usage, was allowed to purchase Jones a certain alleviation of the conditions of his imprisonment. Owen published a lengthy constitution and code of laws for a perfect state of society, apparently with the usual hope. The Land Company's proceedings were centred round the report of the Select Committee. O'Connor addressed meetings and quarrelled. The revolutionary tide had ebbed, and the land scheme no longer inspired. Chartism, in fact, returned to the hopeless position it had occupied four years earlier.

[1] Hansard, Vol. 98, 1848, 1307–12.

APPENDIX TO CHAPTER VIII

DELEGATES TO THE CONVENTION
OF APRIL 4, 1848

J. P. Wilkinson, Exeter.
S. G. Francis, Ipswich.
M. Stevenson, Bolton.
Ernest Jones, Halifax.
Jas. Hutchins, Wigan.
Geo. Buckby, Leicester.
G. J. Harney, Nottingham.
Jos. Jinney, } Birmingham.
J. A. Fussell, }
Samuel Kydd, Oldham.
D. Donovan, } Manchester.
Jas. Leach, }
Edmund Jones, } Liverpool.
Henry Smith, }
Dr. Hunter, } Edinburgh.
Jas. Cumming, }
Jas. Graham, Dundee.
J. T. Lund, Lancaster.
F. Mirfield, Barnsley.
Jas. Watson, Newcastle.
W. Ashton, Northampton.
Thos. Tattersall, Bury.
John West, Stockport.
E. Bevington, } Staffordshire
Edw. Sale, } Potteries.

Jas. Shirren, Aberdeen.
G. W. M. Reynolds, Derby.
Geo. Stevens, York.
Robert Cochrane, Paisley.
Jas. Adams, Glasgow.
C. M'Carthy, Irish Democratic
  Confederation.
Chas. Baldwin, Bath.
D. Lightowler, Bradford.
F. O'Connor, } Leeds.
J. Shaw, }
John Lowery, Carlisle.
D. Thomas, Merthyr.
R. Wild, Ashton-under-Lyne.
Edw. Walter, Worcester.
Wm. Cuffay, }
H. Child, } London.
B. O'Brien, }
J. Petrie, Plymouth.
Dixon, Norwich.
Murphy, Huddersfield.
Tanner, Totnes.
Glenister, Cheltenham.

CHAPTER IX

THE PASSING OF CHARTISM

THE majority of the historical works dealing with the last century regard April 10, 1848, as the day on which Chartism died. Even the massive work of Professor Dolléans deliberately comes to a stop on arriving at this date.

Historians are almost unanimous in regarding Kennington Common as the burial-ground of the movement, and the laugh that went up over the Petition as its funeral sermon. But the date is too early. It overlooks an essential episode in the evolution of the Chartist movement.

On April 8 Lovett attempted to revive the project of uniting the Chartists and the Radical middle-class men. He secured the support of Miall, Parry, Howitt, Vincent, Dr. Epps, Elt, Shaen, Lowery, and Neesom, and the People's League was the outcome. Place sadly remarks to Lovett on April 19 that " it will be some time to come before the words Chartism and Universal Suffrage will meet with favour in the direction you seem to be looking, and F. O'Connor will presently give both a more terrible blow than any or all they have yet received."[1] The People's League died in September, 1849,[2] apparently the result of the competition of its twin-brother, the People's Charter Union, the membership of which was largely duplicate. This organization was virtually the successor of the National Association, which was actually wound up in 1849,[3] after having been in a moribund condition since Lovett's resignation from the secretaryship in 1846. The People's Charter Union

[1] Place Collection, Set 47, 1848, Vol. I, fo. 327.
[2] Lovett, *Life and Struggles*, p. 349.
[3] P. 360.

held its first meeting at the Farringdon Hall on the evening
of April 10, 1848. Cooper was elected president, and Richard
Moore, treasurer. The Council included Hetherington, Watson, Holyoake and Collett. A little later on it was joined by
Dr. Black, who had now become private secretary to Sir William
Molesworth. The Council soon found itself negotiating with
Cobden on the subject of the Stamp Duties. In order to act
with greater freedom, ten members of the Council, on Cobden's
advice, formed themselves into an independent body, the
Newspaper Stamp Abolition Committee. This was in March,
1849. The ten co-opted Dr. Black and appointed Collett
secretary and Francis Place treasurer, Moore becoming chairman, and subsequently added to their number by the accession of prominent members both of the People's Charter Union
and of the N.C.A. Among these were Holyoake and James
Stansfeld, afterwards Chairman of the Local Government
Board. Black and Place prepared appeals and provided
statistical information. Little by little the Committee won
over the more progressive M.P.'s. In February, 1851, it decided to expand, and became the Association for the Repeal
of the Taxes on Knowledge, and invited members not necessarily belonging to the Chartist Movement. Milner-Gibson,
M.P., became President. Dr. Bowkett, John Bright, M.P.,
R. Cobden, M.P., Passmore Edwards, W. Ewart, M.P., Joseph
Hume, M.P., Thornton Hunt, G. H. Lewes, and several other
Radicals, in and out of Parliament, went on the Committee.
The Association gained its first victory in 1853, when the advertisement duty was repealed. The compulsory stamp on newspapers was repealed two years later. The paper duty followed
in 1861. Finally the last restrictions were removed in 1869,
and the year after the Committee met for the last time in the
house in Hart Street, Bloomsbury, where Richard Moore,
chairman for twenty-one years, had lived since his first participation in the Chartism Movement.[1]

Now this episode is of considerable importance, for it gives
the Chartist movement a definite character. We have read

[1] The complete story is to be found in C. D. Collet's *History of the
Taxes on Knowledge*, 2 vols, 1899.

Place's account of the evolution of the W.M.A., from the little Committee presided over by Place and Black, which had come into existence to fight the newspaper taxes. From the agitation against " the taxes on knowledge," intellectual working-class Chartism had arisen. To the agitation against the same taxes, intellectual working-class Chartism, eleven years later, returned. The same agitation, the same Committee. Place and Black, Hetherington, Watson and Moore all follow the same path. And we may be sure that Lovett and Vincent were with them, although they played no prominent parts in the renewed campaign. More than any other fact of the movement, this emergence from and return to the agitation against " the taxes on knowledge " marks Chartism as a protest against ignorance. Chartism had failed because the masses were not yet intelligent enough to realize the necessity of political enfranchisement. This, at least, was the view of the intellectual leaders of Chartism. Just as Lovett had given up political agitation for the far more wearing occupation of educating the young, so the other leaders gave up their parts in the struggle in order to secure that essential to the education of the people—a free press. For the next year or two Chartism, as an organization of the people, was quiescent. O'Connor's influence was waning. The other leaders of the N.C.A. were exhibiting an extraordinary quarrelsomeness, into the details of which it is not necessary to enter. On July 3, 1849, O'Connor moved that the " House do adopt the principles embodied in the People's Charter." Exactly forty members were present during the early part of the discussion. Once again the old assertions were repeated, and met by the old denials. O'Connor's speech on this occasion was one of his most closely-reasoned performances. Among his arguments he adduced that of the inadequate representation of working-class interests in a House constituted on the existing lines, and the unequal representation of the towns. Lord John Russell[1] replied at great length, and made out a case which was not merely negative, but was in fact a statement of the advantages of government by a social hierarchy as against government by

[1] Hansard, 1849, Vol. 106, 1268–1306.

the whole people. " I therefore meet the proposition of the Hon. Gentleman with a direct negative, conceiving that, if adopted, it would tend to the greatest evils, and that in adopting it we should run the risk of losing the liberties which we now possess, and that to do so would be a most foolish and unwise proceeding." On the division fifteen members, including tellers, supported the measure, and 224 voted against it.

On March 16, 1850, the National Reform League for the Peaceful Regeneration of Society came into existence, and at last Bronterre O'Brien had an organization to help him in the propagation of his views, which, incidentally, had by this time received the official assent of the N.C.A. and the Fraternal Democrats. The programme is too long to quote in full : it contains an assertion of the principles laid down in the Charter, a demand for the repeal of the Poor Law, a claim for the generous treatment of paupers, land nationalization and colonization, the National Debt to be paid off by a mortgage on the real estate of the country, nationalization of mines, fisheries, etc., a system of national credit to enable the people to borrow from national funds in order to set up as a cultivator, public market places, fixed prices, paper money based " either upon a corn or a labour standard," and a hint at wider schemes of nationalization, especially of railways, canals, bridges, docks, gasworks, waterworks, a more human code of laws, etc.

On July 11, 1850, O'Connor, once more and for the last time, brought forward a motion in support of the Charter, with a more than usually Socialist preamble. The motion, in fact, consisted in a series of postulates leading up to the Six Points. Just before O'Connor's discussion of this resolution, the House had refused leave by a small majority of the small number of Members present to William Ewart to bring in a Bill to abolish the punishment of death. O'Connor's first argument in support of his motion was that one way of putting an end to the crime of murder was to place the representative system on such a sound and representative basis as that every person in the kingdom should be represented in the House. He was not allowed to continue long in this strain ; the attendance had diminished beyond the requisite forty, and the House was counted out.[1] So, ingloriously, ended the parliamentary career of the Charter.

In the same month O'Connor began a great effort to revive Chartism and addressed meetings all over the country. Arnott, perhaps with a better grasp of the situation, raised the question of uniting into one body the N.C.A., the Fraternal Democrats, and the National Reform League.[2] A little later on a round table conference of these three bodies, in addition to the ephemeral Social Reform League, was suggested, but nothing came of this.[3] In August the Haynau affair took place. The Austrian General, whose behaviour in Italy and Hungary, especially his flogging of women, had gained for him a reputation in England which he probably did not suspect, happened to visit London. Anxious to see sights, he obtained through a friend an invitation to go over Barclay and Perkins's Brewery, Bankside. He arrived, accompanied by a nephew and an interpreter. The draymen, discovering his identity, inflicted a severe flogging upon the General, who escaped with great difficulty, and spent the brief remainder of his stay in England in bed. This incident, as it were, brought home to the English democracy the idea that there is a democracy of action and instinct, as of politics. It received an enormous amount of attention in Chartist papers and on Chartist platforms, and, in fact, throughout the English press, with the exception of the *Times* and the *Morning Chronicle*.

The election figures of the 1851 Executive are sadly smaller than those of earlier occasions ; they illustrate, too, O'Connor's fall from his once unchallenged position : Reynolds, 1,805 ; Harney, 1,774 ; Jones, 1,757 ; Arnott, 1,605 ; O'Connor, 1,314 ; Holyoake, 1,021 ; Davis, 818 ; Grassby, 811 ; Milne, 709. Thornton Hunt and Linton were unsuccessful candidates. Robert Owen, O'Brien, Cooper, Gerald Massey, and Kydd were nominated but refused to stand.[4] Davis resigned immediately after the election, and Hunt took his place. Manchester Chartism, feeling that the London Executive did not represent

---

[1] Hansard, Vol. 112, 1282–84.   [2] *Northern Star*, July 20, 1850.
[3] *Northern Star*, August 10, 1850.
[4] Ib., December 21, 1850.

it, virtually declared its independence, and held a conference
in January which, although solemnly repudiated by the Executive, turned out to be a small and harmless affair.   O'Connor
attended it, and was warmly received.   In London another
National Convention was arranged.   As before, there were to
be forty-nine delegates who were duly elected, and turned out
to be quite undistinguished.   The N.C.A., in fact, no longer
had room for enterprising Chartists, who now habitually formed
themselves into new societies which, on account of their small-
ness, had an appallingly high rate of mortality.   In addition
to those just named, we find references in 1851 to the National
Charter League (containing M'Grath, Clark, Dixon, and Doyle),
the Political and Social Propagandist Society, the Political
and Social Tract Society, and the Democratic and Social Conference.   The membership of the Convention, consisting of the
petite bourgeoisie of the movement, makes its performance the
more remarkable.

The main part of the work of the Convention was the adoption, bit by bit, of a programme of social reform.[1]   This began
with the demand for the establishment of a Board of Agriculture, and the restoration of " poor, common, church, and crown
lands to the people."   Land was to be purchased by the
Government, not confiscated.   The Church was to be separated
from the State, and disendowed of all its accessions made up
to the time of the Reformation.   Here, it will be seen, the
Chartists, drafting a confessedly ideal programme, hesitated
to go as far as the modern Church Disestablishers.   Education
was to be " national, universal, gratuitous, and to a certain
extent compulsory."   This compromise was arrived at after
much discussion, several of the delegates objecting to compulsory education, adducing arguments beneath which tacit
hositilty to the State as State can be detected.   All education,
from the University downwards, was to be free, the status of
co-operative societies was also discussed, and freedom of
association was claimed for them.   The National Debt was
repudiated ; no more interest was to be paid, but the capital
was to be repaid as interest.   Standing armies were condemned

[1] *Northern Star*, April 5, 1851.

on democratic principles, but recognized as unfortunate necessities, subject to considerable changes in the status of the private soldier. Universal training in the use of arms was next recommended. The question of compulsion and the conscientious objector came up on this point. The Convention decided that there should be no compulsion in this respect ; one delegate suggested that Quakers and others who shared their views on the use of arms should be given the opportunity of forming fire brigades. State support for the unemployed, pensions for the aged and infirm, to allow them to be kept in their own homes, provision of work for the unemployed, and if necessary, settlement upon the land, were proposed as measures which might take the place of the Poor Law, which was to be abolished. During the second week the Convention discussed a variety of matters, strongly opposed the death penalty, authorized a fund for the recall of Frost, Williams, and Jones, and so on. Finally another attempt was made to reorganize the N.C.A., and the Convention dissolved on April 10. A Committee set to work on the resolutions and knocked them into shape, making a neat programme out of them. Another National Petition was to be organized, but this time there were to be no fraudulent signatures ; simultaneous meetings were to be held, and the Chairmen were to count the number of those voting for the resolutions. Communications with the Trade Unions were to be initiated. In its final form the Chartist programme called for the nationalization of the land, and claimed that, as " labour was the creator of a nation's wealth," co-operative associations should have every encouragement. All taxation was to be upon land and accumulated property. A change in currency laws was demanded, but no details were provided : finally, measures making for the complete freedom of the press were recommended.

This programme was duly printed by the *Times*,[1] and Chartism, was reintroduced, after a lapse of three years, to the attention of the middle classes. Although by this time the membership of the N.C.A. had diminished to something in the neighbourhood of 4,000, both to the *Times* and

[1] *Times*, May 3, 1851.

the *Spectator* the adoption of the programme appeared to presage a renascence. The *Spectator* finished its review of the situation with these words : " Although standing with practical England in the remote and shadowy regions of ' isms,' neither Chartism or Socialism is quite the bugbear that it once was : common sense begins to regard each as a rude husk containing some kernel of truth, that may be worth analysis : a process in which even the *Times* begins to assist in a slashing bantering fashion."[1]

The adoption of this programme by the Convention is very remarkable in view of its personnel. The leaders were absent : O'Connor, on account of illness, put in but a few ineffective appearances, O'Brien was not a delegate. Thornton Hunt, Harney, Reynolds, Jones, and Holyoake, the most intellectual persons present, had previously given few signs of statesmanship. The delegates were not men committed to doctrinaire views on anything outside the Six Points. Certain unimportant amendments indicated a desire that Chartism should not be identified with any particular philosophy. Yet these men in these unpromising conditions agreed upon a programme which future generations of reformers spent much time, not in reshaping, but in laboriously rediscovering. One clause, not mentioned above, is of special interest. " Municipal and Parochial power should be vested in the hands of the people, since disenfranchisement in local matters is as unjust as the restriction of the elective franchise." Chartists were recommended, wherever possible, to contest local and municipal elections. But by this time the movement was in a state of flaccid senility, and unable to absorb strong new doctrines.

After the Convention the Chartist movement followed a downward path which had no obstacles. Lord John Russell was beginning to hint at reform, and his promises, added to the performances of Hume, now strongly agitating, in good middle-class company, for household suffrage and the ballot, satisfied the milder elements of the Chartist movement. The great Exhibition opening on May 2, 1851, was seriously expected by innumerable optimists to be the immediate precursor of

[1] April 26, 1851.

universal peace among the nations, and so attracted a good deal of attention away from the apparently unobtainable Charter. Feargus O'Connor was now clearly seen to be losing his hold upon the movement, and upon himself. In August he ceased to write the leading article in *The Northern Star*, contenting himself with occasional very short letters. Harassed by creditors, real and imaginary, and by the impossibility of paying the steadily accumulating expenses of winding up the Land Company, he went abroad for some two months, and returned about the middle of October. This happened to be a few days before the arrival in England of the recently liberated Kossuth. The coming of the Hungarian patriot evoked immense excitement among the working classes, and a tumultuous series of receptions and demonstrations was immediately arranged to take place all over the country. In this movement O'Connor took as prominent a part as the state of his health and mind permitted. Before many weeks had passed, however, his behaviour at one of the numerous Kossuth banquets made his mental state obvious to all. Kossuth, fearing a repetition of O'Connor's eccentric behaviour towards himself, asked that he should be excluded from other demonstrations in his honour. It fell upon Holyoake and Hunt to put this desire into effect, and from them the Chartists learned that the current rumour as to their leader's mind was indeed true. At the end of December *The Northern Star* was sold to William Rider, its printer and publisher. Although O'Connor was re-elected to the Executive of the N.C.A. for 1852, he was no longer in a position to be of any use to it. In the early part of the year he paid the briefest of visits to the United States.

The remaining events of O'Connor's life may be conveniently described here. Justin MacCarthy gives a pathetic recollection of meeting O'Connor during this last period in Covent Garden market. His hair had turned white, his movements were restless and uncertain. He rambled from stall to stall, muttering to himself, handling the fruit, bursting into meaningless laughs and walking on.[1]

[1] *Reminiscences*, Vol. 2, p. 261.

On June 8, 1852, O'Connor's behaviour in the House became excessive ; he was named by the Speaker, and apologized to him and the House. On the 14th a Petition was received from his sister, expressing her belief that her brother was of unsound mind.[1] He then was removed to a private asylum in Chiswick, kept by one Dr. Harrington Tuke. In August, 1855, Miss Margaret O'Connor, the sister of the unfortunate man, became dissatisfied with his treatment and effected his removal to her own house in Albert Terrace, Notting Hill, virtually by force. O'Connor was then in a perfectly helpless condition, and the circumstances of his removal hastened his end, which took place on August 30, ten days later. He was penniless at the time of his death ; even the cost of his funeral had to be defrayed by his friends, a committee of whom afterwards got up a public subscription for a memorial. On the day of his burial London was in a highly excited state on account of the long-awaited news of the fall of Sevastopol. A long procession followed him to Kensal Green, where William Jones, a Liverpool workman, and cousin of the deceased, delivered an impassioned graveside speech.[2]

To return to the N.C.A., the voting for the 1852 Committee gave the following results : Ernest Jones, 900 ; John Arnott, 720 ; Feargus O'Connor, 600 ; T. Martin Wheeler, 566 ; John Grassby, 565 ; John Shaw, 502 ; W. J. Linton, 470 ; J. J. Bezer, 456 ; and G. J. Holyoake, 336. Thornton Hunt (282) and P. M. M'Douall (198) were among the unsuccessful candidates.[3] Ernest Jones immediately retired, expressing himself as " unable to sit on an Executive Committee like the present,"[4] and insisting that the movement could not go on without the active co-operation of such men as Harney, Cooper, and Kydd. Linton also refused to act unless the Committee approved of union with the middle classes—which it did not. Wheeler cleared out at once, partly because of a lack of confidence in Arnott as secretary, partly because Holyoake had expressed

---

[1] Hansard, Vol. 122.

[2] *The People's Paper*, September 15, 22, 29, and October 6, 1855, contains biography. See also *Reynolds's Newspaper*, September 16, 1855.

[3] *Northern Star*, January 3, 1852. [4] January 10, 1852.

a lack of confidence in Wheeler, having once seen him drunk. The depleted Committee, foreseeing the worst, gave up its office at 14, Southampton Street, Strand ; appointed Grassby its temporary honorary secretary in place of Arnott, and thenceforth held its meetings at his house at 96, Regent Street, Lambeth. The Committee was in debt for a sum of between £30 and £40, and honourably spent its last efforts in raising this amount—a feat which took about six months for its accomplishment. After this we hear no more about the Executive of the N.C.A.

Ernest Jones, however, did not despair of the movement, and attempted to revive it in Manchester. There a minute Conference was held from May 17–21, 1852, attended by local and midland delegates, and by Jones and James Finlen from London. This assumed the guidance of the N.C.A., revised its constitution, reduced the size of the Executive to three, who were to be paid 30s. weekly and travelling expenses. As missionaries it was hoped that they would revive the movement. The Executive was to be elected for a period of six months. The result of the first election was Gammage,[1] 922 ; Finlen, 839 ; Jones, 739. These went on tour for some months and worked prodigiously. Jones started a weekly, *The People's Paper*, and for a while all went well, but the conduct of this paper, the management of its finances, and the alleged ambition of its editor to be the dictator of the Chartist movement soon caused a quarrel. As the result of this, the next contested election of the Executive, in March 1854, was accompanied by immense gerrymandering, according to Gammage, who was pushed out of the triumvirate.[2] In any case, Jones, Finlen and John Shaw were declared elected on a second count, which presented gigantic discrepancies from the first. Jones's vote rose from 759 to 942, Gammage's place fell from third to fourth.

---

[1] R. G. Gammage, the author of *The History of the Chartist Movement*, was a self-educated man, who rose from coach-building to be a doctor. He had taken an energetic but uninfluential part in the Chartist movement since 1842, and was a strong admirer of O'Brien and (until the events recorded above) of Jones.

[2] Gammage, *History*, p. 397, etc.

Shaw does not appear to have done very much after his election, and Jones and Finlen, in effect the former, carried the banner single-handed against the gale.

The Northern Star policy in the hands of its new owners was only intermittently sympathetic with Chartism. A leading article suggests that " As a system, Chartism has degenerated, its ranks have been disbanded, and the principles cast upon the wide world for every would-be statesman to mock and sneer at. This is the present of Chartism. For all moral effects, it is practically deceased. Its carcase stinks in the nostrils of men."[1] In January, 1852, it attempted to woo the Trade Unions by publishing Strike news and reports of meetings. Much attention is paid to the co-operative movement, and the Christian Socialists. Matters however went from bad to worse. Every sort of editorial device was called into play to keep the paper going. In March it became the *Star and National Trades' Journal*. Two months later it became the *Star of Freedom*, and lowered its price to 4½d. Harney bought the paper cheaply and for the second time was the editor. In August he changed the format and the type, giving the *Star* a pleasant appearance similar to that of the *Spectator* but with slightly larger pages. But his readers would not hear of Chartism. In vain he gave the public what it wanted. At the moment the working classes were feverishly excited over Australian gold diggings. So Harney wrote up Australian gold. The public resolutely refused to have any connexion with any paper with a Chartist taint, and in November, 1852, the *Star* appeared for the last time. Harney promised that its demise would be of a temporary nature, but the promise was unredeemable. In its last issues it contained attacks by Harney on Jones. That no two prominent Chartists could work together for more than a year or so without quarrelling is one of the tragedies of their movement.

The People's Paper at threepence weekly was naturally a contributing cause to the breakdown of *The Northern Star*. The new paper was published ostensibly in the interests of the N.C.A., declared to be, in the first number, " the greatest and

---

[1] *Northern Star*, November 22, 1857.

noblest benefit society of the world." Jones gave far more attention to Chartist doings than his competitor, and gave special prominence to the Metropolitan Delegate Council, a nominally representative body of London Chartists, which, while completely ineffective, staved off the hour of dissolution for an unexpectedly long time. A peculiar interest is given to *The People's Paper* by the fact that Marx, who apparently enjoyed the complete confidence of Jones, gradually became the acknowledged source of its editor's ideas and information. The paper had not been established many weeks when articles in support of land nationalization and other distinctively Socialist tenets began to appear. By the beginning of 1853 it was urging the " nationalization of credit," by which was apparently meant State loans to incipient co-operative undertakings. Early in 1853, Thomas Cooper returned for a while to the movement, but merely to lecture to it, not to guide it. In March, 1853,[1] there was an interesting article entitled " Sutherland and Slavery " by " Dr. Charles Marx," describing the manner in which the Sutherland family had acquired its domains. Other articles, apparently from the same pen, are signed with the initials " M." or " C. M.," or are introduced as by " a well-known foreign politician, at present in London." The outward and visible signs of Marx are, however, less clear than the inward meaning of the paper's teaching. Articles on the class struggle and surplus value (not yet so called) alternate with others on the history of the National Debt and emigration. In 1853 *The People's Paper* begins to develop a bitterly anti-Russian tone. For this, too, Marx was probably very largely responsible. David Urquhart, now a Member of Parliament, had by no means learned to mitigate his hatred of Russia. Considered insane by many, he became a bosom friend of Marx, who, doubtless, passed on his opinions to Ernest Jones. So, between one doctrine and another, *The People's Paper* laboriously managed to rise to a circulation of some three or four thousand within a few years. This was by dint of immense efforts on the part of Jones, who was scarcely ever

[1] *People's Paper*, March 3, 1853.

in a position to say with certainty that he could keep the paper going for another month.

In 1854 an episode took place of some interest as illustrating the tendency of Chartist evolution, although of little direct importance. This was the " Mass Movement," with which Jones was prominently associated. The idea was one of the innumerable anticipations of the General Federation of Trade Unions. On March 6, 1854, the Labour Parliament met in Manchester. The Conference which had adopted this grandiloquent title was a gathering of Chartist and Trade Union delegates, who gave the Mass Movement an organization and a programme. The principal object of the Movement was the raising of a strike fund. The great Engineering lock-out of 1852, and the unsuccessful strikes of the Preston cottonspinners, and the Kidderminster carpet weavers the following year, had made such a fund greatly to be desired. The Labour Parliament wished the fund to be used for other additional purposes, of which one was the purchase of estates to be sublet to trade unionists, as a remedy for unemployment. A long programme was drawn up in support of several items of labour legislation, but, curiously enough, labour representation was not demanded, or even mentioned. On the proposal to buy land, Joseph Harrison, a Nottinghamshire farmer, declared that since the failure of the National Land Company, 300 land schemes had sprung up, and there were half a dozen around Nottingham.[1] Marx and Louis Blanc had been invited to attend as honorary members, but both sent polite letters regretting their inability to be present. The Labour Parliament concluded its proceedings by electing an executive of five : Finlen heading the poll. Jones was appointed honorary member of the executive. Three of the five (including Finlen) were set to work as missionaries and sent out to tour the country. The first and only thing the executive attempted was the formation of the United Brothers' Industrial, Sick, Benefit, and Life Assurance Company, which was to give slightly larger benefits than other insurance companies. The Mass Movement did not live long. For a month or two, about

[1] *People's Paper*, March 11, 1854.

£20 flowed in weekly, then the current slackened. The second
Labour Parliament, which was to have met in Nottingham, in
August, never materialized.

The Crimean War was now occupying the attention of the
British public. Jones and Finlen promulgated the " Soldiers'
Charter," demanding promotion from the ranks, better pay,
abolition of flogging, and higher pensions to ex-soldiers. In
February, 1855, Jones had another access of internationalism,
as one result of which he quarrelled with Finlen ; the two were,
however, soon reconciled, and co-operated in organizing an
international meeting at St. Martin's Hall, on February 27,
1855, to commemorate the revolutions of 1848. At this
meeting Herzen was the most distinguished of the foreign
speakers. Victor Hugo had promised to be present, but the
death of a brother at the last moment forced him to remain in
Jersey. He sent along a written oration, however, a deluge of
exclamation marks, which was read to the meeting. Perhaps
the most noteworthy sentiment it contained was " the least
possible amount of governing, is the formula of the future."[1]
Saffi, one of the Roman triumviri with Mazzini, also sent a
written speech.

In July, 1855, Jones, in deference to N.C.A. branch opinion,
held an election for the executive, as the result of which he,
Finlen, and Abraham Robinson were elected " by large majorities," and John Shaw lost his seat. The numbers voting are
not given, but from certain figures[2] it is fairly obvious that a
few score votes only were cast. Jones and Finlen showed no
disposition to allow Robinson a share in the management, such
as it was, of the movement. The Manchester Chartists protested against the exclusive character of the Jones-Finlen
régime, but were answered as follows :[3] " with respect to the
third member; we should be happy to have his aid—but we
would decline to associate in our plans any one we had not first
tried and deeply tested. . . ." The two then went on to
explain that a movement was much better governed by two
than by three and suggested that the ideal arrangement was

[1] People's Paper, March 10, 1855.
[2] Ib., September 1, 1855.
[3] Ib., March 22, 1856.

that two be " in office on good behaviour, with no polling lists, no show of strength or weakness." If the other Chartists did not like it they could hold another Convention and elect another executive. The dispute ended with the adoption by Jones and Finlen of the motto " Personal confidence under popular control."[1]

In 1856 John Frost returned to England. He had been liberated two years earlier, on condition that he did not set foot in British dominions, and had gone to America. Now at last he was allowed to return. His coming caused something of a revival among the " Old Guards," but not to the extent expected by Jones. Frost, now seventy years old, was much more deeply interested in procuring a reform of the transportation system under which he had suffered, than in Chartist propaganda, and was virtually lost to the movement. He died in 1877, aged well over ninty. The Crimean War continued to hold the attention of the public. Jones used *The People's Paper* to popularize the ideas of the National Sunday League. In February, Finlen settled in Glasgow as a newsagent, became reconciled with Gammage, with whom on account of the disparaging references to Jones in Gammage's *History of the Chartist Movement* a quarrel had taken place a year or two earlier, and the two ex-associates made preparations to publish a new *Northern Star*, to the intense fury of Jones. He stood for Nottingham as Chartist candidate in the General Election of March, 1857, but was badly beaten by Paget and Walter, the Palmerstonian Liberal sitting Members.

In the early autumn of this year Jones made his last effort to galvanize the defunct organization of Chartism back to life. He announced another Conference, advertising it as widely as the resources of *The People's Paper* allowed. Long lists were printed of the well-known ex-Chartists, middle-class sympathizers and others who were to be invited. Frost was asked to preside, but refused. The response was feeble, but Jones persisted, and at last was able to hold the conference.

The last Conference of Chartist delegates was held in St. Martin's Hall, London, and lasted the whole week beginning

---

[1] *People's Paper*, April 5, 1856.

February 8, 1858. Although some forty delegates were present, their total constituency, according to *Reynolds's Newspaper*,[1] only amounted to about 500. Certainly a few at least of those present could only be said to represent by stretching the usual meaning of the term. Apparently Bubb, the delegate for Bermondsey, and treasurer of the Conference, was elected by a meeting of five, of whom two voted against him. Ernest Jones and Holyoake were the only Chartists present whose names convey anything. The object of the proceedings was to effect that political union of the working and middle classes on the basis of a common agitation which had been striven for by so many Chartists since the intervention of Sturge. The middle classes, however, hardly responded to the Chartist appeal. Samuel Morley and Robert Owen appear to have been the only non-Chartists of the one hundred and fifty invited middle-class politicians who took part in the discussion. The Conference passed resolutions supporting the union, and appointed a new executive to carry on the movement. After some controversy as to the most efficient size of this body, the Conference decided that an executive of one would best meet the exigencies of the case. Ernest Jones was thereupon elected the Chartist executive. He might equally well have been appointed the movement's executor. The most interesting speech at this assembly was made by Robert Owen, now eighty-seven years old. As reported in *The People's Paper*, " He was there as a delegate, and he was there as an invited guest. He was in favour of the whole of the Charter. As a Chartist he recommended them not to give up a single point. As a friend of the working classes, he advised them as a matter of expediency to accept what the middle classes offered in reason. The best thing that could be done for the working classes would be to give them a highly beneficial education."[2] The Conference decided to raise a £100 fund for lecturers. The object for which it had met was achieved, in theory, by the

---

[1] February 14, 1858. The *People's Paper* of February 13 gives quite another account, and the week later attacked *Reynolds's Paper* for its falsehoods.

[2] *People's Paper*, February 13, 1858.

formation of the Political Reform League, as a compromise between the Chartists and the middle-class reformers. The programme was an acceptance of three points, a mitigation of two, and the deletion of the remaining one. It consisted of manhood suffrage, the ballot, abolition of the property quali-fication, triennial parliaments, and rearrangements of electoral districts. Jones for some months scoffed at this compromise, but finally yielded to necessity. *The People's Paper* became in May the property of the Political Reform League, and its treasurer J. Baxter; Langley its editor. Chartist news was cut down to occupy only a few columns. Jones, having left *The People's Paper*, once again tempted the fates by starting the *London News* in the very month of his departure. *The People's Paper* died in September; the *London News* survived it only by two months.

Of those present at the pathetic Conference of February, 1858, there came some as delegates of trade unions. *Reynolds's Newspaper* suggests that Chartism was by no means as dead as this Conference would appear to indicate, but implies rather that the great body of Chartist opinion as ever averse to the proposed union was deliberately excluded by the organizers of the Conference. If this was the case the singular inertness of the un—or misrepresented section of the movement can only be explained by the theory that about this time it died noiselessly and peacefully in its sleep. After 1858 the references to Chartism in *Reynolds's Newspaper* occur principally in obi-tuary notices. Organized Chartism may be said to have died just before reaching years of discretion. The attitude of *Reynolds's Newspaper*, which we have called to witness, was now hostile to the movement, because of the personal hostility of G. W. M. Reynolds to Jones. In July, 1859, this led to a libel action, when Jones was awarded damages from Reynolds for an accusation, made in the defendant's paper, of having pilfered from the funds of *The People's Paper*. After this time Jones earned his living at the Manchester bar.

By imperceptible degrees the agitations for the Six Points (now five) had split up into fragments; in 1858 and the follow-ing years, Miall, Muntz and other reformers in and about the

House of Commons were running the Parliamentary Reform Committee, which held meetings and organized public opinion in support of household suffrage. About the same time Perronet Thompson, M.P., now a Major-General, was at the head of the Ballot Society, whose name explains its object. John Bright was the most active of all in the propaganda of franchise reform, both in and out of Parliament. Annual Parliaments had vanished from the list of things desired by the working classes. The theory that a General Election should be an annual performance had a distant and respectable origin. When old age reduced Bentham's writings to all but insurmountable masses of neologisms and incomprehensible formulas, his disciples had taken upon themselves the editing of his books. Francis Place, himself by no means the most incisive of writers, had knocked into shape Bentham's plan of Parliamentary Reform, which urged " Annuality of Parliaments."

By the beginning of the eighteen sixties, a new group of young men was coming forward to take the lead in English industrial politics. George Odger, William Allan, Randal Cremer (subsequently knighted), George Howell, Robert Applegarth and their associates remodelled the trade union movement, made a beginning of labour representation, and with Karl Marx in 1864 founded the International Working Men's Association, that great stimulating force of the late 'sixties. Jones makes a thin link between this group and organized Chartism. In April, 1864, it happened that Garibaldi visited England, in an interval of his great struggle for Italian unity. Jones, Odger, Howell, and Edmond Beales attempted to hold a welcome meeting on Primrose Hill, but the Government were extremely nervous on account of Garibaldi's presence in the country : too many young men were professing republicanism to suit Palmerston. Garibaldi was therefore spirited out of the country ; and, acting on the same principle, the Primrose Hill meeting was broken up by the police. The Committee did the wisest thing possible in the circumstances : it retired to a public-house.[1] Here the Reform League was started, for

---

[1] Howard Evans, *Life of Sir R. Cremer*, p. 42 : B. Wilson, *Struggles of an Old Chartist*, p. 26. Finlen was one of the first lecturers and agents appointed by the League.

the purpose of obtaining manhood suffrage and the ballot. This new body attracted to itself the remaining energetic Chartists. Prominent among these was J. B. Leno, a young printer-poet, who had come forward in 1850, and who had about 1858 started a little Society called the Propagandists, a circle of youthful Chartists, whom he now swept into the Reform League. This organization was responsible for the demonstration of July 23, 1866, for ever to be remembered as the occasion when the Hyde Park railings were pushed down by the crowd.[1]

Jones died in 1868, on the eve of the General Election, at which Manchester had offered him a safe seat. Our vision of him, as of so many of his associates, is distorted by the incessant quarrels in which he was concerned. Yet, it is impossible to deny to Jones the possession of a quite extra-ordinarily developed gift of political sagacity. Like O'Connor and many others, he gave up all he had for the Cause. " It was said that Mr. Jones and other Chartist lecturers were making plenty of money out of us, but there was not a worse paid lot of men in the country than they were . . . Mr. Harney often lecturing in this district (Halifax) . . . sent for a Mr. Burns, a tailor, to mend his trousers whilst he remained in bed. Mr. Kydd . . . had to sit in a shoemaker's shop in this town whilst his shoes were repaired. On one of Mr. Jones's visits . . . the person who had his boots to clean noticed that his boots were worn out . . . on another occasion we had to buy him a new shirt and front before he could appear at the meeting."[2] It appears that an uncle disinherited Jones of £2,000 a year on account of his opinions. Such men as Jones

---

[1] Out of the Reform League there grew, in February, 1866, the London Working Men's Association, the membership of which was largely composed of trade unionists. The secretary was Robert Hartwell, one of the original members of the original W.M.A. and a delegate to the 1839 Convention, a compositor by trade. It was Hartwell who first raised the subject of Labour Representation, and organized the first labour candidatures. He himself stood unsuccessfully at Lambeth and elsewhere, and was virtually ruined by election expenses. (Chapter iii, A. W. Humphrey, *A History of Labour Representation*.)

[2] B. Wilson, *Struggles of an old Chartist*, p. 20.

T

cannot be dismissed as merely quarrelsome and self-centred; their tenacity alone outweighs these characteristics.

We have now followed the main stem as far as is practicable. The remaining filiations of Chartism are at least as important. The end of a great social or political movement is never its death. The history of a theory does not follow a path from birth to death, but a transition from rather more error to rather more truth. The growth and reproduction of truth bears an exact resemblance to the methods of propagation of the more primitive micro-organisms, for like them ideas are fissiparous and therefore for all practical purposes immortal. That is why no movement ever really dies, and the reason why no satisfactory date or definition can be given to the latter end of Chartism, which shaded off into other movements, of which the most important are to be described.

"In 1851 Mr. Holyoake first made use of the term Secularist as more appropriate and distinctive than Atheist, and in 1852 he commenced organizing the English free-thinkers according to the principles of Secularism."[1] For a time Thomas Cooper helped him, until one day in January, 1856, he had been engaged to give a course of Sunday lectures at the Secularist head-quarters, the Hall of Science, Old Street, London, E.C., on the different countries of Europe. He had spoken on the first occasion on Russia and the Russians, on the second it was to be the turn of Sweden and the Swedes.[2] On the evening in point he struggled hard to articulate, but had to give it up. He could not talk about Sweden, he had been converted and felt compelled to give testimony then and there. Thereafter Cooper became a Baptist and preached his newly-acquired religion for many years all over the country, incidentally debating the subject in public with his former friend Holyoake. Cooper died in harness in 1892, aged eighty-seven. Neesom also became a full-time secularist in 1853, and remained one until his death in 1861.[3]

Holyoake and Bradlaugh (although they differed between

---

[1] Flint, *Anti-Theistic Theories*, p. 510.
[2] *Life of Thomas Cooper*, p. 353.
[3] *National Reformer*, July 20, 27, 1861.

themselves) stand out as two phenomena due entirely to the Chartist movement. Through it they harked back to the agitation in the early part of the century, when Carlile and Hone were struggling for free-thought. The old secularist movement had one peculiar characteristic which distinguishes it from whatever can claim to be its successor. The old free-thinkers really did stand for freedom of thought. The early and mid-Victorian atheists were not merely men who raised their voices against God : they struggled against blasphemy laws and the dead hand of a temporarily inert and apathetic State Church. They were undoubtedly sincere, even though their insistent claim to call their souls their own took the eccentric form of denying that they had souls at all. When the Church had reformed itself, and the press had become comparatively free, secularism drooped and disappeared. To-day the forces of organized free-thought would scarcely make a decent funeral cortège for the last of its leaders. We have apathy and spiritual deadness, but the man who attempts to convince his fellows that there is no God has practically vanished from society. It is characteristic of the two figures named above as typical products of Chartism that they should have quarrelled early and often.

The chief instrument in the transition from Chartism to Republicanism is W. J. Linton. In his *English Republic* [1] he gives a brief history of Chartism, and entitles the concluding section " What Remains ? " He calls the remaining Chartists to action. History, giving the meaning of thirty years' Chartism (so long existing, although unnamed), will say : " It was the utterance of a general want, a people's protest—nothing more. Very necessary the protest ; but to stop there. Thirty years' continual word-pouring and vociferation of a million and a quarter of men may surely be judged sufficient prologue to the work they declare necessary. . . . Begin now to prepare for work. The Chartist movement is as good as dead. . . We need now, not merely Chartists, but Republican Associatons.

" ' You would, then, oppose the present Chartist Associ-

[1] P. 83, 1851.

ations ? ' Not so ; but would form Republican Associations of the best men among them ; and so in time, I hope, supersede the present Associations by a more vital, a further-purposed and more powerful organization." Inspired by his friendship with Mazzini, Ledru-Rollin, and republican Poles without number, Linton failed to communicate his personal sentiments to any large number of followers. The Republican idea reached the people, to the slight extent to which they were reached by it, through other channels. Yet the Republican idea had never been completely absent from the Chartist movement. We read that in 1838,[1] " on Thursday evening, the 28th June (Coronation Day), a party of forty gentlemen, to show their contempt of the illuminations, and all the degraded foolery of coronations, invited that stern Republican, Dr. John Taylor, to a public supper in the Black Boy Tavern." After the events of 1848 the Republican sentiment could not well remain latent. But it lacked suitable propagandists, and until Bradlaugh had arrived at the fullness of his powers, the British working man was as apathetic towards the abolition of the monarchy as to the constitutional changes embodied in the People's Charter. And Bradlaugh came too late. He had listened to Lovett and fought with Holyoake on the question of an Atheist's duties towards himself and his neighbour, and occupied himself with other things until the impulse of 1848 had vanished. The events which took place in Paris in 1871 inflated English Republicanism for a brief while. The London Republican Club was founded on May 12, 1871, with Bradlaugh as president. But the Republicanism of this leader was too deeply imbued with his own individuality and his own individualist theories ever to take root. The slight " boom " in Republicanism which is noted as a feature of that time is connected with the Mordaunt case and *The Coming K*——. " The Republican movement in England was an eddy rather than a current."[2] The writer has been told by one of Bradlaugh's most trusted lieutenants that Bradlaugh confidently expected that the alleged misbehaviour of the Prince of Wales would lead to the refusal of

[1] *Northern Star*, July 7, 1838.
[2] H. A. L. Fisher, *The Republican Tradition in Europe*, p. 56.

the nation to allow him to succeed to the throne. Then, of course, the turn of Republicanism would come, and if Bradlaugh was offered the first Presidency, well then——. But, unfortunately for the scheme, Queen Victoria survived Bradlaugh, and at her death not a single voice was raised against her successor. And it must be admitted that the subsequent conduct of Edward VII was never conducive to the success of Republican propaganda, even had it been possible to revive that completely defunct movement.

Linton carried on Republican propaganda from Brantwood (afterwards the home of John Ruskin) until 1855, when he returned to London and the service of art, gaining a reputation as " the best wood engraver of the day." In 1866 he went to the United States, where he settled, giving himself entirely to the theory and practice of his art, and to producing charming little books of verse. He returned to England in 1887, but went back to the States and died there in 1895. His second wife was Mrs. Lynn Linton, the well-known novelist and antifeminist writer. Walter Crane was one of Linton's pupils.

Harney, working through different channels, did much to direct Chartist thought towards Republican ideals. After he had ceased his connexion with *The Northern Star*, Harney edited the *Democratic Review*, a monthly which kept alive from June, 1849, to September, 1850. This was succeeded by the short-lived *Red Republican*, noteworthy because it contained the first English translation of the Communist Manifesto of Marx and Engels. For many years Harney managed to keep a body and soul together by editing obscure periodicals, in England and the Channel Islands. He was always to the fore when any Republican business was afoot : thus we find him in Newcastle in April, 1854, among a local deputation which presented Garibaldi with a sword.[1] Harney, like Linton, his fellow-propagator of Republicanism, emigrated to the United States, but returned and worked for some years in the editorial office of the *Newcastle Daily Chronicle*. He died in Richmond, Surrey, in 1897.[2]

[1] Duncan's *Life of Joseph Cowen*, p. 24.
[2] G. J. Holyoake in *Notes and Queries*, 1902.

In the course of this study little mention has been made of Socialism, although many of the doctrines maintained by Chartist leaders have a distinctly Socialist flavour. Two facts must be borne in mind in this connexion. The word Socialism and Communism have exchanged their meanings since the Chartist period ; in those days Socialism was the generic term for schemes tending to establish a better state of Society by private action, independent of the State. The idea of a State in the hands of the people going beyond its earlier functions for the benefit of the people, now known as State Socialism, was not yet acclimatized. It came with Marx and Bronterre O'Brien, and required a generation to make the slightest impression on the mind of the working class. O'Brien is the first preacher of Socialism in the modern sense, although its economics had been invented in England and slightly diffused a generation earlier.[1] His Reform League did not live many years. For a time O'Brien edited Reynolds's Newspaper ; after he gave up this post he barely existed by lecturing for a few years, and died, in absolute poverty, at the end of 1864. Like him P. M. M'Douall, who had been another of the most popular men in the Chartist movement, died in extreme poverty ; in fact, about 1855, a fund had to be raised to keep his widow and child out of the workhouse.

Reference has already been made to the United Brothers Insurance Society. In its last stages Chartism produced a small crop of insurance and friendly societies.[2] John Shaw had in 1831 founded the Friend-in-Need Benefit and Burial Society, which was reconstructed in 1853 when T. M. Wheeler was one of the directors. In 1852 the British Industrial Association

---

[1] See Menger's Right to the Whole Product of Labour.

[2] The histories of industrial insurance and of building societies in Great Britain have not yet been written. Their roots cannot be traced to any particular Chartist theory or utterance, but are nevertheless apparently fixed in the Chartist period. John Shaw, originally an East End undertaker, and the whole group of N.C.A. members specially associated with the Land Company, were, as we have seen, strongly in favour of these schemes for improving the position of the working class. Dr. Bowkett, a friend of O'Brien, was the author of several works urging the importance of building societies.

was started, Wheeler being its London manager for the first year. The Association quarrelled with the Friend-in-Need, but the latter outlived it. The Friend-in-Need absorbed another society, the National Assurance Friendly Society, which Thomas Clark had founded. Doyle and Dixon, according to Gammage, also went into insurance after the downfall of the Land Company. It is curious to find the group of men specially connected with O'Connor's scheme going into this business with such unanimity. Shaw and Clark died in 1857 and Wheeler in 1862, still convinced that the Land Scheme had been rightly conceived in spite of the year 1847–8 he had spent on his two-acre allotment at O'Connorville.

The Rev. Henry Solly *connects Chartism with another movement. After the decline and fall of Chartism he threw himself with extraordinary energy into the task of founding working men's clubs, and in 1862 formed and became a joint honorary secretary of the Working Men's Club and Institute Union. His enthusiasm is said to have made Fawcett declare that " Solly thinks heaven will be composed of working men's clubs." In the same year he gave up the pulpit to become the paid secretary of the new organization which still exists and thrives. Solly, as we have seen, had participated in the Chartist agitation. In an historical jubilee book of the union the secretary, Mr. B. T. Hall, gives Chartism as the exciting cause of the devotion to the club movement of Hodgson Pratt and other of its pioneers.[1] Although the club organization was consistently non-party—no club in fact registered under the Friendly Societies Act of 1884 may have any political objects—it could hardly prevent the clubs from becoming centres of political discussion. The history of the Socialist movement between 1880 and 1890 is largely the story of men who went out and gave lectures at clubs to apathetic groups of working men, in an atmosphere of beer and tobacco-smoke. Solly had been a friend of Lovett, and both had probably vaguely anticipated Bagehot's demonstration that free discussion is an essential factor of progress. Lovett's district halls and Solly's working men's clubs were both inspired by

[1] B. T. Hall, *Our Fifty Years*, p. 264.

this idea, as also by the need for making educational facilities accessory to the halls or clubs. Solly spent over forty years in the furtherance of his union and in agitation for technical instruction. He died in 1903, aged eighty-nine.

It is possible that readers will regard Christian Socialism a product of Chartism. Charles Kingsley, it is true, addressed himself to Chartists, but had no part in their movement. The day before the great demonstration of April 10, Kingsley had come to London and taken counsel with F. D. Maurice.[1] On April 11 all London was posted with a placard addressed to working men, containing a long and flatulent, if politically sound, manifesto. " You think the Charter would make you free—would to God it would ! " it screamed. " But will the Charter make you free ? Will it free you from the slavery to £10 bribes ? Slavery to gin and beer ? . . . A nobler day is dawning for England, a day of freedom, science, industry ! But there will be no true freedom without virtue, no true science without religion, no true industry without the fear of God, and love to your fellow citizens. Workers of England, be wise and then you must be free, or you will be fit to be free." This document was signed, " a working parson," and is, according to the historians of Christian Socialism, the seed of that movement.

It is usual to speak of Christian Socialism as proceeding from Chartism. This view is fallacious. The group of Christian Socialist leaders wished, it is true, to graft their principles on to Chartism, but their principles owed nothing to Chartism. In May, 1848, they began to bring out a weekly paper, *Politics for the People*, addressed to Chartists, in which Kingsley wrote a series of " Letters to Chartists," over the signature of Parson Lot, declaring in the first epistle that his " only quarrel with the Charter is that it does not go far enough in reform." The paper only lasted for three months ; the Chartists, as already indicated, had other and more exciting things to occupy their attention. The next move of Kingsley, Morris, Ludlow, and Hughes was the establishment of the Working Men's College, which has risen from a humble beginning in a yard off Great

[1] *Christian Socialism*, p. 7.

Ormond Street to a fine home in Crowndale Road, St. Pancras. For a year this occupied the energies of the little group, which rapidly succeeded in attracting the attention and co-operation of an able and finely intentioned middle-class circle. In 1849 the Christian Socialists started on the venture with which their name is perhaps most commonly associated. On the initiative of J. M. Ludlow, they founded the Society for Promoting Working Men's Associations, on the French model, which sprang from the teachings of Buchez. This organization financed twelve associations of working men, and intending to be self-supporting and on lines similar to those on which, as we have seen, various unsuccessful associations of producers had come into being under the Chartist ægis.[1] Three associations were of tailors, three of shoemakers, two of builders, and one each of piano-makers, printers, smiths, and bakers. These began by being self-governing, but this form of management soon broke down. By 1854 the last of these associations of producers had failed. Other similar bodies came to the same end. It was found that in practice the employees in their governing capacity invariably quarrelled with a manager who only held his post on their sufferance.[2] Workshops, on the other hand, owned by working people, but only governed by them as shareholders, not as employees, were opened about this time by the Rochdale and other co-operative stores, and prospered.

The incursion of the Christian Socialists may be taken as evidence in support of the contention that the Chartists never had any genuine middle-class support. Sturge attempted to organize it and failed. Kingsley and Maurice tried to draft their theories into Chartism and failed. J. S. Mill, with all his Socialist sympathies, never even attempted to approach Chartism. Carlyle alone of his class was sufficiently attracted by the subject to write a little book about it. His *Chartism* is a pitiful contribution of sympathy with a misunderstood

---

[1] Beatrice Potter (Mrs. Sidney Webb), *The Co-operative Movement*, pp. 118–125, describes in full the genesis and work of this body.

[2] The British Museum contains a bound volume of prospectuses of such associations, formerly the property of F. J. Furnival, one of the first Christian Socialists (08278 35).

cause attempting to domesticate itself upon a misunderstanding public. He meant well, but the Chartists would have none of him. In the minute books of the Working Men's Association we find an amusing reference to this splutter of Carlyle. In 1843 the Committee decided to form a small library, and a short select list was drawn up of books to be purchased. *Chartism* was amongst them, but the Committee, on consideration, struck it out.[1] In a review of a review in the *British and Foreign Review*, a writer in *The Northern Star* says, " Neither Mr. Carlyle nor his reviewer know what Chartism is."[2] Neither moral nor physical force Chartists, in fact, would have anything to do with the book. The Appendix to Chapter VI contains several condensed expressions of middle-class opinion :

It should be remembered that Lord John Russell was not above misrepresenting Chartism for the furtherance of his own plans. Cobden complained in 1849 that the Monmouthshire riots were immediately after their occurrence made by Russell the basis of a proposal for a temporary increase of 5,000 men to the Army. But when tranquillity returned, no corresponding reduction was made.[3] Treated in this manner by those in authority, Chartism became all the more difficult for the middle classes to understand. As a working-class protest, to use Linton's word, Chartism was completely inaccessible to middle-class sympathy. Hence the breakdown of Sturge's endeavour of 1842, which he made no attempt to repeat.

Joseph Sturge died in 1859, the year after he had been elected president of the Peace Society. His most ambitious scheme of reconciliation was an attempt to stave off the war with Russia. In company with two other Quakers he travelled to Russia and had an interview with Nicholas I, beseeching him, on moral and religious grounds, not to enter into war. After

---

[1] British Museum, Additional MSS. 37,776.

[2] *Northern Star*, November 6, 1841.

[3] Speech delivered in the Free Trade Hall, Manchester, January 10, 1849 : included in *Free Trade and other Fundamental Doctrines of the Manchester School*, edited by F. W. Hirst, p. 296.

the war, hearing of the destruction caused on the Finnish coasts by the bombardment of the British Fleet, Sturge organized a fund for the relief of the distressed Finns ; his effort being, as usual, based on his personal knowledge gained from a visit to the devastated coastal towns immediately after the declaration of peace. His connexion with Chartism, brief as it was, had been conceived in a spirit which made it one of the finest episodes of the movement.

We now pass on to chronicle the deaths of the leaders of Chartism. The real hero of the movement is Lovett. Perhaps the best clue to his character is his belief, probably derived from Owen, in the virtue of ideas. To him it was sufficient to have given birth to an idea ; if it was right it would prevail in the end. This side of his character is curiously illustrated by his autobiography, which is mainly composed of the addresses drafted by him in the course of his various secretaryships. In 1846 he resigned the secretaryship of the National Association, but retained virtual possession of the National Hall, which he gradually succeeded in converting into a school. He was for a time (1846–9) publisher of *Howitt's Journal,* and had Mazzini, the Howitts, W. J. Fox, Linton, Harriet Martineau, and several other distinguished writers among its contributors. After he had given up his secretaryship, he published an Appeal to the Friends of Progress, calling for a union of the reform parties. But the popularity and success of political associations is apparently in inverse ratio to the extent of the schemes they set out to establish, on which hypothesis the failure of all Lovett's schemes (and those of Owen), and especially of this last one, and, conversely, the success attending so many of Place's undertakings, are to be explained. In 1848 a presentation was made to him, chiefly on the initiative of W. J. Fox and J. H. Parry, but Lovett used a good deal of his testimonial money the following year to enable the National Association to die free of debt. He then taught himself anatomy and physiology, in order to be able to instruct the young, writing a successful and well-reviewed textbook on the subject in the process. In 1850 he was put on the Working Class Committee of the Great Exhibition, other members of this being Dickens,

Thackeray, Lord Ashley, and Vincent. In 1853 he published a book, *Social and Political Morality*, with the object of teaching the English the importance of stability in " the morals of our population." The comment he makes on this book's reception is characteristic of his faith in ideas : " I regret to say that it was not circulated so as to effect the object aimed at."[1] In 1857 he was swindled out of his National Hall, and that home of ideas was in the course of time converted into the Holborn Empire Music Hall.

Lovett continued to teach natural history, anatomy, and physiology at schools, for many years, taking little part in political movements. He died in 1877, and was buried at Highgate, Holyoake making a speech by the graveside.

Lovett's organizations had predeceased him by many years. The Working Men's Association had never taken a prominent part in Chartist politics after Lovett's imprisonment. Its minute book from 1843–1847 [2] shows us an organization resembling that of a Fabian Society in reduced circumstances. In many respects there is, in fact, an analogy between the W.M.A., and the Fabian Society. Both produced ideas, and left the task of forcing them upon the attention of an apathetic country to other larger bodies. The W.M.A. looked after the social side of the Chartist movement and the education of its own members to a larger extent than the other societies having the same ultimate knowledge. If it were possible to recover some of the minute books of the N.C.A., we should be unlikely to find in them any evidence of a desire to be accommodated with a library, or to provide social amenities. The minutes close with an expression of opinion in favour of the purchase of a piano, at a committee meeting held on October 4, 1847. So the W.M.A. glides modestly into the realms of recordless things.

The National Association minute books record a calm series of discussions and formal business for many years. New members were rare comers. The excitements of April 10, 1848,

---

[1] *Life and Struggles*, p. 367.
[2] British Museum, Additional MSS. 37,776.

brought in some six new adherents. The minute books break off on June 4, 1849. The total amount owing by the Association was then £434 5s. 3d. A month earlier a subscription list had been opened to defray old debts. The school, now attended by 200 pupils, was handed over to Lovett, Parry, Shaen, and one or two others, and the National Association ceased to exist.[1]

James Watson died in November, 1874, having fought side by side with Moore in the struggle for a free press until the final victory.

Richard Moore, Watson's nephew-in-law, died four years later, having for many years earned his living as a master woodcarver. Holyoake spoke at his funeral.

Henry Vincent died at the end of 1878. He had married, in 1841, a daughter of John Cleave. Between 1841 and 1852 he contested seven parliamentary elections with optimism, but without success. He earned his living for many years as a lecturer, chiefly on moral subjects, his audiences consisting chiefly of Free Church congregations. There must be few lecturers or audiences in our days which would make a success of Vincent's subjects, which were *inter alia* " Home Life : its Duties and Pleasures," and " The Philosophy of True Manliness." In 1866 he went on a lecturing tour to the United States ; this was extremely successful and was repeated several times. Cleave appears to have died in 1847.

Henry Hetherington died of cholera in August, 1849. He had lived just long enough to see that section of the Chartist movement which meant most to him return to the work which had been especially his own for twenty years. Towards the end of his life he had accepted Owen's system, and had done a good deal for the Institute in John Street. He had also become a Director of the Poor for the parish of St. Pancras. Holyoake preached over his grave at the funeral in Kensal Green.

Holyoake, having literally buried the movement, died in

[1] The Minute Books of the National Association are in the British Museum, Additional MSS. 37,774–5, wrongly described as Vols. II–III of the Minute Books of the Working Men's Association.

1906, after a long lifetime devoted to the service of co-operation and secularism. A sturdy common sense, and an ape-like inability to understand spiritual things came to his aid in these movements. He was the author of a vast number of books and pamphlets on subjects connected with his propaganda, frequently inaccurate in detail, and always with a strong autobiographical element.

Were the demands of the People's Charter impracticable ? In the absolute sense, certainly they were not. One state— and one only—has, probably unintentionally, incorporated as many as five of the six points in its constitution. The little Central American Republic of Salvador (population about 1,250,000), for the two generations following its extrication from the Central American Union, zealously followed the quest of the perfect constitution. The sixth attempt, made in 1886, has to the present resisted the forces which would substitute for it a seventh. In Salvador there is universal manhood suffrage, and a Salvadorean becomes a man for this purpose on his eighteenth birthday, or on his wedding day, whichever comes first. There are annual parliaments, elected every February. Voting is by ballot, there are no property qualifications for members of the Assembly, who are paid ten Salvadorean dollars a day during the session. It will be seen therefore that the only Chartist Point not conceded is equality of constituencies, but as this was demanded for England in order to rectify certain striking disproportions, which apparently do not exist in Salvador, the omission would readily be forgiven by the Chartists. Certain other arrangements would certainly be approved by them. By way of preventing the Salvadorean's visits to the voting booths from becoming less than annual, voting is made compulsory and citizens who do not fulfil this obligation are fined. Candidates must reside habitually in the department which they seek to represent ; [1] thus the carpet-bagger is eliminated. The constitution is uni-cameral, the President is elected for four years and may not serve consecutive periods, and there are only four Cabinet Ministers. The Salvadoreans who are of pure white descent number only $2\frac{1}{2}$

[1] Except at the Universities.

per cent. of the total population, and are mainly recruited, it appears, by reason of the absence of all extradition treaties with other nations. To draw a moral for British use therefore would be futile. We can only say it has been done, and leave it at that.

The steps taken by Parliament towards democracy as the Chartists saw it have followed one on the other with a curious halting consistency. In 1858, Lord Derby abolished the property qualification : it had long been a dead letter to the ingenious. In 1867, after several false starts, a certain amount of redistribution took place, chiefly to the advantage of the boroughs, and later of Scotland. At the same time household suffrage was conceded to the boroughs, and in 1868 the Scottish Occupation Franchise and the Irish Borough Franchise were reduced. In 1872 the ballot-box became part of the electoral machinery, and although its inclusion in the annual Expiring Laws Continuation Bills in theory makes its continued presence in the Statute Book liable to a sudden and unforeseen termination, it has now become in practice to be regarded as almost an essential part of the constitution. More redistribution and enfranchisement took place in 1884 and 1885, yielding working approximation to both universal suffrage and equal representation. Payment of members came, in a remarkably casual manner in 1911, in the same year as the Parliament Act limited the duration of Parliaments from seven to five years—a limitation to be subsequently hung up for the benefit of the very Parliament which had enacted it ! None of the Six Points therefore has retained its original urgency. What has not been conceded has been compromised.

Throughout this work, Chartism has been used synonymously with the Chartist movement. This is due to the exiguity of the language, which contains no other word for that concatenation of political tendencies, working in all directions, than movement. But these tendencies may possibly work simultaneously in opposite directions. The word movement, in fact, may have to be used to describe a number of conflicting movements, or stagnation itself. We should not overlook the fact that there were several Chartist movements ; several

bodies of activity, that is, associated with the People's Charter.
These acted concurrently ; but as a history has to be written
consecutively, there is a distinct danger that the student will
be unable to separate the interdigitating tendencies and events
covered by the term Chartism. Let us roughly analyse the
entire group of these. We begin in 1837–38 with a Radical
movement in London, associated with the Working Men's
Association, a body of labour intellectuals deriving their ideas
directly from Owen, Bentham, the Mills, and the other fountain-
heads of political doctrine. From this group proceeds the
People's Charter published on May 8, 1838. At the same time
another group of Radicals has crystallized in Birmingham
around the personality of the local M.P., Thomas Attwood. This
group has imbibed both Attwood's political and economic
faith ; in particular it is committed to currency reform.
Lastly there is a large and unorganized mass of people in
Lancashire and Yorkshire, Radical out of opposition to Toryism,
inflamed by the terrible industrial conditions from which they
are themselves the chief sufferers, and inspired with revolutionary sentiments by Stephens and Oastler. The Charter is
published ; the two groups not responsible for it immediately
accept it as a programme. Birmingham tries to take the lead
and is partly successful. The Convention is held ; repression
begins, acting upon the leaders of all three groups, who spend
the next year or two in jail. Reorganization then begins ;
resolving itself by 1843 into two movements ; the pacific C.S.U.
plus National Association movement which avoids class bitterness ; and the N.C.A., which dozes for a while, revives, adopts
the Land Scheme and collapses, more gradually than is generally supposed. The Lovett-Place-Sturge movement has
bursts of activity for some years, but slowly wanes and died
with its founders. A closer analysis would reveal a larger
number of Chartisms ; in 1842 the student would find beside
these just described a teetotal-cum-feminist variety in Bristol.
Bath, and the West, the Shakespearean brigade of Chartist.
in Leicester, decorative, emotional, and under the discipline
of a uniformed " General," and a teetotal-cum-religious Chartism in the Lowlands of Scotland. If one force more than

another inspired the Chartist movement, it was that which proceeded from philosophic Radicalism. From Place and the W.M.A., the opinions emanating from Cobbett and Paine, the Malthusian controversy, the current political economy, the press of the well-to-do, the pulpit and the magistrate's bench, there drifted down to the minds of the working class a practical Radicalism, adapted to their needs, and guaranteed to mitigate their sufferings.

Even before the publication of the People's Charter, a Radical paper of Newcastle-on-Tyne once attempted to answer the question, What is a Radical ? [1] " The True Radical is best described by first saying what he is not. " He is not a God-winite, nor an Owenite, nor a Benthamite, nor a Cosmopolite. . . . He has no passion for democracy, because it *is* democracy, but looks to what it produces. He thinks imagination has nothing to do with politics, and passion as little. Liberty may sound well upon the stage, but that is no argument for him that it must therefore necessarily be good. . . . He has no idea that the framework of society can be altered suddenly, or that such attempts can do any good ; but he praises a government rather for what it does not do than for what it does ; and goes to negations rather than the contrary in all that respects dealing with the people. He thinks, in short, that government the best which meddles least and takes least from the pockets of the people. If it be an economical one, it cannot, in his opinion, as long as it is so, be a bad one, be its name and form what it may. He . . . advocates democracy only because it seems most likely to prefer and perpetuate a system of this kind. . . . He cannot, for the life of him, understand how any man with a love of freedom and justice . . . can tolerate the Malthusians and their Poor Law. . . . He is for universal suffrage, annual parliaments, and vote by ballot, and thinks Whigs and Tories equally worthless as politicians. Though accused of violent inclinations and inten-tions, and called a savage and a firebrand, he is full of the milk of human kindness, and would not in his greatest rage hang more than a dozen loan-mongers, or set fire to anything

[1] *Northern Liberator*, April 28, 1838.

U

unless perhaps the Stock Exchange, the Poor Law Bastiles, or the Bank."

This is the best contemporary example we have seen of the Radical Credo. Chartism is both an acceptance and an attempted evasion of the implications of this faith. The Radical working man of the 'sixties, 'seventies, and 'eighties with his dislike of Socialism, is a result of a movement which both rejected Socialism and gave it shape ; a movement which set out to destroy the socialism of Owen and ended by accepting, on its death-bed, the socialism of Marx.

Foreign studies on Chartism invariably conclude with a section entitled, Why was the Movement a Failure ? or something of similar effect. The example, set by innumerable authors, does not seem to be worth copying, as it begs the question, Was the Movement a Failure ? An answer in the negative, the author ventures to suggest, is contrary only to superficial evidences. Chartism was an episode in that concatenation of aspirations and struggles which is vaguely spoken of as the working-class movement. What are the essential objects of this movement, as distinguished from the immediately attainable and ostensible objects of which the Six Points are specimens ? There is but one essential object—the awakening of class-consciousness, the better organization of the working class in its struggle for greater economic and political power. No body of opinions which fails to stimulate class consciousness can be said to be strictly necessary to the working-class movement, just as no set of doctrines or practices which fail to stimulate the consciousness of nationality can be integrally connected with nationalism. The Chartist movement with its derivations, its appeals to " blistered hands and fustian jackets," its actual tenets of class antagonism, its association with industrial unrest, and its inability to accept the advances of middle-class sympathizers, was the first organized effort to stir up class consciousness on a national scale. The movement's failures lay in the direction of securing legislation, or national approbation for its leaders. Judged by its crop of statutes and statues, Chartism was a failure. Judged by its essential and generally overlooked purpose, Chartism was a success. It achieved, not the Six Points, but a state of mind. This last achievement made possible the renascent trade union movement of the 'fifties, the gradually improving organization of the working classes, the Labour Party, the co-operative movement, and whatever greater triumphs labour will enjoy in the future.

BIBLIOGRAPHY

Alton Locke. Kingsley.
Anti-Theistic Theories. Flint.
Attwood, Life of Thomas. C. M. Wakefield.
Autobiography of John Bowes.
Babeuf's Conspiracy, History of. Buonarotti.
Briefwechsel. Engels-Marx.
British Radicalism. Walter Phelps Hall.
Bygones Worth Remembering. G. J. Holyoake.
Chartism. Carlyle.
Chartism : a New Organization of the People. Lovett and Collins.
Chartisme, Le. Prof. Dolléans.
Chartist Movement, History of the. R. G. Gammage.
Chartisten-Bewegung, Die. Schluter.
Christian Socialism.
Cobbett, William : a Biography. Edward Smith.
Cobden, Life of. Morley.
Conditions of the English Working Class in 1841. Engels.
Conservative Science of Nations. Sommerville.
Cooper, The Life of Thomas.
Co-operation, History of. G. J. Holyoake.
Co-operative Movement, The. Beatrice Potter (Mrs. S. Webb).
Cowen, Life of Joseph. Duncan.
Cremer, Life of Sir R. Howard Evans.
Crimes of the Clergy. William Benbow.
Crisis, The.
Decline and Fall of the Roman Empire. Gibbon.
Defensive Instruction to the People. Col. Francis Maceroni.
Dictionary of National Biography.
Early Correspondence of Lord John Russell.
Economic Annals of the Nineteenth Century. W. M. Smart.
English Local Government. S. and B. Webb.
English Philanthropy, a History of. B. Kirkham Gray.
English Radicals, The. C. R. B. Kent.

English Republic. W. J. Linton.

Essay on Population, An. Malthus.

Exercises. Col. Perronet Thompson.

Flugschriften literatur des Chartistenhewegung, Der.

Forty Years' Recollections. Thomas Frost.

Free Trade and Other Fundamental Doctrines of the Manchester School. F. W. Hirst.

Genesis of Parliamentary Reform, The. G. S. Veitch.

Geschichte des Socializmus in England. Beer.

Girlhood of Queen Victoria, The.

Gladstone. Morley.

Greville Memoirs. Charles Greville.

History of England in the Eighteenth Century, A. W. E. H. Lecky.

Holyoake, Life and Letters of G. J. J. MacCabe.

Hunt, Life of Henry.

John Frost and John Watkins.

Labour Representation, A History of. A. W. Humphrey.

Life and Letters. Major Cartwright.

Life and Struggles of William Lovett.

Lovett, William: an Autobiography.

Memories of an Ex-Minister. Lord Malmesbury.

My Memories. W. J. Linton.

Mill, James: a Biography. Bain.

Mill, Letters of J. S.

Napier, Life of Charles James. Lt.-Gen. Sir W. Napier.

Notes and Queries. G. J. Holyoake.

O'Connor, The Trial of Feargus, and Fifty-eight others at Lancaster.

Our Fifty Years. B. T. Hall.

Owen, Life and Labours of Robert. Lloyd Jones.

Owen, Robert. Frank Podmore.

Passages in the Life of a Radical. Samuel Bamford.

Peace, History of the. Harriet Martineau.

Pitt, William, and the Great War. Dr. Holland Rose.

Place, Life of Francis. Graham Wallas.

Place MSS. and Collection.

Practical Work on the Management of Small Farms. Feargus O'Connor.

Recollections and Reflections. Lord John Russell.

Reflections on the Revolution in France. Burke.

Reminiscences. Justin MacCarthy.

Republican Tradition in Europe, The. H. A. L. Fisher.

Right to the Whole Produce of Labour. Anton Menger.
Rights of Man, The. Thomas Paine.
Rights of Nations. Anonymous.
Rise and Fall of Chartism in Monmouthshire.
Robespierre, Life of. B. O'Brien.
Rochdale Pioneers, History of the. G. J. Holyoake.
Rough Types of English Life. J. C. Symons.
Sixty Years of an Agitator's Life. G. J. Holyoake.
Social and Political Morality. William Lovett.
Spen Valley: Past and Present.
Stephens, Life of J. R. G. J. Holyoake.
Struggles of an Old Chartist. B. Wilson.
Sturge, Memoirs of Joseph. Henry Richard.
Taxes on Knowledge, History of the. C. D. Collet.
Thelwall, John. C. Cestre.
Thelwall, John, Life of.
These Eighty Years. Rev. H. Solly.
Trade Unionism, History of. S. and B. Webb.
Victoria, Letters of Queen.
Village Labourer, The. J. L. and Barbara Hammond.
Vincent, Henry: a Biographical Sketch. William Dorling.
Vindication of the Rights of Man. Mary Wollstonecraft.
Vindication of the Rights of Woman. Mary Wollstonecraft.
Watson, Life of. W. J. Linton.
Wealth of Nations. Adam Smith.
Wellington. G. Lathom Browne.
Wellington, Life of. Maxwell.
West Indies, The. Joseph Sturge.
Wheeler, Life of. Stevens.

For further details, references to newspapers, periodicals, etc.,
see Index.

INDEX

301